Web Service Imp.

Transaction Script (134)	How can developers quickly implement web service logic?
Datasource Adapter (137)	How can a web service provide access to internal resources like database tables, stored procedures, domain objects, or files with a minimum amount of custom code?
Operation Script (144)	How can web services reuse common domain logic without duplicating code?
Command Invoker (149)	How can web services with different APIs reuse common domain logic while enabling both synchronous and asynchronous request processing?
Workflow Connector (156)	How can web services be used to support complex and long-running business processes?

Web Service Infrastructures

Service Connector (168)	How can clients avoid duplicating the code required to use a specific service and also be insulated from the intricacies of communication logic?
Service Descriptor (175)	How can development tools acquire the information necessary to use a web service, and how can the code for Service Connectors be generated?
Asynchronous Response Handler (184)	How can a client avoid blocking when sending a request?
Service Interceptor (195)	How can common behaviors like authentication, caching, logging, exception handling, and validation be executed without having to modify the client or service code?
Idempotent Retry (206)	How can a client ensure that requests are delivered to a web service despite temporary network or server failures?

Web Service Evolution

Single-Message Argument (234)	How can a web service with an *RPC API* (##) become less brittle and easily accommodate new parameters over time without breaking clients?
Dataset Amendment (237)	How can a service augment the information it sends or receives while minimizing the probability of breaking changes?
Tolerant Reader (243)	How can clients or services function properly when some of the content in the messages or media types they receive is unknown or when the data structures vary?
Consumer-Driven Contracts (250)	How can a web service API reflect its clients' needs while enabling evolution and avoiding breaking clients?

Service
Design Patterns

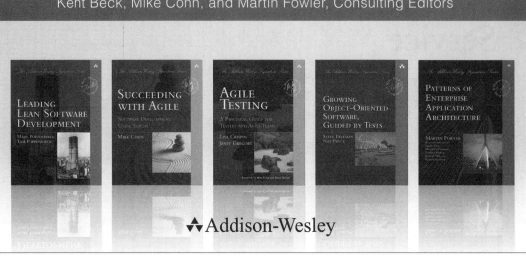

The Addison-Wesley
Signature Series

Kent Beck, Mike Cohn, and Martin Fowler, Consulting Editors

LEADING LEAN SOFTWARE DEVELOPMENT — MARY POPPENDIECK, TOM POPPENDIECK

SUCCEEDING WITH AGILE — Software Development Using Scrum — MIKE COHN

AGILE TESTING — A Practical Guide for Testers and Agile Teams — LISA CRISPIN, JANET GREGORY

GROWING OBJECT-ORIENTED SOFTWARE, GUIDED BY TESTS — STEVE FREEMAN, NAT PRYCE

PATTERNS OF ENTERPRISE APPLICATION ARCHITECTURE — MARTIN FOWLER

♦♦Addison-Wesley

Visit **informit.com/awss** for a complete list of available products.

The **Addison-Wesley Signature Series** provides readers with practical and authoritative information on the latest trends in modern technology for computer professionals. The series is based on one simple premise: Great books come from great authors. Books in the series are personally chosen by expert advisors, world-class authors in their own right. These experts are proud to put their signatures on the covers, and their signatures ensure that these thought leaders have worked closely with authors to define topic coverage, book scope, critical content, and overall uniqueness. The expert signatures also symbolize a promise to our readers: You are reading a future classic.

♦♦Addison-Wesley   **Cisco Press**   EXAM/**CRAM**   **IBM Press.**   que   ⁞⁞ PRENTICE HALL   **SAMS** | Safari"

Service Design Patterns

Fundamental Design Solutions for SOAP/WSDL and RESTful Web Services

Robert Daigneau

✦Addison-Wesley

Upper Saddle River, NJ • Boston • Indianapolis • San Francisco
New York • Toronto • Montreal • London • Munich • Paris • Madrid
Capetown • Sydney • Tokyo • Singapore • Mexico City

Many of the designations used by manufacturers and sellers to distinguish their products are claimed as trademarks. Where those designations appear in this book, and the publisher was aware of a trademark claim, the designations have been printed with initial capital letters or in all capitals.

The author and publisher have taken care in the preparation of this book, but make no expressed or implied warranty of any kind and assume no responsibility for errors or omissions. No liability is assumed for incidental or consequential damages in connection with or arising out of the use of the information or programs contained herein.

The publisher offers excellent discounts on this book when ordered in quantity for bulk purchases or special sales, which may include electronic versions and/or custom covers and content particular to your business, training goals, marketing focus, and branding interests. For more information, please contact:

U.S. Corporate and Government Sales
(800) 382-3419
corpsales@pearsontechgroup.com

For sales outside the United States, please contact:

International Sales
international@pearson.com

Visit us on the Web: informit.com/aw

Library of Congress Cataloging-in-Publication Data
Daigneau, Robert.
    Service design patterns : fundamental design solutions for SOAP/WSDL and restful Web services / Robert Daigneau.
        p.   cm.
    Includes bibliographical references and index.
    ISBN-13: 978-0-321-54420-9 (hardcover : alk. paper)
    ISBN-10: 0-321-54420-X (hardcover : alk. paper)
    1. Web services. 2. Web site development. 3. Simple Object Access Protocol (Computer network protocol) I. Title.
    TK5105.88813.D35 2012
    006.7'8—dc23

                                                                2011033436

ISBN-13: 978-0-321-54420-9
ISBN-10:   0-321-54420-X

Text printed in the United States on recycled paper at Courier in Westford, Massachusetts.
First printing, October 2011

For John, Alice, Heather, and Michelle

Contents

Foreword

by Martin Fowler

One of the inevitable truisms of enterprise applications is that they are not islands. You may be focused on solving a particular business problem, but in order to do that you won't be able to capture all the data you need yourself, or develop all the processing. Even if you had the time, that data and processing is being done elsewhere, and duplication is both wasteful and leads to messy inconsistencies. As a result, almost all enterprise applications need to communicate with other applications. These foreign systems are often not in the same organization, but are provided by some third-party organization.

For many years, one of the hardest parts of this kind of collaboration was just to get some kind of communication path. Often these applications were written on different platforms, with different languages, on different operating systems supporting different communication protocols. But in the past decade, the web has appeared as a solution to the connection problem. Almost all systems can open port 80 and talk text over it.

But that still leaves many questions around how they should talk. Should they use an RPC-style API, a message-oriented API, or this fashionable REST stuff? Should logic be embedded in services directly or delegated to underlying objects? How can we change services that are already in use without breaking clients?

Generally in my series, the books have featured topics that haven't been covered much elsewhere, but there have already been too many books about various aspects of web services. As a result, when a draft of Robert's book came to me across the ether, I didn't think I would be interested in it. What changed my mind was that it brings together these key questions into a single handbook, in a style that I like to see in a technical book that's worth the effort of reading.

First, he takes the approach of breaking up the topic area into patterns, so we have vocabulary to talk about these topics. Then he goes into each pattern, explaining how each one works and how to choose between them. As a result, you are able to see the various approaches to web service design and decide what will work for you in your context. He provides code examples, so you can see how these patterns might work in practice, yet the patterns are general enough to apply to many technology stacks.

The result is a book that collects the important design decision points for using web services in a style that focuses on principles that are likely to be valuable despite changes in technology.

Martin Fowler
http://martinfowler.com

Foreword

by Ian Robinson

Distributed application development often starts well. And just as often it ends badly. *Point, add web reference, click:* That's the sound of a developer pointing a loaded client at your carefully crafted service interface. By substituting tooling for design, we somehow turned all that loose coupling into plain irresponsible promiscuity; come release time, we all have to join the lockstep jump.

In a more cautious era, we'd have just said: "No. Don't distribute." And in large part that advice still holds true today. A layer is not a tier. Blowing a three-layered application architecture out to distributed proportions is foolishness writ large, no matter how many open standards you implement.

But today's applications are rarely islands. Where a business's capabilities are scattered across organizational boundaries, so too are the systems that automate them. Some form of service orientation, both within and between companies, is necessary if we are to support the distributed nature of the modern supply chain.

The web, or rather, the technology that underpins the web, has proven enormously resourceful in this respect. Whether or not you're aware of—or even carelessly indifferent to—the web's prominent place in the history of distributed systems, there's inevitably something of the web about a sound majority of the services you've built or used. For all its purported transport agnosticism, SOAP, in practice, has tended to ride the HTTP train. Hidden, but not forgotten, the web has shouldered the services burden for several years now.

When we look at the web services landscape today, we see that there are at least three ways to accommodate the web in the software we build. The web has succeeded not because of the overwhelming correctness of its constituency, but because of its tolerance for the many architectural styles that inhabit and sometimes overrun its borders. Some services and applications are simply *behind* the web. They treat the web as an unwelcome but nonetheless necessary narrow gateway through which to access objects and procedures. Adjust your gaze, and you'll see that some services are *on* the web; that is, they treat HTTP not as a brute transport, but rather as the robust coordination and transfer protocol described in RFC 2616. Last, you'll see some (very few) that are *of* the web. These use the web's founding technologies—in particular, URIs and HTTP and generalized hypermedia representation formats such as HTML—to present a web of data, including data that describes how to access and manipulate more data, to consumers.

This book brings together the need for caution and defensive design when distributing systems with the several ways of using the web to enable distribution. As a compendium of sound strategies and techniques, it rivals the hard-won experience of many of my friends and colleagues at ThoughtWorks. It's a book about getting things done on the web; it's also a book about not backing yourself into a corner. By balancing the (necessary) complexity of shielding a service's domain and data from that army of cocked clients with the simplicity that begets internal quality and service longevity, it may just help you avoid the midnight lockstep deployment.

Ian Robinson

Preface

When I started working on this book I wasn't entirely sure what SOA and REST were. I knew that I wasn't the only one who felt this way. Most discussions on these topics were rife with ambiguity, hyperbole, misinformation, and arguments that appealed to emotion rather than reason. Still, as a developer who had struggled with distributed object technologies, I was fascinated by web services. I saw them as a pragmatic way to integrate systems and reuse common business logic.

Since then, REST has gained significant momentum, WS* services have established a solid foothold, and SOA was proclaimed dead [Manes]. Through it all, my fascination with web services never waned. As mobile, cloud, and Software-as-a-Service (SaaS) platforms cause software to become increasingly distributed, the importance of web services will only continue to increase. We live in exciting times indeed!

What Is This Book About?

This book is a catalogue of design solutions for web services that leverage SOAP/WSDL or follow the REST architectural style. The goal was to produce a concise reference that codifies fundamental web service design concepts. Each pattern describes a known and proven solution to a recurring design problem. However, the patterns are not meant to be recipes that are followed precisely. In fact, a given pattern might never be implemented in exactly the same way twice. This catalogue also doesn't invent new solutions. Rather, the patterns in this book were identified over long periods of time by developers who noticed that certain problems could be solved by using similar design approaches. This book captures and formalizes those ideas.

Services can be implemented with many different technologies. SOA practitioners, for example, often say that technologies as diverse as CORBA and

DCOM, to the newer software frameworks developed for REST and SOAP/ WSDL, can all be used to create services. This book focuses exclusively on web services. Unfortunately, this term is somewhat overloaded as well. Some use it to refer to any callable function that uses WSDL. The term has also been used to describe RESTful services (re: [Richardson, Ruby]). This book uses the term *web service* to refer to software functions that can be invoked by leveraging HTTP as a simple transport over which data is carried (e.g., SOAP/WSDL services) or by using HTTP as a complete application protocol that defines the semantics for service behavior (e.g., RESTful services).

Who Is This Book For?

This book is aimed at professional enterprise architects, solution architects, and developers who are currently using web services or are thinking about using them. These professionals fall into two distinct groups. The first group creates software products (e.g., commercial, open source SaaS applications). The second develops enterprise applications for corporate IT departments. While this catalogue is tailored for software professionals, it can also be used in academia.

What Background Do You Need?

Pattern authors often provide code examples to illustrate design solutions. Most catalogues aren't meant to be platform-specific, but the author must still choose which languages, frameworks, and platforms to use in the examples. While a plethora of new languages have become popular in recent years, I decided to use Java and C# for two reasons. First, these languages have a significant market share (i.e., a large installed base of applications) and are quite mature. Second, most readers probably use or have used these languages and are therefore familiar with their syntax. I will assume that the reader has an intermediate to advanced understanding of these languages and of several object-oriented programming (OOP) concepts.

The patterns in this catalogue make heavy use of a few web service frameworks popular with Java and C# developers. These frameworks encapsulate the most common functions used by web service developers. This book does not identify the patterns used within these frameworks. Instead, it identifies patterns that developers use when leveraging these frameworks to build web services. Here are the frameworks that are used in this book:

- SOAP/WSDL frameworks:
  - The Java API for XML Web Services (JAX-WS)
  - Apache CXF
  - Microsoft's Windows Communication Foundation (WCF)
- REST frameworks:
  - The Java API for RESTful Web Services (JAX-RS)
  - Microsoft's WCF
- Data-binding frameworks:
  - The Java Architecture for XML Binding (JAXB)
  - Microsoft's `DataContractSerializer` and other serializers (e.g., `XmlSerializer`)

It is assumed that the reader will at least have a basic acquaintance with the following:

- JavaScript Object Notation (JSON)
- Extensible Markup Language (XML)
- XML Schema Definition Language
- XML Path Language (XPath)
- Extensible Stylesheet Language Transformation (XSLT)
- The Web Services Description Language (WSDL)

Organization of This Book

Following a general introduction in Chapter 1, the patterns in this catalogue are grouped into six chapters.

- **Chapter 2, Web Service API Styles:** This chapter explores the primary API styles used by web services. The ramifications of selecting the right style cannot be underestimated because, once a style is chosen, it becomes very hard to change direction.

- **Chapter 3, Client-Service Interactions:** This chapter presents the foundations for all client-service interactions. These patterns may be used with any service design style. Given an understanding of these patterns, you can devise complex conversations in which multiple parties exchange data about a particular topic over short or extended periods of time.

- **Chapter 4, Request and Response Management:** Software applications are frequently organized into layers that contain logically related entities. This chapter identifies the common *Service Layer* [POEAA] entities that are used to manage web requests and responses. The intent of these patterns is to decouple clients from the underlying systems used by the service.

- **Chapter 5, Web Service Implementation Styles:** Services may be implemented in various ways. They may have intimate knowledge of resources such as database tables, they may coordinate the activities of an Object Relational Mapper (ORM) or direct calls to legacy APIs, or they may forward work to external entities. This chapter looks at the ramifications of each approach.

- **Chapter 6, Web Service Infrastructures:** Certain tasks are so generic that they can be used over and over again. This chapter discusses some of the most common and basic infrastructure concerns pertinent to client and service developers. A few patterns common to corporate SOA infrastructures are also reviewed.

- **Chapter 7, Web Service Evolution:** Developers strive to create services that will remain compatible with clients which evolve at different rates. This goal, however, is quite difficult to achieve. This chapter reviews the factors that cause clients to break and discusses two common versioning strategies. You'll also see how services can be augmented to meet client requirements while avoiding a major software release.

Supporting information is provided in the Appendix, Bibliography, and Glossary.

The Pattern Form Used in This Book

There are many ways to present patterns, from the classic style of Christopher Alexander [Alexander] to the highly structured forms of the Gang of Four [GoF] and *Pattern-Oriented Software Architecture* [POSA] books. The convention used in this book was influenced by the Alexandrian form and the style used in *Enterprise Integration Patterns* [EIP]. Hopefully you will find that the conversational style makes the patterns easy to read. Only a few recurring headers are used to demarcate content. Each design pattern is described using the following conventions.

- **Pattern name:** The pattern name describes the solution in a few words. The name provides a handle or identifier for the solution, and is a part of the larger pattern language presented in the book. The goal was to use evocative names that can be easily understood and used in everyday conversations. Many of the pattern names in this book are already quite common.

- **Context:** The context follows the pattern name and is expressed in no more than a few sentences. It identifies the general scenario in which the pattern might apply. Of course, all of these patterns apply to web services, but some are only relevant to certain situations. This section may refer to other patterns to help set the context.

- **Problem:** The problem to solve is stated as a single question. You should be able to read the problem and quickly determine if the pattern is relevant to the design challenge you are facing. This section is marked off between two horizontal bars.

- **Forces:** The forces provide more detail on the problem. This section, which follows the problem definition, explores some of the reasons why the problem is difficult to solve and presents alternative solutions that have been tried but may not work out so well. The goal of this narrative is to naturally lead you to the solution.

- **Solution summary:** This section provides a brief description of the design solution, in a few sentences. Despite its terseness, you should be able to quickly understand how the problem can be solved. The solution summary typically describes the primary entities that comprise the design, their responsibilities and relationships, and the way they work together to solve the problem. The solution is not meant to be an absolute prescription that has one and only one implementation. Rather, it should be viewed as a general template that can be implemented in many different ways. The written summary is usually accompanied by a diagram to supplement the narrative. The primary mechanisms used in this book include sequence diagrams and class diagrams. In some cases, the solution is modeled through nonstandard graphical depictions. This section is demarcated by two horizontal bars, just like the problem section. The intent was to make it easy for readers to quickly find the problem and solution summary.

- **Solution detail:** This section presents several aspects of the solution in a prosaic style. It expands on the solution summary to explore how the primary elements of the solution are employed in order to solve the problem and resolve the forces. Since every solution has benefits and drawbacks, this section reviews the consequences and additional factors you may need to consider. I also point out related patterns that may be found elsewhere in this book or in other pattern catalogues. This is done for a variety of reasons. Some of the patterns in this book are actually specializations of existing patterns, and I felt that it was only right to acknowledge the original source. Other patterns are complementary to the pattern being discussed, or may be considered as an alternative.

- **Considerations:** This section discusses additional factors you may need to consider when using the pattern. Such factors include design considerations, related technologies, and a variety of other pertinent topics. Bulleted lists are used to help the reader skim this section and hone in on specific topics of interest. This section does not occur in each and every pattern.

- **Examples:** This section is meant to supplement the prior sections. You should be able to understand the essence of a pattern without having to read this section. Some patterns offer several examples to help you understand the many ways in which the pattern may be implemented. Other patterns only provide a few examples to facilitate understanding.

    The examples in this book take many forms. The most common form is Java and C# code. Other examples use XML, JSON, XSD, and WSDL. All attempts were made to keep the examples as simple as possible, so a number of things were left out (e.g., exception-handling blocks, thread management, most queuing and database-related logic, etc.). In some cases, the examples only include enough code to convey the basic idea of the pattern. In other cases, the code examples provide much more detail because I felt that omitting such detail would have left the reader with too many questions.

    Please note that this is not meant to be a book on how to use a specific API; there are many great books out there for such matters. Rather, these code samples are provided to deepen your understanding of abstract design solutions. Furthermore, just as the pattern descriptions provide a template, so too do the code examples. This means that you probably won't want to copy any code verbatim.

Pattern Categories Not Covered

A vast array of topics has been included under the umbrella of service design. However, many of these subjects are quite deep and have already been covered extensively in other works. The content of this catalogue has therefore been constrained to only include the most fundamental solutions relevant to web service design. The following topics have been avoided or only covered lightly.

- **Enterprise integration patterns:** While web services provide a great way to integrate disparate applications, the topic of integration is exceedingly deep. Hohpe and Woolf's book, *Enterprise Integration Patterns: Designing, Building, and Deploying Messaging Solutions* [EIP], does a great job of showing how integration can occur through middleware solutions that primarily leverage queuing technologies. This book builds on and refers to many of their patterns.

- **Workflow/orchestration:** Workflow technologies provide the means to define the flow of execution through a set of related activities managed by a central controller. Workflows are frequently triggered by web services and often interact with external web services to send or receive data. Workflows may be relatively short in duration (i.e., a few seconds), or may transpire over days, weeks, or even months. The subject of workflow is far beyond the scope of this book, and is addressed by such catalogues as http://workflowpatterns.com [van der Aalst, et al.].

- **Event-driven architecture:** An alternative to the "command and control" architectural style exemplified by workflows is event-driven architecture (EDA). With EDA, there is no centralized controller. Instead, clients and services communicate with each other in a much more fluid, dynamic, and often unpredictable way when specific events occur within their respective domains. Sometimes the rules for EDA are described through choreography. For more information on this topic I recommend the following:

  www.complexevents.com/category/applications/eda/

- **Choreography:** Choreography, like EDA, is not a "command and control" architectural style. Instead, it suggests that parties adopt a rules-based approach that declares the sequence of allowed exchanges between parties as if seen by an external observer. This concept has yet to see wide adoption.

- **Security:** Matters such as authentication, authorization, data confidentiality, data integrity, nonrepudiation, techniques used to harden network infrastructures, and other security concerns are not discussed in any detail as these subjects are incredibly deep and have been covered extensively in other works.

Supporting Web Site and contact information

Companion information for this book may be found at

www.ServiceDesignPatterns.com

Acknowledgments

I'd like to acknowledge everyone who has assisted in this project. I could not have done this without you.

I am indebted to a number of people from the Pattern Languages of Programming Conference (PLoP) held in 2008. Kyle Brown played an instrumental role by pointing me toward an effective pattern form. He instilled in me a strategy for setting up the problem, forces, and constraints. I'd also like to thank my PLoP 2008 workshop mates for their feedback on early versions of a few patterns and my writing style. This group included Paul Austrem, Philipp Bachmann, Geert Monsieur, Mark Mahoney, Lise Hvatum, Bobby Woolf, and John Liebenau.

Bobby Woolf, Rebecca Wirfs-Brock, and Michael Stiefel volunteered to review early versions of a few chapters. Your feedback helped steer me in the right direction. John Liebenau and Uwe Zdun also offered help in those early days.

My biggest thanks go to my official team of technical reviewers. Jim Webber was incredibly gracious with his time and proved to be a reliable REST resource. Eric Newcomer offered thoughts on how to fine-tune the book's scope. Marc Hadley kept me honest on several Java Specification Requests (JSRs), and provided great input in several other areas. Scott Ambler offered several suggestions to help make the patterns more readable. Elliotte Rusty Harold's expertise is world renowned, and his critiques were thought provoking. Ian Robinson made a huge contribution by offering a very important pattern to the book. Rebecca Wirfs-Brock, more than anyone else, recognized my strengths and weaknesses. Her measured feedback was invaluable. I am, of course, extremely grateful to Martin Fowler for accepting me into this prestigious series and working with me to sharpen the book's content.

Last but not least, I must thank my editorial team, Chris Guzikowski, Raina Chrobak, Chris Zahn, Julie Nahil, and Audrey Doyle. Without your patience, support, and a little prodding, I would have never reached the finish line.

About the Author

Robert Daigneau has more than twenty years of experience designing and implementing applications and products for a broad array of industries from financial services, to manufacturing, to retail and travel. Rob has served in such prominent positions as Director of Architecture for Monster.com, and Manager of Applications Development at Fidelity Investments. He has been known to speak at a conference or two.

Rob can be reached at rob@ServiceDesignPatterns.com.

Chapter 1

From Objects
to Web Services

Web services have been put into practical use for many years. In this time, developers and architects have encountered a number of recurring design challenges related to their usage. We have also learned that certain design approaches work better than others to solve certain problems. This book is for software developers and architects who are currently using web services or are thinking about using them. The goal is to acquaint you with some of the most common and fundamental web service design solutions and to help you determine when to use them. All of the concepts discussed here are derived from real-life lessons. Proven design solutions will also be demonstrated through code examples.

Service developers are confronted with a long list of questions.

- How do you create a service API, what are the common API styles, and when should a particular style be used?

- How can clients and services communicate, and what are the foundations for creating complex conversations in which multiple parties exchange data over extended periods of time?

- What are the options for implementing service logic, and when should a particular approach be used?

- How can clients become less coupled to the underlying systems used by a service?

- How can information about a service be discovered?

- How can generic functions like authentication, validation, caching, and logging be supported on the client or service?

1

- What changes to a service cause clients to break?

- What are the common ways to version a service?

- How can services be designed to support the continuing evolution of business logic without forcing clients to constantly upgrade?

These are just a few of the questions that must be answered. This book will help you find solutions that are appropriate for your situation.

In this chapter, you'll learn what services are and how web services address the shortcomings of their predecessors.

What Are Web Services?

From a technical perspective, the term **service** has been used to refer to any software function that carries out a business task, provides access to files (e.g., text, documents, images, video, audio, etc.), or performs generic functions like authentication or logging. To these ends, a service may use automated workflow engines, objects belonging to a *Domain Model* [POEAA], commercial software packages, APIs of legacy applications, Message-Oriented Middleware (MOM), and, of course, databases. There are many ways to implement services. In fact, technologies as diverse as CORBA and DCOM, to the newer software frameworks developed for REST and SOAP/WSDL, can all be used to create services.

This book primarily focuses on how services can be used to share logical functions across different applications and to enable software that runs on disparate computing platforms to collaborate. A platform may be any combination of hardware, operating system (e.g., Linux, Windows, z/OS, Android, iOS), software framework (e.g., Java, .NET, Rails), and programming language. All of the services discussed in this book are assumed to execute outside of the client's process. The service's process may be located on the same machine as the client, but is usually found on another machine. While technologies like CORBA and DCOM can be used to create services, the focus of this book is on web services. **Web services** provide the means to integrate disparate systems and expose reusable business functions over HTTP. They either leverage HTTP as a simple transport over which data is carried (e.g., SOAP/WSDL services) or use it as a complete application protocol that defines the semantics for service behavior (e.g., RESTful services).

Terminology

Web service developers often use different terms to refer to equivalent roles. Unfortunately, this has caused a lot of confusion. The following table is therefore provided for clarification and as a reference. The first column lists names used to denote software processes that send requests or trigger events. The second column contains terms for software functions that respond or react to these requests and events. The terms appearing under each column are therefore synonymous.

Client	Service
Requestor	Provider
Service consumer	Service provider

This book uses the terms *"client"* and *"service"* because they are common to both SOAP/WSDL services and RESTful services.

Web services were conceived in large part to address the shortcomings of distributed-object technologies. It is therefore helpful to review some history in order to appreciate the motivation for using web services.

From Local Objects to Distributed Objects

Objects are a paradigm that is used in most modern programming languages to encapsulate behavior (e.g., business logic) and data. Objects are usually "fine-grained," meaning that they have many small properties (e.g., FirstName, LastName) or methods (e.g., getAddress, setAddress). Since developers who use objects often have access to the internals of the object's implementation, the form of reuse they offer is frequently referred to as white-box reuse. Clients use objects by first instantiating them and then calling their properties and methods in order to accomplish some task. Once objects have been instantiated, they usually maintain state between client calls. Unfortunately, it wasn't always easy to use these classes across different programming languages and platforms. Component technologies were developed, in part, to address this problem.

Components were devised as a means to facilitate software reuse across disparate programming languages (see Figure 1.1). The goal was to provide a means whereby software units could be assembled into complex applications much like electronic components are assembled to create circuit boards. Since developers who use components cannot see or modify the internals of a component, the form of reuse they offer is called black-box reuse. Components group related objects into deployable binary software units that can be plugged into applications. An entire industry for the Windows platform arose from this concept in the 1990s as software vendors created ActiveX controls that could be easily integrated into desktop and web-based applications. The stipulation was that applications could not access the objects within components directly. Instead, the applications were given binary interfaces that described the objects' methods, properties, and events. These binary interfaces were often created with platform-specific interface definition languages (IDLs) like the Microsoft Interface Definition Language (MIDL), and clients that wished to use components frequently had to run on the same computing platform.

Objects were eventually deployed to remote servers in an effort to share and reuse the logic they encapsulated (see Figure 1.2). This meant that the memory that was allocated for clients and distributed objects not only existed in separate address spaces but also occurred on different machines. Like components, distributed objects supported black-box reuse. Clients that wished to use distributed objects could leverage a number of remoting technologies like CORBA, DCOM, Java Remote Method Invocation (RMI), and .NET Remot-

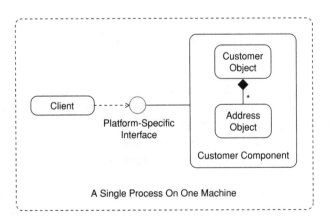

Figure 1.1 *Components were devised as a means to facilitate reuse across disparate programming languages. Unfortunately, they were often created for specific computing platforms.*

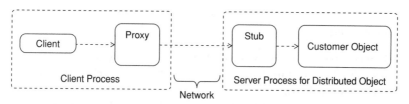

Figure 1.2 *Objects were frequently used in distributed scenarios. When a client invoked a method on the proxy's interface, the proxy would dispatch the call over the network to a remote stub, and the corresponding method on the distributed object would be invoked. As long as the client and distributed object used the same technologies, everything worked pretty well.*

ing. The compilation process for these technologies produced a binary library that included a *Remote Proxy* [GoF]. This contained the logic required to communicate with the remote object. As long as the client and distributed object used the same technologies, everything worked pretty well. However, these technologies had some drawbacks. They were rather complex for developers to implement, and the process used to serialize and deserialize objects was not standardized across vendor implementations. This meant that clients and objects created with different vendor toolkits often had problems talking to each other. Additionally, distributed objects often communicated over TCP ports that were not standardized across vendor implementations. More often than not, the selected ports were blocked by firewalls. To remedy the situation, IT administrators would configure the firewalls to permit traffic over the required ports. In some cases, a large number of ports had to be opened. Since hackers would have more network paths to exploit, network security was often compromised. If traffic was already permitted through the port, then it was often already provisioned for another purpose.

Distributed objects typically maintained state between client calls. This led to a number of problems that hindered scalability.

- Server memory utilization degraded with increased client load.

- Effective load-balancing techniques were more difficult to implement and manage because session state was often reserved for the client. The result was that subsequent requests were, by default, directed back to the server where the client's session had been established. This meant that the load for client requests would not be evenly distributed unless a sophisticated infrastructure (e.g., shared memory cache) was used to access the client's session from any server.

- The server had to implement a strategy to release the memory allocated for a specific client instance. In most cases, the server relied on the client to notify it when it was done. Unfortunately, if the client crashed, then the server memory allocated for the client might never be released.

In addition to these issues, if the process that maintained the client's session crashed, then the client's "work-in-progress" would be lost.

Why Use Web Services?

Web services make it relatively easy to reuse and share common logic with such diverse clients as mobile, desktop, and web applications. The broad reach of web services is possible because they rely on open standards that are ubiquitous, interoperable across different computing platforms, and independent of the underlying execution technologies. All web services, at the very least, use HTTP and leverage data-interchange standards like XML and JSON, and common media types. Beyond that, web services use HTTP in two distinct ways. Some use it as an application protocol to define standard service behaviors. Others simply use HTTP as a transport mechanism to convey data. Regardless, web services facilitate rapid application integration because, when compared to their predecessors, they tend to be much easier to learn and implement. Due to their inherent interoperability and simplicity, web services facilitate the creation of complex business processes through service composition. This is a practice in which compound services can be created by assembling simpler services into workflows.

Web services establish a layer of indirection that naturally insulates clients from the means used to fulfill their requests (see Figure 1.3). This makes it possible for clients and services to evolve somewhat independently as long as *breaking changes* do not occur on the service's public interface (for more on breaking changes, refer to the section What Causes Breaking Changes? in Chapter 7). A service owner may, for example, redesign a service to use an open source library rather than a custom library, all without having to alter the client.

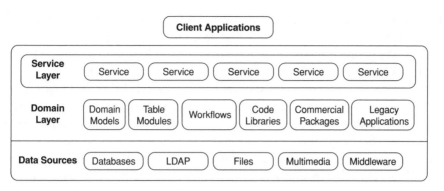

Figure 1.3 *Web services help to insulate clients from the logic used to fulfill their requests. They establish a natural layer of indirection that makes it possible for clients and domain entities (i.e., workflow logic, Table Modules, Domain Models [POEAA], etc.) to evolve independently.*

Web Service Considerations and Alternatives

While web services are appropriate in many scenarios, they shouldn't be used in every situation. Web services are "expensive" to call. Clients must **serialize** all input data to each web service (i.e., the request) as a stream of bytes and transmit this stream across computer processes (i.e., address spaces). The web service must **deserialize** this stream into a data format and structure it understands before executing. If the service provides a "complex type" as a response (i.e., something more than a simple HTTP status code), then the web service must serialize and transmit its response, and the client must deserialize the stream into a format and structure it understands. All of these activities take time. If the web service is located on a different machine from the client, then the time it takes to complete this work may be several orders of magnitude greater than the time required to complete a similar in-process call.

Possibly more important than the problem of latency is the fact that web service calls typically entail distributed communications. This means that client and service developers alike must be prepared to handle partial failures [Waldo, Wyant, Wollrath, Kendall]. A partial failure occurs when the client, service, or network itself fails while the others continue to function properly. Networks are inherently unreliable, and problems may arise for innumerable reasons. Connections will occasionally time out or be dropped. Servers will be overloaded from time to time, and as a result, they may not be able to receive or process all requests. Services may even crash while processing a request. Clients may crash too, in which case the service may have no way to return a response. Multiple strategies must therefore be used to detect and handle partial failures.

In light of these inherent risks, developers and architects should first explore the alternatives. In many cases, it may be better to create "service libraries" (e.g., JARs, .NET assemblies) that can be imported, called, and executed from within the client's process. If the client and service have been created for different platforms (e.g., Java, .NET), you may still use a variety of techniques that enable disparate clients and services to collaborate from within the same process. The client may, for example, be able to host the server's runtime engine, load the services into that environment, and invoke the target directly. To illustrate, a .NET client could host a Java Virtual Machine (JVM), load a Java library into the JVM, and communicate with the target classes through the Java Native Interface (JNI). You may also use third-party "bridging technologies." These options, however, can become quite complex and generally prolong the client's coupling to the service's technologies.

Web services should therefore be reserved for situations in which out-of-process and cross-machine calls "make sense." Here are a few examples of when this might occur.

- The client and service belong to different application domains and the "service functions" cannot be easily imported into the client.

- The client is a complex business process that incorporates functions from multiple application domains. The logical services are owned and managed by different organizations and change at different rates.

- The divide between the client and server is natural. The client may, for example, be a mobile or desktop application that uses common business functions.

Developers would be wise to consider alternatives to web services even when cross-machine calls seem justified.

- MOM (e.g., MSMQ, WebSphere MQ, Apache ActiveMQ, etc.) can be used to integrate applications. These technologies, however, are best reserved for use within a secured environment, far behind the corporate firewall. Furthermore, they require the adoption of an asynchronous communications style that forces all parties to tackle several new design challenges. MOM solutions often use proprietary technologies that are platform-specific. For complete coverage of this topic, see *Enterprise Integration Patterns:*

Designing, Building, and Deploying Messaging Solutions [EIP]. Web services often forward requests to MOM.

- A certain amount of overhead should be expected with HTTP due to the time it takes for clients and servers to establish connections. This added time may not be acceptable in certain high-performance/high-load scenarios. A connectionless protocol like User Datagram Protocol (UDP) can be a viable alternative for situations like these. The trade-off, however, is that data may be lost, duplicated, or received out of order.

- Most web service frameworks can be configured to stream data. This helps to minimize memory utilization on both the sender's and receiver's end because data doesn't have to be buffered. Response times are also minimized because the receiver can consume the data as it arrives rather than having to wait for the entire dataset to be transferred. However, this option is best used for the transfer of large documents or messages rather than for real-time delivery of large multimedia files like video and audio. For situations like these, protocols such as Real Time Streaming Protocol (RTSP, www.ietf.org/rfc/rfc2326.txt), Real Time Transport Protocol (RTP, http://tools.ietf.org/html/rfc3550), and Real Time Control Protocol (RTCP, http://tools.ietf.org/html/rfc3605) are usually more appropriate than HTTP.

Services and the Promise of Loose Coupling

Services are often described as being loosely coupled. However, the definitions for this term are varied and cover a broad array of concerns. Coupling is the degree to which some entity (e.g., client) depends on another entity. When the dependencies are many, the coupling is said to be high or tight (e.g., high coupling, tightly coupled). Conversely, when the dependencies are few, coupling is considered to be low or loose (e.g., low coupling, loosely coupled).

It is certainly true that web services can eliminate the client's dependencies on the underlying technologies used by a service. However, clients and services can never be completely decoupled. Some degree of coupling will always exist and is often necessary. The following list describes a few forms of coupling that service designers must consider.

- **Function coupling:** Clients expect services to consistently produce certain results given certain types of input under particular scenarios. Clients are therefore indirectly dependent on the logic implemented by web services. The client will most certainly be affected if this logic is implemented

What about
SOA?

incorrectly or is changed to produce results that are not in accordance with the client's expectations.

- **Data structure coupling:** Clients must understand the data structures that a service receives and returns, the data types used in these structures, and the character encodings (e.g., Unicode) used in messages. If a data structure provides links to related services, the client must know how to parse the structure for that information. The client may also need to know what HTTP status codes the service returns. Service developers must be careful to refrain from including platform-specific data types (e.g., dates) in data structures.

- **Temporal coupling:** A high degree of temporal coupling exists when a request must be processed as soon as it's received. The implication is that the systems (e.g., databases, legacy or packaged applications, etc.) behind the service must always be operational. Temporal coupling can be reduced if the time at which a request is processed can be deferred. Web services can achieve this outcome with the *Request/Acknowledge* pattern (59). Temporal coupling is also high if the client must block and wait for a response. Clients may use the *Asynchronous Response Handler* pattern (184) to reduce this form of coupling.

- **URI coupling:** Clients are often tightly coupled to service URIs. That is, they often either have a static URI for a service, or follow a simple set of rules to construct a service URI. Unfortunately, this can make it difficult for service owners to move or rename service URIs, or to adopt new patterns for URI construction since actions like these would likely cause clients to break. The following patterns can help to reduce the client's coupling to the service's URI and location: *Linked Service* (77), *Service Connector* (168), *Registry* (220), and *Virtual Service* (222).

What about SOA?

Many definitions for Service-Oriented Architecture (SOA) have been offered. Some see it as a technical style of architecture that provides the means to integrate disparate systems and expose reusable business functions. Others, however, take a much broader view:

> *A service-oriented architecture is a style of design that guides all aspects of creating and using business services throughout their lifecycle (from conception to retirement).* [Newcomer, Lomow, p. 13]

Service Oriented Architecture (SOA) is a paradigm for organizing and utilizing distributed capabilities that may be under the control of different ownership domains. [OASIS Ref Model]

These viewpoints suggest that SOA is a design paradigm or methodology wherein "business functions" are enumerated as services, organized into logical domains, and somehow managed over their lifetimes. While SOA can help business personnel articulate their needs in a way that comes more naturally than, say, object-oriented analysis, there are still many ways to implement services. This book focuses on several technical solutions that may be used to create a SOA.

Summary

By eliminating coupling to specific computing platforms, web services have helped us overcome one of the main impediments to software reuse. However, there are many ways to go about designing services, and developers are confronted with a long list of questions that must be resolved. This book will help you find the solutions that are most appropriate for your situation.

Chapter 2

Web Service API Styles

Introduction

In the book *Patterns of Enterprise Application Architecture*, Randy Stafford describes how a *Service Layer* [POEAA] can be used to create a distinct Application Programming Interface (API) for multiple client types. Stafford describes how this API is composed of a set of services that establish a clear boundary between one or more clients and a target domain or application. Web services are an effective way to provide exactly this type of boundary. By behaving like *Facades* [GoF], they also insulate clients from the underlying execution technologies. This makes it easier for various clients to reuse the service's logic. It also becomes easier for service owners to alter the domain logic as needed. Furthermore, web services provide a convenient point at which common behaviors like transaction management and client authentication may be applied.

This chapter explores the most common API design styles for web services, the merits of each, and their trade-offs. Table 2.1 provides an overview of these styles.

Table 2.1 *Web Service API Styles*

Pattern Name	Problem	Description
RPC API (18)	How can clients execute remote procedures over HTTP?	Define messages that identify the remote procedures to execute and also include a fixed set of elements that map directly into the parameters of remote procedures. Have the client send the message to a Uniform Resource Identifier (URI) designated for the procedure.

Continues

13

Design
Considerations
for Web Service
APIs

Table 2.1 *Web Service API Styles (continued)*

Pattern Name	Problem	Description
Message API (27)	How can clients send commands, notifications, or other information to remote systems over HTTP while avoiding direct coupling to remote procedures?	Define messages that are not derived from the signatures of remote procedures. These messages may carry information on specific topics, tasks to execute, and events. Have the client send the message to a designated URI. Once the message is received at the server, examine its contents to determine the correct procedure to execute.
Resource API (38)	How can a client manipulate data managed by a remote system, avoid direct coupling to remote procedures, and minimize the need for domain-specific APIs?	Assign all procedures, instances of domain data, and files a URI. Leverage HTTP as a complete application protocol to define standard service behaviors. Exchange information by taking advantage of standardized media types and status codes when possible.

The ramifications of selecting the right style for your needs cannot be underestimated. The decision you make regarding the service API style may be one of the most important decisions you will make. Once a style is chosen, it becomes very hard to migrate to one of the alternatives.

Design Considerations for Web Service APIs

Regardless of the chosen style, the following factors should be considered when designing service APIs.

- **Encapsulation:** Services should generally hide implementation details. The client should never know if, for example, the service accesses a database directly or uses a *Domain Model* [POEAA]. This helps to prevent clients from becoming directly coupled to the means used to fulfill requests. Additionally, service designers should consider the consequences of carrying domain model, database table, and stored procedure designs forward to the API. Such design practices cause clients to become directly coupled to internal entities. If the domain models and table designs ever need to change, then the client must change as well. It might be said that we are designing from the "bottom up" when we create APIs that simply make internal domain entities accessible to external clients. Service APIs should, in most cases, be designed from the "top down." This means that the architect should create an API that is driven by client needs, and this API should reflect the use cases required by the various client applications [re: *Consumer-Driven Contract* (250)]. APIs like these tend to hide internal entities fairly well. Consequently, they provide a level of indirection that enables internal entities to evolve or even be replaced while at the same time minimizing the impact on clients.

Design
Considerations
for Web Service
APIs

- **The Service Contract:** A Service Contract can be thought of as an agreement that specifies how clients and services may interact. Each API style has its own perspective on this concept. Regardless, all service APIs should be designed with an emphasis on what type of information needs to be exchanged, when such exchanges may occur, and at what rate. If the service designer focuses on these external obligations, the API design often arrives naturally. Developers should also consider what conditions must be true before the service can be called (i.e., the pre-conditions), and what should happen when the service completes (i.e., the post-conditions and expected service behaviors) [Meyer, Bertrand]. Nontechnical requirements (a.k.a. Quality of Service or QoS requirements) for matters such as client authentication, data privacy, service response time, hours of operation, and up-time (i.e., availability) should also be clarified. This information provides the context necessary to produce an API that meets the needs of its clients. Given this information, the developer can proceed to create the logic behind the external API.

    It is important to note that machine-readable contracts like WSDL can only capture the most basic information required to use a service. Indeed, information such as a detailed explanation of what the service really does, when to use it, how to prepare requests, and how to handle failures is often described through prose and in unit tests.

- **Autonomy:** Consistent and reliable outcomes are more likely when the service controls its own execution and has few dependencies on outside forces. One implication is that web service APIs should usually discourage or even prohibit distributed transactions (i.e., WS-Atomic Transactions). When web service APIs allow for distributed transactions, service autonomy is compromised because the outcome is partially determined by external entities (e.g., another service). Furthermore, distributed transactions tend to inhibit service scalability because the locks a service places on internal entities (e.g., database tables) are often held for inordinate periods of time. This is due, in part, to network latency, but may also be caused by other factors (e.g., another service enlisted in the transaction has dropped its connection, causing the entire transaction to hang). Compensation provides a reasonable, though imperfect, alternative to distributed transactions. It is frequently used when data is exchanged between business organizations, or when services take minutes, hours, days, weeks, or longer to complete. Web service developers can support compensation by providing pairs of services that function as logical inverses of each other. For example, a customer account management system may provide "debit" and "credit" services. If a debit to a customer's account must be reversed, the client may invoke the "credit service" to compensate for the debit. One must, however, recognize that the data shared between collaborating systems may not be completely synchronized.

• **Latency:** Service and client developers alike must keep in mind that the latency, or time it takes for a client to receive a response from web services, will be significantly higher than calling similar in-process functions, even when the service is located on the same machine. This is due to the fact that all requests must be serialized as a stream of bytes, transmitted across process boundaries, intercepted by a server process, deserialized on the receiving end, and dispatched to the appropriate handler. A similar process occurs when the service provides a response. The implication is that web service developers should create APIs that minimize the number of network round-trips required to get work done. Every attempt should be made to design messages and media types that carry all of the information required to complete a given use case. The downside is that this may result in "larger" data payloads being sent back and forth. Nonetheless, latency can usually be reduced when the service API favors the exchange of a few "chunky messages" versus a "chatty conversation" wherein several smaller messages must be exchanged to accomplish the same objective.

• **Partial failures:** Web service calls typically entail distributed communications wherein a local process (i.e., the client) attempts to call a remote process (i.e., the service) over a network connection. Clients must be prepared for services to fail, and vice versa, and each must be ready to handle situations in which the network fails or becomes saturated with traffic. Developers are far more likely to implement the necessary precautions (e.g., exception-handling blocks for communication errors, *Idempotent Retry* [206], etc.) when a clear distinction is made between local and remote processes. The *Message API* (27) and *Resource API* (38) styles tend to emphasize this distinction. In contrast, the *RPC API* style (18), especially when used in conjunction with a *Service Proxy* (168), attempts to provide the impression that a client is invoking a local procedure.

- **Binary message encoding of text-based data:** The information exchanged through *RPC APIs* (18) and *Message APIs* (27) is generally text-based. Nonetheless, this text-based information may be encoded as binary data before it is serialized as a stream of bytes and transmitted over the network. Binary encoding has significant advantages. Consider XML Infosets, which can be quite large. Binary encoding causes these payloads to be compressed, thus helping to conserve network bandwidth and reduce latency. Most web service frameworks enable developers to configure whether or not a service should use binary encoding. When binary encoding is selected, the framework will automatically convert text-based messages to binary data and back again. Of course, additional processing time is required on both the client and the server to encode and decode binary message payloads, but it is often worth it. The only way to really know is to measure total response time.

RPC API

A client application consumes or manipulates text-based information managed by a remote system.

▼

How can clients execute remote procedures over HTTP?

▲

It's not easy for clients to invoke remote software functions. They may establish connections to remote systems through "low-level" protocols like the BSD Socket API. However, developers that use these mechanisms must convert the data types defined on the remote computing platform to corresponding types on the local platform. This can be a daunting task because different platforms use different character encoding schemes (e.g., ASCII, EBCDIC, UTF-8, UTF-16, Endianness) to represent and store data types. Developers that work at this level must therefore understand how the remote platform encodes data and how it interprets any byte stream received.

Remoting technologies like CORBA and DCOM have made it much easier to share and use remote procedures. While they have abstracted away many lower-level concerns, issues with interoperability can arise when the parties use different technologies. For example, a distributed object exposed through CORBA cannot be easily accessed by a client running on the .NET platform, and vice versa. Third-party products may be used to bridge disparate platforms, but they tend to be expensive and complex. Additionally, the TCP ports used by different vendors aren't standardized, so network administrators must often open up nonstandard ports to allow external traffic through the firewall.

HTTP mitigates many of these issues because it enables clients and servers that run on different computing platforms to easily communicate by leveraging open standards. But how can clients use HTTP to execute remote procedures? One approach is to send messages that encapsulate the semantics for procedure invocation.

Define messages that identify the remote procedures to execute and also include a fixed set of elements that map directly into the parameters of remote procedures. Have the client send the message to a URI designated for the procedure.

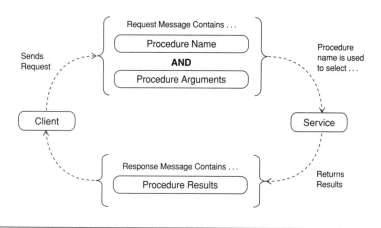

The core concept behind *RPC APIs* is the idea of a Remote Procedure Call (RPC). With RPC, the client sends a message to a remote server process and blocks while waiting for a response. The request message identifies the procedure to be executed, and also includes a fixed set of parameters that map directly to the parameters of the remote procedure. When a message arrives at the server, a server process inspects the message, invokes the procedure (i.e., service) whose name is found in the message, and maps the message parameters directly into the service's input arguments. These tasks are usually performed by service frameworks like JAX-WS and WCF. Once the service has been invoked, it may process the client's request and return a response. The client can then extract the results and resume execution.

This is the default service design style for many because it is relatively easy to understand and implement. Developer productivity can be attributed, in part, to the code generation capabilities of tools that come with popular frameworks like JAX-WS and WCF. These frameworks enable developers to create web services in languages like Java or C# without having to know much about structural formats (e.g., XML, JSON, etc.), encoding strategies (e.g., text versus binary, character encodings like UTF-8, etc.), or *Service Descriptors* (175) like WSDL. Frameworks like these make it possible for developers to expose class methods as web services by simply annotating methods with keywords. For frameworks that leverage XML, such annotation also enables the automatic generation of

XSDs that describe the service's input and output messages. For instance, if the name of an annotated class method is GetStockQuote, then the framework may generate XSDs that describe input and output messages named GetStockQuote and GetStockQuoteResponse, respectively. From this, one may infer that messages for *RPC APIs* are tightly coupled to the remote procedure (i.e., the service), and the client, through association, becomes coupled to the procedure as well.

There are two basic ways to define Service Contracts when following this API style. The most common approach uses the XML Schema Language to define reusable data types and messages, Web Services Description Language (WSDL) to provide *Service Descriptors* (175), and specifications like WS-Policy and WS-Security to define various rules on how the client should be authenticated, how data should be encrypted, and so forth. The second approach for RPC Service Contract definition includes the entire universe of non-XML approaches. This includes specifications like JSON-RPC, and a plethora of proprietary frameworks offered by various organizations, open source communities, and vendors.

Considerations

Service developers who implement RPC APIs should consider the following issues.

- **An inclination to create flat APIs:** Developers that use this style are often tempted to create service signatures that look like the signatures of normal class methods. These signatures often have long parameter lists that look like this:

```
@WebMethod(operationName = "ReserveRentalCar")
public RentalOptions ReserveRentalCar (
  @WebParam(name = "RentalCity")  String RentalCity,
  @WebParam(name = "PickupMonth") int PickupMonth,
  @WebParam(name = "PickupDay")   int PickupDay,
  @WebParam(name = "PickupYear")  int PickupYear,
  @WebParam(name = "ReturnMonth") int ReturnMonth,
  @WebParam(name = "ReturnDay")   int ReturnDay,
  @WebParam(name = "ReturnYear")  int ReturnYear,
  @WebParam(name = "RentalType")  String RentalType
)
{
  // implementation would appear here
}
```

The problem with this type of API is that it is inherently inflexible and fragile. Clients must send procedure arguments in an exact order, and if the need ever arises to add, remove, or reorder parameters, one can't avoid a breaking change. However, increased flexibility is possible if the service's signature is designed to only receive a *Single-Message Argument* (234). With this pattern, the service developer may refrain from imposing a strict element sequence and may instead design the message to contain optional or repeating elements.

- **Proxies and service descriptors:** Client applications typically use *Proxies* (168) to connect to services that use this style. The purpose of proxies is to make services easier to use by insulating the client from the network communications logic that interacts with the service. Rather than connecting directly to the service, clients select proxy methods whose names correspond to the remote procedures. From the client's perspective, it often looks like a local call. Instead, the proxy actually establishes a connection to the remote server and dispatches a message on behalf of the client. Proxies are typically generated by client-side tools capable of reading *Service Descriptors* (175). These artifacts describe how clients may call one or more services. The most common descriptor language for web services is WSDL. These must be synchronized to reflect the signatures of the services they describe. Therefore, if a change occurs on a service signature, then the descriptor must be updated (and vice versa). This implies that proxies must be updated whenever the descriptor changes. Figure 2.1 illustrates this relationship. While it is true that proxies must be regenerated whenever a breaking change occurs on the descriptor, there are a few occasions when a descriptor may change and the proxy won't need to be updated. For example, the service owner can add new operations to a WSDL port (or interface), and clients would only need to re-create their proxies if they wanted

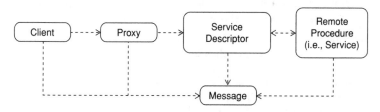

Figure 2.1 *Since a bidirectional dependency exists between* Service Descriptors *(175) and remote procedures, each must be regenerated when the other changes.* Proxies *(168) may also need to be re-created when the descriptor changes.*

to use those operations. (For more information on breaking changes, see the section What Causes Breaking Changes? in Chapter 7.)

- **Location transparency and proxies:** Another hallmark of RPC and *RPC APIs* is the concept of Location Transparency. Some interpret this principle to mean that the true location of a service should be completely hidden, and client developers should write roughly the same code to invoke local or remote procedures. The thought is that, if the client application is unaware of a service's location, then the service can be moved as the need arises. The implication, however, is that additional mechanisms must be used to help the client locate and connect to the service. One approach is to store the service's location in a configuration file or database table that is queried whenever a proxy method is invoked. For more coverage on this topic, please see the *Service Connector* pattern (168).

  Unfortunately, the application of this principle often obscures the ability of client developers to recognize distributed service interactions. The problem typically occurs when client developers use *Service Proxies* (168). In many cases, these proxies make it difficult for client developers to know when they're calling remote procedures. Consequently, they might not implement the necessary logic to handle network-related failures like lost connections, server crashes, and busy services. Fortunately, many developers have learned that the use of a proxy implies distributed communications, and that one must create exception-handling logic around the proxy to handle communication errors.

- **Achieving asynchrony:** Services with *RPC APIs* may use the *Request/ Acknowledge* (59) interaction pattern rather than the default *Request/ Response* pattern (54). With this pattern the request is not processed when it is received. Instead, the service forwards the message to an asynchronous background process and returns a simple acknowledgment to the client. By separating the receipt of the message from the time it is processed, the system is better able to handle unanticipated spikes in request load and can also better control the rate at which messages are processed. After a message has been received, it can be forwarded through a queue or saved to a database that is periodically polled by a background process.

- **How to avoid blocking:** Clients that use *RPC APIs* need not block after sending a message. Rather, they may use an *Asynchronous Response Handler* (184). This enables clients to perform other useful work while the request is being processed.

- **Binary encoding:** The information received or sent from *RPC APIs* may be encoded as binary data, thus causing the payloads to be compressed. This often conserves network bandwidth and helps to reduce latency. Most web service frameworks enable developers to configure whether or not a service should use binary encoding. When this option is selected, the framework will automatically convert binary requests to text-based data, and text-based responses to binary payloads. The downside is that additional processing time is required on both the client and the server to encode and decode these payloads. Developers should therefore measure the response time for each service with and without binary encoding to determine whether or not the additional compute time is justified.

Example: *Using JAX-WS to Create an RPC API in Java*

This example shows how a message uses a Document-Literal-Wrapped SOAP binding style to map parameters directly into a remote procedure. The code that follows shows a WSDL 1.1 port definition for a service that uses this binding. This port contains a single operation named GetFlightSchedules that receives a GetFlightSchedules message and returns a GetFlightSchedulesResponse message.

```
<wsdl:portType name="BargainAirServicePort">
  <wsdl:operation name="GetFlightSchedules">
    <wsdl:input message="GetFlightSchedules"/>
    <wsdl:output message="GetFlightSchedulesResponse"/>
  </wsdl:operation>
</wsdl:portType>
```

The definitions for the messages received and returned from the GetFlightSchedules operation are listed here.

```
<wsdl:message name="GetFlightSchedules">
  <wsdl:part name="parameters"
             element="tns:GetFlightSchedules"/>
</wsdl:message>
<wsdl:message name="GetFlightSchedulesResponse">
  <wsdl:part name="parameters"
             element=" tns: GetFlightSchedulesResponse"/>
</wsdl:message>
```

Each message contains a single "message part" whose name matches the name of the message. The GetFlightSchedules message part identifies a data structure that wraps the input parameters for the remote procedure of the same name. The GetFlightSchedulesResponse message part defines the structure for the response. The following listing shows the XSDs for these messages; the details of the TravelConstraints XSD have been omitted.

```
<xs:element name="GetFlightSchedules">          This is the procedure name
  <xs:complexType>
    <xs:sequence>
      <xs:element name="departConstraints"      This is an argument
                  type="TravelConstraints"/>
      <xs:element name="returnConstraints"      This is another argument
                  type="TravelConstraints"/>
    </xs:sequence>
  </xs:complexType>
</xs:element>


<xs:element name="GetFlightSchedulesResponse">
  <xs:complexType>
    <xs:sequence>
      <xs:element name="GetFlightSchedulesResult"
                  type="TravelOptions"          This is the response type
                  minOccurs="0" nillable="true" />
    </xs:sequence>
  </xs:complexType>
</xs:element>
```

The GetFlightSchedules data structure identifies two input arguments named departConstraints and returnConstraints. The GetFlightSchedulesResponse message identifies the operation's return type as being TravelOptions.

The Java code for the Service Endpoint Interface (SEI) that was generated from the WSDL listed above is shown below. This SEI exemplifies one part of the *Service Controller* pattern (85). Notice how the elements of the GetFlightSchedules document wrapper map directly into the parameters of this procedure.

```
@WebService(name="BargainAirServicePort",
    targetNamespace="http://www.acmeCorp.org/schemas",
    wsdlLocation="WEB-INF/wsdl/BargainAirService.wsdl")

public interface BargainAirServicePort{

    @WebMethod

    @WebResult(name="TravelOptions",
            targetNamespace="http://www.acmeCorp.org")

    @RequestWrapper(localName="GetFlightSchedules",
            targetNamespace="http://www.acmeCorp.org/Schemas",
            className="org.acmeCorp.GetFlightSchedules")
```

RPC API

```
@ResponseWrapper(localName="GetFlightSchedulesResponse",
        targetNamespace="http://www.acmeCorp.org/Schemas",
        className="org.acmeCorp.GetFlightSchedulesResponse")

public TravelOptions GetFlightSchedules(
        @WebParam(name="departConstraints" // argument 1
          targetNamespace="http://www.acmeCorp.org/Schemas")
        TravelConstraints departContraints,
        @WebParam(name="returnConstraints" // argument 2
          targetNamespace="http://www.acmeCorp.org/Schemas")
        TravelConstraints returnConstraints);
}
```

The implementation for the SEI is shown below.

```
@WebService(
    targetNamespace="http://www.acmeCorp.org/schemas",
    endpointInterface="org.acmeCorp.BargainAirServicePort")

public class BargainAirService implements BargainAirServicePort{

    @Resource
    WebServiceContext wscontext;

    public TravelOptions GetFlightSchedules(
            TravelConstraints departContraints,
            TravelConstraints returnConstraints){

        // implementation here

    }
}
```

A C# client that calls the service shown above might look similar to the code that follows. Notice that the client declares and instantiates a proxy; it then calls the proxy's Open method to establish a connection to the service. This makes it clear that a local object is not being used. The client instantiates and populates a request object, then invokes a remote procedure by selecting its name on the proxy.

```
BargainAirServiceClient proxy = new BargainAirServiceClient();

proxy.Open();

GetFlightSchedules request = new GetFlightSchedules();

// set departing and returning constraints here

GetFlightSchedulesResponse response =
                        proxy.GetFlightSchedules(request);
```

The HTTP POST command and SOAP message sent by the proxy may look something like this. These messages can get quite large, so the headers and other tangential data were eliminated to keep the example short.

```
POST /BargainAirService HTTP/1.1
Host: www.acmeCorp.org
Content-Type: application/soap+xml; charset="utf-8"
Content-Length: ####

<s:Envelope xmlns:s="http://www.w3.org/2003/05/soap-envelope">
  <s:Body>
    <GetFlightSchedules> <!-- This is the remote proc name -->
      <DepartConstraints>    <!-- This is argument 1 -->
        <StartCity>Boston</StartCity>
        <DestCity>San Francisco</DestCity>
        <Month>2</Month>
        <Day>22</Day>
        <Year>2011</Year>
        <Date>2011-02-22T00:00:00</Date>
      </DepartConstraints>
      <ReturnConstraints> <!-- This is argument 2 -->
        <StartCity>San Francisco</StartCity>
        <DestCity>Boston</DestCity>
        <Month>2</Month>
        <Day>24</Day>
        <Year>2011</Year>
        <Date>2011-02-24T00:00:00</Date>
      </ReturnConstraints>
      <MatchingFlights />
    </GetFlightSchedules>
  </s:Body>
</s:Envelope>
```

Note that the procedure name is usually identified in the SOAPAction and WS-Addressing headers as well. These are used by most web service frameworks to route the request to the correct web service handler. For more information, see the *Service Controller* pattern (85).

Message API

A client application consumes or manipulates text-based information managed by a remote system.

▼

How can clients send commands, notifications, or other information to remote systems over HTTP while avoiding direct coupling to remote procedures?

▲

Service APIs may be derived from the signatures of remote procedures. The service owner must, however, consider several issues that arise from such a strategy. If the signature of a procedure changes, then the web service API must change, and the client's code must be altered to accommodate that change as well. This may be acceptable if the service and client applications are managed by the same organization. However, such changes require careful planning, a significant degree of collaboration, and a concerted effort from all parties. If the clients and services are managed by different organizations or businesses, this approach could be impractical. This practice also assumes that either the service owner has the authority to define the data structures that are exchanged, or the clients will accept the message structures that are derived from their procedures. However, there are many occasions in which message design cannot be driven entirely by the service owner. This is especially true in large organizations or in scenarios where business partners exchange data. Service developers in situations like these need an API style that recognizes a common set of related messages, but does not tie those messages to specific procedures.

Message API

Define messages that are not derived from the signatures of remote procedures. These messages may carry information on specific topics, tasks to execute, and events. Have the client send the message to a designated URI. Once the message is received at the server, examine its contents to determine the correct procedure to execute.

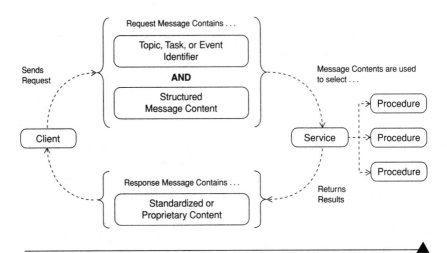

Services that have *Message APIs* (a.k.a. *Document APIs*) receive one or more self-descriptive message types at a given URI. The body of the message contains the data of primary interest. The message may optionally include headers. These may be used to convey "control information" like client authentication credentials, the expiration date of the request, and the URIs where errors should be sent. *Message APIs* often receive or send standardized message formats like SOAP; however, alternatives to SOAP and XML may also be used. *Message APIs* that use XML but eschew both SOAP and XSD are frequently called Plain Old XML (POX) services.

Clients use *Message APIs* by sending messages to a designated URI. Once the message is sent, the client may optionally block while waiting for a response. When a message arrives at the server, a web service deserializes and inspects the message, then selects an appropriate procedure (i.e., handler) to process the request. The web service therefore provides a layer of indirection by insulating the client from the actual handler (i.e., remote procedure). Once the handler has been invoked, it may process the client's request and return a response. The client can then extract the results and resume execution.

The name of this pattern is derived from the emphasis that is placed on message design. In the course of gathering requirements and designing a service

API, the parties identify logical messages they wish to exchange independent of any remote procedure. This approach is frequently used when external entities like industry consortiums drive requirements definition. The most common way to define messages is through the XML Schema Language. However, message structures may be defined through other means as well (e.g., Google's Protocol Buffers).

The web services are typically created once messages have been identified and designed. The API therefore provides a receiving endpoint, and the web service acts as a dispatcher. Clients generally send one of three message types. *Command Messages* [EIP] are used to ask the receiving system to carry out a specific task (e.g., process loan). *Event Messages* [EIP] notify the receiver about interesting events (e.g., inventory was depleted), and *Document Messages* [EIP] are like business documents (e.g., purchase orders). The information used to identify the message type may be found anywhere in the message. It could, for example, be the name of the message itself, the first element in the message body, or a parameter in the body. As you might expect, *Message APIs* provide results through messages as well. These messages may contain the actual results for the client request, or a simple acknowledgment that the request was received and is being processed. The return message might also contain detailed error information if a failure occurred during request processing. *Message APIs* that use SOAP, for example, often return SOAP Faults that are specialized messages for specific types of errors.

Service Contracts for *Message APIs* frequently use the XML Schema Language to define reusable data types and messages. They may optionally use WSDL to define *Service Descriptors* (175), and specifications like WS-Policy and WS-Security to define various rules on how clients should be authenticated, how data should be encrypted, and so forth. *Message APIs* may also define message structures through any one of the countless non-XML-based approaches offered by various organizations, open source communities, and vendors.

Considerations

Message API developers should consider the following issues.

- **Service descriptors and connectors:** *Message APIs* often employ *Service Descriptors* (175) to aid in the generation of code for client-side *Service Connectors* (168). The most common mechanism for service description is WSDL. This meta-language provides the means to define a set of related "service operations" that clients may use. These operations are grouped together into an abstract type (i.e., Port Type in WSDL 1.1 and Interface in WSDL 2.0). Each operation also identifies the relevant XSDs for input and output messages, and additional constraints (i.e., policies) for usage. Examples of policies include the requirements for client authentication and data encryption. Port/Interface types are then bound to a specific transport protocol like HTTP, and exposed at a specific URI. All together, these items define an explicit interface.

- **Delegation of work:** The logic used to process specific message types is often triggered by a *Command Invoker* (149). This pattern may be employed when the logic required to process a given document is sufficiently complicated. In many cases, it becomes easier to manage the message processing logic by separating it out from the receiving web service. One can also alter the web service to receive new messages at the same URI with little effort. An alternative to the *Command Invoker* is the *Workflow Connector* (156). This approach is used when the receipt of a message should trigger a complex or long-running process.

- **Achieving asynchrony:** Services that use *Message APIs* often use *Request/ Acknowledge* interactions (59) rather than the *Request/Response* pattern (54). With this pattern the request is not processed when it is received. Instead, the service forwards the message to an asynchronous background process and returns a simple acknowledgment to the client. By separating the receipt of the message from the time it is processed, the system is better able to handle unanticipated spikes in load and better control the rate at which messages are processed. After a message has been received, it can be forwarded through a queue or saved to a database that is periodically polled by the background process.

- **How to avoid blocking:** Clients that call these services may use an *Asynchronous Response Handler* (184) to avoid blocking after a message has been sent. This enables clients to perform other useful work while the request is being processed.

- **Late binding:** Responses from *Message APIs* often provide addresses to related services clients may use. For more information, see the *Linked Service* pattern (77).

- **Binary encoding of message payloads:** *Message APIs* are able to conserve network bandwidth and reduce latency by encoding the data they receive or send in binary. Web service developers can often configure whether or not binary encoding is used, in which case the framework will automatically convert binary requests to text-based data, and text-based responses to binary payloads. Some frameworks always transmit data in as binary. The downside of binary encoding is that additional processing time is required on both the client and the server to encode and decode message payloads. Developers should therefore measure the response time for each service with and without binary encoding to determine whether or not the additional compute time is justified.

Example: *A Message API That Uses SOAP and WSDL*

This example shows how a service that uses SOAP and WSDL can be used to implement the *Message API* pattern. The first part of this example shows the C# code used to implement the service. After walking through this code, the WSDL associated with the service implementation will be presented.

The first code snippet shows a *Service Controller* (85) written in C#. This class defines an abstract WSDL Port whose definition will be generated automatically at runtime by the WCF framework. Notice that this interface identifies two logical operations named Invoice and Contractor. While operations are often considered to be synonymous with procedures, these are named for the messages they receive. Notice that each operation receives a single message argument. This is one very subtle characteristic that differentiates *RPC APIs* (18) from *Message APIs*. While the former typically receives many arguments, those arguments aren't messages and may, in fact, be primitive data or complex types. In contrast, *Message APIs* that leverage WSDL are specifically designed to receive a single message argument.

```
[ServiceContract(Name = "Dropbox" )]
public interface IDropbox
{
  [OperationContract(Action = "http://acmeCorp.org/Dropbox/Invoice",
    IsOneWay = true)]
  void Invoice(InvoiceMessage invoice);

  [OperationContract(Action = "http://acmeCorp.org/Dropbox/Contractor",
    IsOneWay = true)]
  void Contractor(ContractorMessage contractor);
}
```

The class definition for the InvoiceMessage is shown below. Note that it only contains a single MessageBodyMember (i.e., WSDL Message Part). This is because

the WCF framework, by default, uses a Document-Literal-Wrapped SOAP
binding style.

```
[MessageContract(IsWrapped=false)]
public class InvoiceMessage
{
  [MessageBodyMember]
  public Invoice Invoice { get; set; }
}
```

The complex type used as the message part is shown in the following.

```
[DataContract(Name="Invoice")]
public class Invoice
{
  [DataMember(IsRequired=true,Order=1)]
  public int ContractorId { get; set; }

  [DataMember(IsRequired = true, Order = 2)]
  public string PurchaseOrder { get; set; }

  [DataMember(IsRequired = true, Order = 3)]
  public DateTime StartDate { get; set; }

  [DataMember(IsRequired = true, Order = 4)]
  public DateTime EndDate { get; set; }

  [DataMember(IsRequired = true, Order = 5)]
  public decimal Hours { get; set; }
}
```

A partial implementation for this service follows. Note that this class implements the IDropbox interface. Not only does this force the MessageService class to
implement all of the methods on that interface, but it also wires up communications between the WCF framework and the service implementation. The result
is that the methods on this class will be invoked when specific messages identified on the IDropbox interface are received.

```
public class MessageService : IDropbox
{
  void IDropbox.Invoice(InvoiceMessage invoice)
  {
    // select procedure to process message here
  }

  void IDropbox.Contractor(ContractorMessage contractor)
  {
    // select procedure to process message here
  }
}
```

Now let's turn our attention to the WSDL associated with the above code listings. The first WSDL listing shows the logical operations on the abstract WSDL port definition named DropBox. You should be able to see how these map back to the class methods identified previously.

```
<wsdl:portType name="Dropbox">
  <wsdl:operation name="Invoice">
    <wsdl:input wsaw:Action="http://acmeCorp.org/Dropbox/Invoice"
            name="InvoiceMessage" message="tns:InvoiceMessage"/>
  </wsdl:operation>

  <wsdl:operation name="Contractor">
    <wsdl:input wsaw:Action="http://acmeCorp.org/ContractorInfo"
       name="ContractorMessage" message="tns:ContractorMessage"/>
  </wsdl:operation>
</wsdl:portType>
```

The definition for InvoiceMessage is shown below. Note how this message has a single part that refers to a complex type named Invoice. The definition for the Invoice type and element follows the message definition.

```
<wsdl:message name="InvoiceMessage">
  <wsdl:part name="Invoice" element="tns:Invoice"/>
</wsdl:message>


<xs:complexType name="Invoice">
  <xs:sequence>
    <xs:element name="ContractorId" type="xs:int"/>
    <xs:element name="PurchaseOrder" nillable="true"
                type="xs:string"/>
    <xs:element name="StartDate" type="xs:dateTime"/>
    <xs:element name="EndDate" type="xs:dateTime"/>
    <xs:element name="Hours" type="xs:decimal"/>
  </xs:sequence>
</xs:complexType>

<xs:element name="Invoice" nillable="true" type="tns:Invoice"/>
```

Example: *A Message API That Doesn't Use WSDL*

This example shows how a *Message API* can be implemented without WSDL. This approach may be used with or without SOAP. The decision as to whether or not WSDL should be used often depends on whether you want to leverage WS* specifications like WS-Security or WS-ReliableMessaging.

The first code snippet shows an interface class written in C# for a service that will be deployed to the .NET/WCF framework. This class identifies the URI pattern used to intercept and route messages to a specific handler. In this case, the handler is ReceiveMessage, and the URI pattern is defined by UriTemplate. The RequestFormat annotation tells the WCF framework that the service expects an XML message. The ReceiveMessage operation indicates that it will receive any Stream of data. Therefore, a client may POST a message of virtually any structure to a service that implements this interface.

```
[ServiceContract]
public interface IDropbox
{
  [OperationContract]
  [WebInvoke(Method = "POST",
    RequestFormat = WebMessageFormat.Xml,
    UriTemplate = "/dropbox")]
  void ReceiveMessage(Stream stream);
}
```

The following code shows a rudimentary implementation for MessageService. Note how the ReceiveMessage method receives the byte stream identified in the IDropbox interface. Once this service is invoked, the MessageHelper class is called to convert the incoming stream to an array of bytes. The MessageHelper then uses the array to acquire the msgName (i.e., message name).

```
public class MessageService : IDropbox
{
  public void ReceiveMessage(Stream msgStream)
  {
    OutgoingWebResponseContext responseContext =
      WebOperationContext.Current.OutgoingResponse;

    try
    {
      byte[] msgBytes =
        MessageHelper.GetStreamAsByteArray(msgStream);

      string msgName = MessageHelper.GetRootNodeName(msgBytes);
```

After the message name has been retrieved, the service passes it to the GetMessageProcessor method of the MessageProcessors class. This method returns a class that knows how to process the current message. The details of how this occurs have been excluded. If a class to process the message cannot be found, a null value is returned, and this routine will exit with an HTTP code of 400.

```
      MsgProcessor processor =
        MessageProcessors.GetMessageProcessor(msgName);

      if (null == processor)
      {
```

```
    responseContext.StatusCode = HttpStatusCode.BadRequest;
    return;
}
```

At this point, we have an object that knows how to process the current message. The message service then calls methods on this processor to provide it the byte array for the message, and to invoke message processing. If all goes well, an HTTP code of 200 is returned. If an exception occurs, the service will log information about the error and return a code to indicate something went wrong.

```
    processor.SetByteArray(msgBytes);
    processor.Execute();

    responseContext.StatusCode = HttpStatusCode.OK;
}
catch (Exception ex)
{
    // would usually log error here

    responseContext.StatusCode =
        HttpStatusCode.InternalServerError;

    responseContext.StatusDescription =
        "Your message couldn't be processed. Please contact us";
    }
  }
}
```

The above snippets provided the code for the web service. The following code listings provide details on a few of the classes used by this service. The first class shown is MessageHelper. This class has two methods. The first method takes the incoming byte stream, copies it to a memory buffer, then returns a byte array that is used in subsequent operations. The second method, GetRootNodeName, is critical. This operation uses a fast and efficient XPathNavigator to retrieve the name of the root node in the incoming XML document. This is the key information that is used to determine which object should be called to process the message.

```
public class MessageHelper
{
  public static byte[] GetStreamAsByteArray(Stream stream)
  {
    MemoryStream memStream = new MemoryStream();
    stream.CopyTo(memStream);
    return memStream.ToArray();
  }
```

Message API

```
public static string GetRootNodeName(byte[] byteArray)
{
  XPathDocument doc =
    new XPathDocument(new MemoryStream(byteArray));

  XPathNavigator docNav = doc.CreateNavigator();

  docNav.MoveToRoot();
  docNav.MoveToFirstChild();

  return docNav.LocalName;
  }
}
```

All message processors that handle client requests are defined as child classes of an abstract class named MsgProcessor. This class keeps a byte array for the inbound message and has minimal logic that enables the child class to deserialize the message to a specific type for processing. The details of this class are shown below.

```
public abstract class MsgProcessor:ICloneable
{
  private byte[] msgAsByteArray = null;

  public MsgProcessor() {;}

  public abstract void Execute();

  public object Clone()
  {
    return this.MemberwiseClone();
  }

  public void SetByteArray(byte[] byteArray)
  {
    // Array is copied just in case this class is
    //   forwarded to another process

    msgAsByteArray = new byte[byteArray.Length];
    byteArray.CopyTo(msgAsByteArray, 0);
  }

  protected object DeserializeMessage(Type targetType)
  {
    DataContractSerializer deserializer =
      new DataContractSerializer(targetType);

    return deserializer.ReadObject(
        new MemoryStream(msgAsByteArray));
  }
}
```

This final class illustrates a concrete message processor class that inherits from the base MsgProcessor class. As you can see, the first thing it does is call the base class to deserialize the message to a type that it knows how to process. The design of the invoice message should be assumed to be the same as what was presented in the prior WSDL example. The remaining logic that processes the Invoice is omitted since that is tangential to this example.

```
public class InvoiceProcessor:MsgProcessor
{
  public override void Execute()
  {
    Invoice invoice =
      (Invoice)DeserializeMessage(typeof(Invoice));
    // logic to process the invoice message here
  }
}
```

Resource API

A client application consumes or manipulates text, images, documents, or other media files managed by a remote system.

Resource API

How can a client manipulate data managed by a remote system, avoid direct coupling to remote procedures, and minimize the need for domain-specific APIs?

HTTP makes it relatively easy for clients to reuse logic found in remote procedures while insulating them from underlying technologies. One way to invoke these procedures is to have clients send messages that not only identify the procedure to execute, but also include elements that correspond to the procedure's arguments. When these messages are received at the web server, an underlying service framework typically invokes a procedure given the name found in the message. Web services that use this API style are relatively easy to implement and use thanks to modern development tools, but the messages are tightly coupled to the procedures. If the need ever arises to add, change, or remove procedure arguments, then the related message structures must be updated, and the client's *Proxy* (168) will probably have to be regenerated as well. Developers could instead create a service API that doesn't tie messages directly to remote procedures. These messages identify a topic of interest, an event, or a logical command rather than a specific procedure name that is internal to the receiving system. When they are received at the web server, a service framework or custom code uses the content found in the message to determine what procedure should be invoked. While this loosens the dependencies between messages and remote procedures, other factors should be considered.

Many web services use messages to form their own domain-specific API. These messages incorporate common logical commands like Create, Read (i.e., Get), Update, or Delete. This CRUD approach, however, can lead to a proliferation of messages, even in relatively small problem domains. Consider, for example, a set of services that manages company and contact information. In this scenario, the client developer would have to use eight or more distinct messages, one for each combination of a domain entity (i.e., company or contact) and CRUD operation. An API like this might include messages like "Create-Company", "GetCompany", and so forth. The service owner would also have to create response messages for the various service outcomes (e.g., "Create-CompanyResp", "GetCompanyResp", etc.). Rather than creating a domain-specific API like this, one could leverage the standards defined in the HTTP specification.

Assign all procedures, instances of domain data, and files a URI. Leverage HTTP as a complete application protocol to define standard service behaviors. Exchange information by taking advantage of standardized media types and status codes when possible.

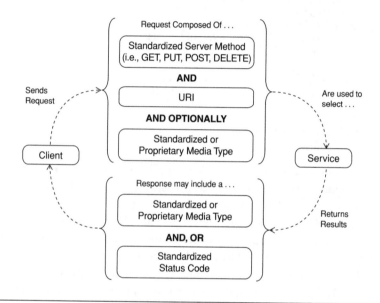

Services that have *Resource APIs* use the requested URI and HTTP server methods issued by the client along with the submitted or requested media type to determine the client's intent. These services often adhere to the principles of Representational State Transfer (REST), but not every *Resource API* can be considered RESTful. A quick review of the REST architectural style is therefore provided, to help you better understand this pattern.

Resource APIs, as the name implies, provide access to resources. A resource may be a text file, a media file (e.g., images, videos, audio), a specific row in a database table, a collection of related data (e.g., products), a logical transaction, a queue, a downloadable program, a business process (i.e., procedure)—almost anything. Clients manipulate the state of these resources through representations. A database table row may, for example, be represented as XHTML, XML, or JSON. Representations typically capture the current or intended state of a resource. A client that receives a representation from a service is usually acquiring the most recent state of that resource. When clients send representations to services, their intent is usually to alter the state of a resource. Resource state is transferred when representations are exchanged between clients and services. This is how the term "Representational State Transfer" was derived. A sample representation that uses Atom Publishing Protocol (APP) is shown below.

```
<?xml version="1.0" encoding="UTF-8"?>
<entry xmlns="http://www.w3.org/2005/Atom">
  <title>Flight Confirmation</title>
  <id>http://bargainair.net/itineraries/JK3N76</id>
  <summary>BargainAir flight confirmation - August 12, 2010
          - New York to London
  </summary>
  <link rel="depart-trip"
        href="http://bargainair.net/itineraries/JK3N76/123"/>
  <link rel="return-trip"
        href="http://bargainair.net/itineraries/JK3N76/456"/>
  <updated>2010-06-09T16:57:02Z</updated>
</entry>
```

This representation shows how a client application may discover the services that return detailed information about a customer's flights. In this case, information on the customer's departing and returning flights can be discovered by following the URIs found in the href tags. Each URI is a logical address to which clients may send requests in order to invoke a service. These URIs may be permanent or transitory addresses that clients may reference, save, bookmark, and share. A business person could, for example, easily forward the URIs shown above to her accounting department for approval. The following listing demonstrates how URIs can be used to identify other resources.

```
http://www.acmeCorp.org/products
```

```
http://www.acmeCorp.org/products/Model205
```

```
http://www.acmeCorp.org/orders/b0d891d1-3ddd-4d1a-a90f-b3138388ae1f
```

The first URI shows how a client might access a collection of products. The second references a specific product, and the last provides access to a customer's order. URI schemes like these make it easy to add new services for different resources as the need arises. For example, acmeCorp.org can easily add a new "store finder service" by receiving requests at a new URI.

A one-to-many relationship may exist between resources and URIs. That is, a resource may have many addresses; much like a person can have a proper name and nicknames. A single URI, however, should only be used to refer to a single logical resource. This provides clients the means to uniquely identify and access specific resources or resource collections. Since each URI refers to a single resource or collection of resources, services can often be added, changed, or removed with minimal impact to other services.

Service Contracts for *Resource APIs* are composed of an application protocol (i.e., HTTP), the media types consumed or produced by the service, the service's status codes, and the URIs and URI schemes or patterns used to identify resources.

Resource APIs use HTTP as an application protocol that prescribes several standard service behaviors. It is expected that all web servers implement the standard HTTP methods, and that all *Resource APIs* will respond to these methods as follows.

- PUT is used to create or update resources.

- GET is used to retrieve a resource representation.

- DELETE removes a resource.

- The behavior of POST varies. It can be used to create a subordinate of the target resource identified in the client's request, or for "nonstandard behaviors" where other methods aren't a good fit. For example, a mutual fund service might accept requests to execute functions like "Exchange Funds", "Sell X Shares", and "Sell Dollar Amount" through POST. This method can also be used as a workaround when PUT and DELETE are disabled on the web server or blocked at the firewall. In this situation, the behaviors that would normally be carried out by other methods are tunneled through POST. Many REST advocates argue against tunneling through POST since it tends to obfuscate the purpose of the request. POSTed requests also can't be cached by intermediaries.

- The OPTIONS verb may be used to discover what HTTP methods are supported at the target URI.

- HEAD is used to acquire metadata about the media types exchanged at a URI. It is similar to GET except that a representation is not returned.

- While the core methods are static, extensions to HTTP have been added (e.g., WebDAV).

Resource APIs should respond to the methods listed above in the prescribed manner. So, if a client issues a GET to acmeCorp.org/products, it should expect the service to execute a Get Products function. Since the semantics are predetermined by HTTP, clients don't have to learn a specialized API. However, they must still know what methods may be used with each URI and when to use each method. Additionally, it's still up to the service developer to implement the function according to the standards. Since the standard behaviors of PUT, GET, and DELETE map roughly to the CRUD paradigm, some believe that *Resource APIs* should only be used for CRUD use cases. This, however, is an incorrect assessment because POST can be used to execute behaviors that don't map well to CRUD.

Resource API

The HTTP specification also identifies which methods should be "safe" and which should be "idempotent." Safe operations are supposed to have no side effects. That is, they should not trigger write operations (i.e., creates, updates, or deletes). GET, HEAD, and OPTIONS are supposed to be implemented as safe operations. Idempotence means that no matter how many times a procedure is invoked with the same data, the same results should occur. GET, HEAD, PUT, DELETE, and OPTIONS are idempotent. POST, on the other hand, is not. Therefore, if a client repeatedly POSTs contact information to the same URI one should expect that information will be written each time. There are times when POST should exhibit idempotent behavior. For example, if a client sends the same order over and over again, the client shouldn't have to worry about duplicate orders. This means that the service must differentiate one POST from another. The easiest approach is to have the client insert a unique key (i.e., identifier) into the request that is examined by the service before executing its main logic. If the service finds that it has already processed a request with the identifier, it can reject the new request. The problem is ensuring that these identifiers will indeed be unique. Another approach is to have the client query a service to retrieve a unique URI that may be used exclusively for the subsequent POST. This pattern is known as *Post-Once-Exactly* [Nottingham, Marc].

Resource APIs usually take advantage of standard HTTP status codes as a mechanism to provide results to the client. For example, rather than returning an XML message, the service could return an HTTP code of 200 to indicate a request has succeeded. If a resource has moved, the service could return a 301 code, and if the client sends a malformed message, the service might return a 400 error code to inform the client that their request isn't understood and can't be processed. A long list of codes that cover common scenarios may be leveraged (re: www.w3.org/Protocols/rfc2616/rfc2616-sec10.html). These codes enable clients and services to communicate in a standard way, and can also help to optimize network utilization because minimal data is returned to the client.

The media types consumed or produced by the service are the most explicit part of a *Resource API* contract. These define the required data structures (i.e., representations using formats like XML or JSON), character encodings (e.g., Unicode, ASCII), rules for parsing data, and standards for linking to other resources. Media types can be altered or extended as long as these data structures, character encodings, rules for parsing, and standards for linking don't incur breaking changes in clients (for more on breaking changes, see the section What Causes Breaking Changes? in Chapter 7). This means that services that use this API style shouldn't suddenly switch to using types that aren't understood by their clients. Indeed, unilateral changes cannot be allowed in "enterprise business applications" where changes must generally be coordinated. Therefore, clients must have foreknowledge of the service's media types and must also know how to process them. All parties should also leverage standardized types (e.g., MIMEs) or use common vocabularies (e.g., Atom Publishing Protocol, Microformats) when possible. However, if existing standardized types or vocabularies cannot be used, then the parties may develop their own proprietary types and vocabularies. Of course, this may limit the audience for the service.

Not every client will understand the media types used by a service. Some clients must delegate the handling of specific media types to specialized agents. A service could, for example, wrap a representation in an "execution engine" (e.g., Java applet, JavaScript) that the client is able to host and run. Other media types may require the use of a plug-in that has specific knowledge of the media type's processing model. In this case, the client must have installed the plug-in and have granted it appropriate execution privileges.

Considerations

Developers who create Resource APIs should consider the following issues.

- **Use with disparate clients:** *Resource APIs* are a great choice when you have a wide mix of clients. Web browsers, feed readers, syndication services, web aggregators, microblogs, mashups, AJAX controls, and mobile applications are all natural clients for this style. This API style can also be used in enterprise integration and workflow scenarios.

  Resource APIs are especially effective when large documents and messages or binary files must be exchanged. The advantage is that media types like these need not be wrapped in message envelopes that require clients and services to use additional protocols (e.g., like the Message Transmission Optimization Mechanism or MTOM) to attach or detach the payload to or from the message.

- **Addressability:** Resource APIs make it easy for clients to save and share links to services. However, service owners must first decide whether or not data should be directly addressable. The problem is that URIs often provide malicious users with clues on how to mine an organization for information.

These "hackable" URIs make it easy for anyone to understand the meaning of each URI segment, and to replace the content of specific segments in an attempt to gain access to information that perhaps he shouldn't see. A URI may, for example, include customer account numbers as URI segments. Such schemes are easy to exploit. The service owner could prevent mischievous users from hacking these URIs by replacing simple account numbers with meaningless UUIDs. This, however, is not enough. Service owners should always implement the appropriate authentication and authorization logic to confirm the identity of the caller and to constrain what each caller can do. Nevertheless, some may consider direct resource addressability to be too much of a security risk, even when the proper authentication and authorization protections have been put into place. The alternative is to funnel all requests through a *Message API* (27) or *RPC API* (18).

- **Code generation of service connectors:** Client developers that use *Resource APIs* often can't take advantage of code generation tools. This is partially due to the fact that most *Resource API* designers prefer not to offer *Service Descriptors* (175). For those who appreciate code generation of client-side *Service Connectors* (168), services that have *Message APIs* (27) or *RPC APIs* (18) may be a better option.

- **Achieving asynchrony:** Resource-oriented services typically use the *Request/Response* pattern (54), but can also use the *Request/Acknowledge* interaction pattern (59). With this pattern the request is not processed when it is received. Instead, the service forwards the request to an asynchronous background process and returns an acknowledgment (i.e., HTTP code 202). By separating the message receipt from the time it is processed, the system is better able to handle unanticipated spikes in load and control the rate at which requests are processed.

- **How to avoid blocking:** Clients that use this API style need not block after sending a message. Rather, they may use an *Asynchronous Response Handler* (184) to enable the client to perform other useful work as soon as a message is sent.

- **Ability to support client preferences:** *Resource APIs* often provide multiple representations of the same logical resource. Rather than using a different URI for each, you can use *Media Type Negotiation* (70) to enable clients to indicate their preferences.

- **Late binding:** Once a service has processed a request, clients often need to call additional services in specific sequences. For example, a client that calls an "Order Creation" service will frequently call "Order Update", "Order Cancel", and "Order Status" services thereafter. The *Linked Service* pattern (77) enables clients to discover related services that may be called after receiving a service response.

- **Ability to leverage commodity caching technologies:** This API style leverages commodity caching technologies designed specifically with HTTP in mind. If, for example, a client requests a product that hasn't changed within the past day, and information on that product can be found in a Reverse Proxy, then the cached representation will be returned and service execution can be bypassed. This reduces the load on the Origin Server, especially in cases where the service would have queried a database or performed a CPU- or memory-intensive computation. *Resource APIs* are therefore well suited for "read scenarios." Clients can also implement caches that may be checked for matching representations before sending messages to services. Figure 2.2 illustrates the possibilities.

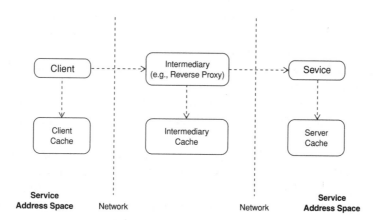

Figure 2.2 *Representations from* Resource APIs *can be easily served up from client, intermediary, and server caches. Whenever a representation can be provided from a cache close to the client, associated performance costs related to network latency can be avoided, and server loads can be minimized.*

- **Resource APIs and REST:** Earlier in this pattern I said that *Resource APIs* often adhere to the principles of REST, but not every *Resource API* can be considered RESTful. REST is an architectural style defined by several constraints [Fielding]. These include the following.

  - **Client/server:** All web services, regardless of the API, meet this constraint.
  - **Stateless:** Not every *Resource API* is stateless. Some developers are less concerned about super scalability and opt to create web services that maintain client state across multiple calls. For more information, see the section Design Considerations for Web Service Implementation in Chapter 5.
  - **Cacheable responses:** Most *Resource APIs* can leverage commodity caching technologies. Whether you should or shouldn't cache response data is another discussion altogether. It should be noted that responses from *RPC APIs* (18) and *Message APIs* (27) can also be cached by intermediaries, but specialized infrastructures must often be used.
  - **Uniform interface:** This is a fairly complex constraint. It suggests that a uniform interface be used between all components (i.e., clients, intermediaries, and servers). For *Resource APIs,* this uniform interface is defined through the HTTP specification. REST practitioners suggest that *Resource APIs* must use the server methods (i.e., GET, PUT, POST, DELETE) exactly as prescribed by the specification. Therefore, an API that relies on POST for all logical operations is not RESTful.

    This constraint also includes four architectural constraints. The first is that all resources must be uniquely identified. This occurs through URIs. The second and third subconstraints state that resources should be manipulated through representations, and that messages must be self-descriptive. *Resource APIs* usually meet these requirements. The last constraint says that hypermedia should be the engine of application state. In short, this means that hyperlinks should be used to guide client applications through various workflow state transitions. Many *Resource APIs* do not meet this requirement. For more information on this topic, see the *Linked Services* pattern (77).
  - **Layered system:** All web services, regardless of the API style, meet this constraint if we look at them from the perspective of the Open Systems Interconnection (OSI) Model.
  - **Code on demand:** This constraint states that client applications can be extended if they are allowed to download and execute scripts or plug-ins that support the media type provided by the service. Adherence to this constraint is therefore determined by the client rather than the API.

Resource API

Example: *A Resource API Implemented in Java and JAX-RS*

This example shows a partial implementation of a *Resource API* for music queries. The class named `MusicGenreController` is a *Service Controller* (85) that maps client requests to a specific request handler. This handler, named `GetArtistsInGenre`, accepts a music genre and the starting characters of an artist's name as input. The controller uses the `MusicSearch` *Command* [GoF] to execute a search for artists. The `Artists` *Data Transfer Object* (94) produces a JSON representation that is returned to the client.

```java
@Path("/genre")
public class MusicGenreController {

  private String NEXT_URI =
    "http://www.acmeCorp.org/MusicService/artists";

  @GET
  @Path("/{genreName}/{artistNameStartsWith}")
  @ProduceMime("application/json")

  public JAXBElement<Artists> GetArtistsInGenre(
      @PathParam("genreName")             String genreName,
      @PathParam("artistNameStartsWith") String startsWith){

    MusicSearch search = new MusicSearch(NEXT_URI);

    Artists artists =
      search.getArtists(genreName, startsWith);

    return new JAXBElement<Artists>(
      new QName("Artists"), Artists.class, artists);
  }
}
```

This service enables clients to issue `GET` requests that look like this:

```
GET /MusicService/artists/genre/rock/roll HTTP/1.1
Host: acmeCorp.org
```

The representation for this resource might look something like this:

```
{"@StartsWith":"roll","@Genre":"rock",
"Artist":
[
{"Name":"Rolling Stones",
"URI":"http://www.acmeCorp.org/MusicService/artists/Rolling&Stones"},
{"Name":"Rollins Band",
"URI":"http://www.acmeCorp.org/MusicService/artists/Rollins&Band"}
]}
```

Example: *Procedure Invocation*

Flickr, the popular image and video hosting web site, provides several APIs (re: www.flickr.com/services/api/). The following are examples of *Resource APIs* that enable clients to upload or replace standard binary photos.

```
http://api.flickr.com/services/upload/
```

```
http://api.flickr.com/services/replace/
```

Clients can also invoke procedures by issuing an HTTP GET or POST to URIs that look like this:

```
http://api.flickr.com/services/rest/?method=X&arg1=Y
```

This cannot be considered a RESTFul API because it doesn't utilize the uniform interface of HTTP. In other words, a client could invoke an operation that has side effects (e.g., a routine that writes to a database) without using PUT or DELETE. Regardless, this API provides a simple way for client developers to execute procedures. It's interesting to note that a specific invocation of a procedure, inclusive of its arguments (as specified by the query strings), can be saved or bookmarked.

Example: *Conditional Queries and Updates*

Clients can often help to minimize latency by specifying that representations should only be returned if something has changed recently. Clients may, for example, use standard HTTP header fields like If-Modified-Since to tell the service to only return a response if the requested entity was modified after the time specified. Here's an example of a client request:

```
GET /products/pricelist HTTP/1.1
Host: acmeCorp.org
If-Modified-Since: Fri, 30 Sep 2010 18:00:00 GMT
```

In this case, the service should only return a representation if the price list has changed since the date indicated in the If-Modified-Since header. If the resource has not been modified, the service may return an HTTP code of 304 to indicate that nothing has changed. This helps to optimize network bandwidth because a full representation isn't sent to the client. However, server load may not be significantly reduced because the service must still execute the necessary logic to retrieve the data and evaluate whether the resource has changed since the date specified in the client's header.

Resource API

The service owner has several options to reduce server load. One option is to use the *Service Interceptor* pattern (195). An inbound interceptor may, for example, be configured to check to see if the requested data can be found in a distributed memory cache that is shared across web servers. If the requested information can be found in this cache, then the information may be returned directly from the interceptor, and the request handler will not be called. Server utilization is optimized somewhat because the handler that would have presumably queried the database and formatted a response is not executed. However, the server still receives the request and, as a result, its load is higher than it might otherwise be. Server load can be reduced by configuring Reverse Proxies to cache responses. In this case, the proxy evaluates the client's criterion against its cache and will return a representation if the criterion is met. Regardless of the caching approach, the service owner must determine how long data may be kept in any cache before it is considered stale.

The Lost-Update Problem can be prevented through a similar conditional statement.

```
PUT /products/pricelist/123 HTTP/1.1
Host: acmeCorp.org
If-Unmodified-Since: Fri, 30 Sep 2011 18:00:00 GMT
```

If requests are sent directly to a service that has no interceptors (including Reverse Proxies), then the request will only be processed if the service determines that the resource has not been modified since the date provided in the client's request. Otherwise, the service will return a 412 status code to indicate that a "precondition" has failed. In this case, the precondition is the modification date. Again, server load can be reduced by using *Service Interceptors* (195) that leverage distributed caches, or with Reverse Proxies.

Chapter 3

Client-Service Interactions

Introduction

All web services must be designed with a particular interaction style in mind.
That is, the developer must consider how a service and its clients will communicate. This chapter presents the most fundamental design patterns that are used
for all web services, regardless of the service's API style (i.e., Message, RPC, or
Resource). Given an understanding of these patterns, one may combine them in
many ways to create complex conversations in which multiple parties exchange
information about a particular topic over short or extended periods of time.
However, before we can approach these patterns, a familiarity with a few concepts must be established.

The use of web services indicates a Client-Server model of distributed computing. In this model, a client program (a.k.a. Requestor, Service Consumer,
Message Sender) sends a request to a server program (a.k.a. Service, Service
Provider, Message Receiver). The client program may have a user interface, or it
may run without user intervention as an unattended background process.
Examples of the latter include Unix daemons and Windows services. Of course,
server programs are always implemented as background processes. When a
server receives a request, it may process that request in its entirety or forward it
to another server. The server may or may not provide a response.

The most basic way clients can communicate with web services is through
point-to-point connections. In other words, the client connects directly to the
service. Once the client has established a connection, the parties may begin to
exchange data. Clients should generally use a single connection for multiple
data exchanges. This helps to minimize the latency associated with establishing
and tearing down the connections. Either party may terminate the connection

51

at any time. Developers must remember that connections may also be dropped due to network disturbances or server faults.

Regardless of what it looks like from the developer's perspective, network traffic is typically routed through intermediaries. A firewall, for example, is usually positioned between public networks and corporate servers. These can be configured to block clients that either don't provide the proper credentials (e.g., X.509 certificates) or don't originate from white-listed (i.e., approved) domains. Reverse proxies are often the next intermediary to intercept traffic. They can be used to balance the load across a web server farm, and are frequently used to manage "perimeter caches" as well. To this end, these intermediaries can be configured to intercept all client requests and check a cache to see if a matching response can be found. If a recent response can be found in the cache, it is returned from the proxy server, thereby avoiding a trip to the web server and reducing its load.

HTTP is a connection-oriented protocol that requires the target server to be available at the time a client sends a request. It is also synchronous because the client's request must be processed, to some extent, when it arrives. The client has a similar time dependency and usually waits for the server to provide a response. These factors illustrate a potential challenge for web services. Developers and architects must ensure high availability for the web servers and the underlying systems (e.g., databases) used by the services, and must also allocate sufficient system capacity (i.e., CPU, memory, internal network bandwidth, etc.) to handle the normal client load and unanticipated spikes in load. The types of client-service interactions that are adopted have a significant influence on system availability and scalability.

This chapter presents the foundational patterns upon which all client-service conversations are built. We'll review synchronous exchanges, and we'll see how web services can be used in asynchronous conversations as well. We'll look at how the data structures that are exchanged can be negotiated, and we'll see how service addresses can be dynamically discovered at runtime. These patterns are previewed in Table 3.1.

Table 3.1 *Client-Service Interaction Patterns*

Pattern Name	Problem	Description
Request/Response (54)	What's the simplest way for a web service to process a request and provide a result?	Process requests when they're received and return results over the same client connection.
Request/Acknowledge (59)	How can a web service safeguard systems from spikes in request load and ensure that requests are processed even when the underlying systems are unavailable?	When a service receives a request, forward it to a background process, then return an acknowledgment containing a unique request identifier.
Media Type Negotiation (70)	How can a web service provide multiple representations of the same logical resource while minimizing the number of distinct URIs for that resource?	Allow clients to indicate one or more media type preferences in HTTP request headers. Send requests to services capable of producing responses in the desired format.
Linked Service (77)	Once a service has processed a request, how can a client discover the related services that may be called, and also be insulated from changing service locations and URI patterns?	Only publish the addresses of a few root web services. Include the addresses of related services in each response. Let clients parse responses to discover subsequent service URIs.

Client-Service Interactions

These patterns may be combined in many ways to create complex conversations that involve multiple data exchanges. In other words, they may be used to create interactions that include two or more parties where the roles of client and server shift based on which system initiates a given exchange. A client may, for example, initiate a conversation in which a request is sent to a service. The service might then become the client by sending a request back to the initiator to get more information. The flow of such conversations is frequently defined in workflows, which may be triggered when a service uses a *Workflow Connector* (156).

Request/Response

A client uses a service to execute a business task, provide access to files or documents, or perform generic functions like authentication or logging. The request must be processed immediately.

Request/
Response

What's the simplest way for a web service to process a request and provide a result?

When a client uses a service, it usually wants the service to carry out its orders immediately. If, for example, a traveler clicks on a link for the current weather conditions in Munich, the intent is to see that information now. If a job seeker uses a service to find local job openings, the goal is to see a listing after the query is sent. In both of these scenarios, the service must provide an immediate response to a specific client instance.

These are examples of the most basic type of client-service interaction. However, as trivial as it may seem, the act of invoking a remote service is far more involved than calling a local method. Information must be sent from the client process to the service process and back again to the client. Information may also need to be returned to a specific client thread. There are, of course, many ways to do these things. The simplest approach that can work should generally be considered first. How can a service provide immediate results to a client with minimal complexity?

Process requests when they're received and return results over the same client connection.

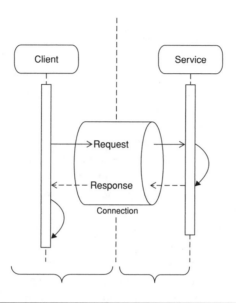

Request/Response is the most basic and common of the client-service interaction patterns. It's easy to understand, and is the default pattern used by web service frameworks and related APIs. It is used when the client must have an immediate response or wants the service to complete a task without delay. *Request/Response* begins when the client establishes a connection to the service. Once a connection has been established, the client sends its request and waits for a response. The service processes the request as soon as it is received and returns a response over the same connection. This sequence of client-service activities is considered to be synchronous because the activities occur in a coordinated and strictly ordered sequence. Once the client submits a request, it cannot continue until the service provides a response. It is often assumed that these activities will complete within a few seconds.

Considerations

The following issues should be considered before selecting a *Request/Response* interaction style.

Request/
Response

- **Temporal coupling:** In this pattern, the client generally assumes that the service can always fulfill a request when it is received, and that a response will be returned once the request has been processed. The implication is that the underlying systems used by the service must always be operational. If the service or systems it uses have crashed or have been brought down for planned maintenance, then the client's request may be rejected. This highlights the effect of temporal coupling, or the dependency on timing, in this interaction. Since requests must be processed immediately and responses returned without delay, temporal coupling is high. If these time constraints can be loosened, then the risks associated with temporal coupling can be mitigated.

    Problems in meeting the client's expectations for a timely response can occur even when all of the systems used by the service are operational. Since this pattern requires requests to be processed right away, a large volume of concurrent requests could overwhelm the system's capacity. Service architects must therefore understand the typical workload of the service and scale the servers, databases, and network resources accordingly to handle the expected loads. This may include "scaling up" by adding additional processors or memory to servers, or "scaling out" by adding additional servers to a cluster.

    One may need to migrate away from *Request/Response* in order to mitigate the aforementioned risks. Availability and scalability issues can be addressed through patterns like *Request/Acknowledge/Poll* (62) or *Request/Acknowledge/Callback* (63). Both of these separate in time the receipt of the request, the processing of the request, and the delivery of the response. The former enables the client to submit a request and poll for a response at its leisure. The latter requires the client to provide its own service that receives callback messages. The downside with these patterns is that they are much more complex to implement and debug than is *Request/Response*.

    Temporal coupling has other implications too. If the request takes more than a few seconds to process, the client's connection may time out, and the response will be lost. The reasons for why this might occur are numerous. The input data may incur activity that is compute- or I/O-intensive.

Sometimes the service can be refactored for greater efficiency, and at other times performance cannot be improved. High levels of network traffic can also cause responses to be delayed. *Request/Response* should therefore only be used when the average time to process a request and return a response is "relatively short" and the client is designed to tolerate lost responses. Otherwise, one should consider using the previously named patterns.

Request/
Response

- **Client-side blocking:** By default, clients of *Request/Response* services block and wait for responses. The time the client spends waiting may be better spent working on other things. Fortunately, the client can overcome this obstacle by using an *Asynchronous Response Handler* (184). This enables the client to dispatch requests and receive responses on an alternative thread apart from the "main client thread." The client may then attend to other work on the main thread while the request is being processed. Unfortunately, the connection could still time out, in which case the response may be lost.

- **Intermediaries:** Regardless of the fact that *Request/Response* involves a point-to-point connection between a client and service, intermediaries can be positioned between the two. Proxy servers, for example, may be used to cache query results for *Resource APIs* (38). When a request passes through a proxy, the proxy can check to see if the requested data can be found in its cache. Data is returned from the cache rather than the service if it fulfills the client's query. Firewalls are another type of intermediary. These are used to block or filter network traffic and check client credentials. One may, for example, define a firewall rule to check for the presence of an X.509 certificate attached to a request. If the certificate is found, then the request will be forwarded to the service; otherwise, it is blocked.

- **Request/Response is not RPC:** Some equate *Request/Response* with Remote Procedure Calls (RPCs). While they are similar in some ways, there are some important differences. With classic RPC technologies like CORBA and DCOM, the client usually waits for a response after the remote procedure is invoked. Clients that use *Request/Response* services don't have to wait. Instead, they may leverage *Asynchronous Response Handlers* (184) as was explained above. RPC protocols also require clients to submit a fixed set of parameters. However, neither *Resource APIs* (38) nor *Message APIs* (27) make this stipulation, and both of these can use *Request/Response*.

Example: *An RPC API That Uses the Request/Response Pattern*

The following C# code shows a service that uses *Request/Response*. The class FlightChecker encapsulates the flight search algorithms.

```csharp
[ServiceContractAttribute]
public interface IBargainAirService
{
  [OperationContractAttribute]
  [FaultContract(typeof(SafeFault))]
  TravelOptionsMessage GetFlightSchedules(
                          TravelOptionsMessage request);
}

public class BargainAirService : IBargainAirService
{
  public TravelOptionsMessage GetFlightSchedules(
                          TravelOptionsMessage request)
  {
    TravelOptionsMessage response = null;

    FlightChecker checker = new FlightChecker(
                                request.DepartConstraints,
                                request.ReturnConstraints);

    response.MatchingFlights = checker.GetMatchingFlights( );

    return response;
  }
}
```

This service has very little logic of its own. Its primary responsibility is to provide a publicly addressable endpoint that clients may call, to select the class that fulfills the client's request, and to return a response. This demonstrates a clear separation of responsibilities (i.e., separation of concerns).

A Java client for this service is shown below. Notice that the client waits for a response when it calls getFlightSchedules.

```java
BargainAirService proxy = new BargainAirService();

BargainAir port = proxy.getBargainAirPort();

TravelOptionsMessage request = new TravelOptionsMessage();

// populate request here

TravelOptionsMessage response = port.getFlightSchedules(request);

// do something with the response message
```

Request/Acknowledge

A client would like to manipulate a file or document, launch a business task, or notify a system about an interesting event. Requests don't need to be processed right away. If a response is required, it doesn't need to be delivered as soon as the request has been processed.

How can a web service safeguard systems from spikes in request load and ensure that requests are processed even when the underlying systems are unavailable?

A key consideration in the design of any web service is the degree of temporal coupling that should exist between the client and service. Temporal coupling is considered to be relatively high when the request must be processed as soon as it's received. The implication is that the systems (e.g., databases, legacy or packaged applications, etc.) behind the service must always be operational. If systems have been taken offline, perhaps for maintenance reasons, then client requests will be rejected. High temporal coupling also leaves systems vulnerable to the effect of unanticipated spikes in request load. Since the capacity of a system (i.e., memory, CPU, disk, network bandwidth, number of database connections) is usually based on average loads, a spike can cause excessive resource utilization leading to systemic failures.

Temporal coupling is also high when the client blocks and waits for a response. This can be a concern if the client could have spent the time waiting for a response on other activities. Web service clients may use the *Asynchronous Response Handler* pattern (184) to mitigate this issue, but more significant problems remain. A client's connection may time out if the request takes more than a few seconds to process. This usually means that the response will be lost. Additionally, if a web service launches a process that transpires over hours, days, or months, then it's just not feasible to have the client wait. All of these issues can be abated if temporal coupling is reduced. This suggests the adoption of an asynchronous request processing paradigm. In other words, clients may send requests to web services, but they should not expect those requests to be processed immediately, nor should they wait for responses.

The traditional way to support asynchronous processing is through network-addressable message queues (i.e., Message-Oriented Middleware or MOM). These technologies allow clients to send messages to remote systems at any time, regardless of the operational state of the target system. Messages are stored in the remote queue until the target system decides to retrieve them. If the client can't connect to a remote queue, the client's queuing infrastructure usually saves the message to its own local queue and repeatedly attempts to send the message until it finally succeeds. Distinct queue readers in the target system can also protect remote system resources from spikes in request load by throttling or controlling the rate at which requests are processed. Queues can also be used to receive requests to execute long-running processes. Unfortunately, while queues can help to reduce temporal coupling, they are best reserved for use within a secured network, far behind the corporate firewall. One may mitigate some security concerns by establishing a queue entry point on a hardened gateway, but the business partner must use the same queuing technologies. If queues shouldn't be exposed beyond the corporate firewall, how can asynchronous processing be supported and temporal coupling reduced?

The web service could attempt to mimic the fire-and-forget characteristics of queues by not returning a response (a.k.a. the *One-Way* or *In-Only* message exchange pattern). In this approach, the service receives a request, processes it, but doesn't provide a response. While this eliminates the problem of client-side blocking, it doesn't let the client know whether or not a request has been received and if it will be processed. It also doesn't alleviate problems related to unavailable resources (e.g., databases) or request spikes. How, then, can a web service behave like a queue while also providing immediate client feedback?

When a service receives a request, forward it to a background process, then return an acknowledgment containing a unique request identifier.

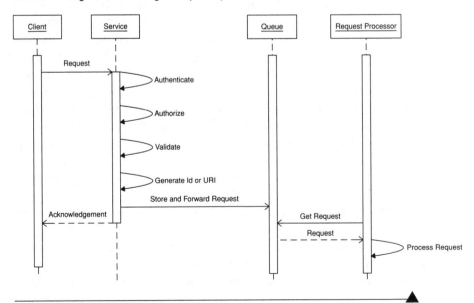

Request/Acknowledge may be used as an alternative to *Request/Response* (54). The service typically performs the following steps.

1. Receive the request.

2. Authenticate client credentials (optional).

3. Authorize the client for the requested operation (optional).

4. Validate the request (optional).

5. Generate a Request Identifier or URI.

6. Store and forward the request.

7. Return an acknowledgment.

Request/ Acknowledge

When the service receives a request, it typically authenticates and authorizes the client, then validates portions of the request to ensure that it can be processed. The service may use *Service Interceptors* (195) to complete these tasks. If the client can't be authenticated or is not authorized for the requested operation, or if the request is invalid, then the service will return a Negative Acknowledgment (NAck) indicating the nature of the error and terminate. *Resource APIs* (38) frequently return NAcks as HTTP status codes, while services with *RPC APIs* (18) or *Message APIs* (27) generally return *Document Messages* [EIP] containing error information. A very specific type of document message used to convey errors for the latter two API styles is the SOAP Fault. If a client receives a NAck, it may try to fix the problem and resubmit the message, or it may decide to end the conversation.

If the client is authenticated and authorized, and if the request is valid, then the service usually generates a Request Identifier or URI. This is a unique key that can be used by all parties to refer to the request in future interactions. Once this identifier is created, it is attached to the request, which is then forwarded to an asynchronous background process by way of a queue or database table. These processes (a.k.a. request processors) read and process each client's request. After the service has forwarded the request, it returns an Acknowledgment (Ack) to the client and terminates. The acknowledgment might only be a status code. A *Resource API* (38), for example, might only return an HTTP 202 code to indicate that the request has been received but has not yet been processed. The acknowledgment could also be a document message containing the request identifier somewhere in its body.

Considerations

In many cases, the client's interaction with the service will end when the acknowledgment is sent. There are, however, scenarios in which the client must receive a response or periodic updates. A customer may, for example, want to know when the status of an order changes. The client application might also want to receive the outcome from a long-running process. A traveler might, for example, use a service to create a comprehensive travel package, but may not receive confirmation for several hours or days. In both of these situations, it's not feasible to have the client maintain a connection to the service and wait for the process to complete. It must have another way to receive updates and results. The client might also want to have information relayed to other interested parties. A hotel, for example, might call a web service to update its room availability. It may wish to have this information relayed to one or more travel web sites.

There are three ways by which *Request/Acknowledge* can provide updates or final results. The client can poll, callback messages can be sent to the client, or messages can be relayed to interested parties. These variations are discussed in the following list.

- **Polling:** The *Request/Acknowledge/Poll* variation of this pattern has been discussed by many over the years (e.g., [Brown 1], [Snell]), and is probably the easiest variation of *Request/Acknowledge* to implement. This pattern requires the client to periodically poll a second web service for updates or final results. Clients must first retrieve the prerequisite information from the acknowledgment. *Resource APIs* (38) usually return URIs for the web services that clients may poll. These URIs frequently contain the request identifier somewhere in the path. *RPC APIs* (18) and *Message APIs* (27) can provide the value of the request identifier anywhere in the acknowledgment. In this case, the request identifier is extracted by the client and is usually included as a parameter in the request to the polled service. Clients may poll at their leisure and don't have to poll on the same thread that issued the request. Even if the client crashes, it can retrieve the final results after a restart as long as the polling information was extracted from the acknowledgment and saved before the crash. Figure 3.1 illustrates the general sequence of activities in the *Request/Acknowledge/Poll* variation of this pattern.

  Request/Acknowledge/Poll has a few drawbacks. If the client doesn't poll frequently enough, there may be a significant delay between the time updates or final results are ready and the time they are retrieved. If the cli-

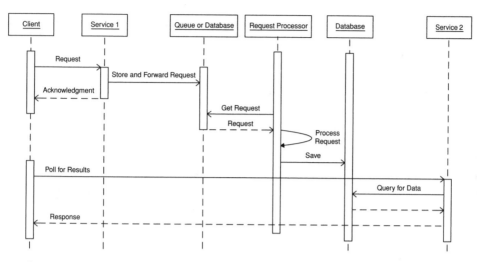

Figure 3.1 Request/Acknowledge/Poll *enables clients to poll for results at their leisure.*

ent polls too often, then excessive load may be placed on the web server, and an inordinate amount of network traffic may be generated.

Request/Acknowledge/Callback can mitigate these problems, and can also be used to deliver results in a more timely fashion.

- **Callbacks and relays:** *Request/Acknowledge/Callback* is equivalent to *Request/Acknowledge/Poll* with one exception. Rather than having the client poll a second service for results, a request processor (i.e., background process) pushes information back to the client or forwards it to other parties. This latter variation may be called *Request/Acknowledge/Relay.* To make this happen, the client and server must switch roles. In other words, the system that received and processed the request becomes the client, and the system that sent the original request must offer a Callback Service that receives results. Figure 3.2 depicts the general flow of events in the *Request/Acknowledge/Callback* variation of this pattern.

  In the *Request/Acknowledge/Callback* variation of this pattern, a list of callback services must be acquired after the request has been processed. This list could be retrieved from a local data store, or it might be passed in with the original request itself. In the former approach, the request processor would first extract a key value from the request. This could be a customer or account identifier, for example. The request processor would then use this key to retrieve a list of callback services. The information

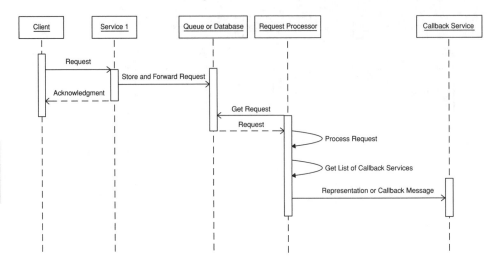

Figure 3.2 Request/Acknowledge/Callback *can be used when the status updates or final results for a request must be delivered as soon as possible to one or more recipients. In this variation of* Request/Acknowledge, *the request processor pushes a Representation or Callback Message to a Callback Service.*

used to create this list may have been keyed in manually, uploaded from files, or registered by the client through some other web service (e.g., a "subscription service"). The callback service list can also be passed in with the original request. Clients of *Resource APIs* (38) might, for example, send requests containing the URIs for their callback services. Clients of *RPC APIs* (18) and *Message APIs* (27) can leverage WS-Addressing headers for a similar purpose. However, when callback recipients are identified in the request, special precautions must be taken to ensure that they cannot be seen or altered by anyone except the authorized parties. The easiest way to protect the request is through Transport Layer Security (TLS). WS-Security can also be used to digitally sign and encrypt requests. This latter approach is typically used when the request is passed through multiple intermediaries. Once a callback list has been procured, the request processor is able to dispatch updates or results for the original request. Sometimes the same results will be sent to each service. At other times the results must be formatted specifically for each target. The request processor may have to implement the *Idempotent Retry* pattern (206) if there's a chance that callback services might be unavailable.

There are several things to consider before selecting *Request/Acknowledge/Callback*. It is more complex to implement and debug than is *Request/Acknowledge/Poll*. Capacity planning is also more challenging. If there's a one-to-one correspondence between requests and callback services, then the level of system resources (e.g., CPU, memory, etc.) required to process requests for *Request/Acknowledge/Callback* may only be slightly higher than for *Request/Response* (54). However, if a single request generates multiple updates, if the results of a single request must be delivered to many callback services, or if the updates or results must be formatted in a variety of ways for each recipient, then the system resources required can be orders of magnitude higher.

The *Request/Acknowledge/Callback* pattern cannot be used if the originating client is unable or unwilling to provide a publicly addressable callback service. Some originating clients will not consider this pattern because they would have to open a port to receive inbound traffic. While various security measures (e.g., firewalls, X.509 certificates, SAML tokens, private networks) could be leveraged to protect against unauthorized traffic, some organizations do not wish to take the risk or allocate the necessary funds. If this is the case, the only option to receive responses is *Request/Acknowledge/Poll*.

- **A foundation for Publish/Subscribe:** Publish/Subscribe is a classic design pattern in which a Message Sender (i.e., Publisher) transmits messages to an intermediary (e.g., web service) that enables interested parties (i.e., Subscribers) to receive this information while keeping them ignorant of one another. Each published message may have one or many Subscribers.

  Request/Acknowledge/Relay and *Request/Acknowledge/Poll* provide two different ways to realize this pattern. The former is more closely aligned with what many consider to be the classic implementation of the Publish/Subscribe pattern. In this approach, a web service receives messages from Publishers and pushes information to one or more Subscribers. In the latter approach, a web service receives messages, and information extracted from these messages is persisted (e.g., to a database) by the service. Subscribers must then pull information from another web service (e.g., an Atom Syndication feed) that queries the data persisted by the first web service.

Example: *A Service That Implements Request/Acknowledge*

The following listing shows how a Java service can use JMS to forward requests. These are picked up by asynchronous background processes designed to pull requests from a queue and process them.

Request/
Acknowledge

```java
@WebService(name="BargainAirService")
public class BargainAirService {
  @WebMethod()
  public TripReservationAck ReserveTrip(
                            @WebParam(name = "request")
                            TripReservation request))
  {
    String requestId = System.currentTimeMillis().toString() +
                       java.util.UUID.randomUUID().toString();

    request.setIdentifier(requestId);

    FlightReservationsGateway.SendMessage( request );

    TripReservationAck response = new TripReservationAck();

    response.setRequestId(requestId);
    return response;
  }
}

public class FlightReservationsGateway {


  public static void SendMessage(TripReservation request){

    Context context = new InitialContext();

    ConnectionFactory factory =
      (ConnectionFactory)context.lookup("queueConnFactory");

    Queue queue = (Queue) context.lookup("flightReservations");

    Connection conn = factory.createConnection();

    Session session = conn.createSession(true,
                                  Session.AUTO_ACKNOWLEDGE);

    MessageProducer sender = session.createProducer(queue);

    TextMessage msg = session.createTextMessage( request.toString() );

    sender.send( msg);
  }
}
```

Example: *A Resource API That Implements Request/Acknowledge/Poll*

This example shows how a *Resource API* (38) implemented in Java could support polling. The OrdersResourceController is a *Service Controller* (85) that maps HTTP POST and GET requests to request handlers named PlaceOrder and GetOrder, respectively. The first receives an order request and returns an acknowledgment containing the URI of the service that should be polled. This URI is mapped by the controller to the GetOrder method.

```
@Path("/orders")
public class OrdersResourceController {

  private static String BaseURL =
                "http://orders.acmeCorp.com/";

  public OrdersResourceController() {;}

  @POST
  @ConsumeMime("application/xml")
  @ProduceMime("text/plain")
  public String PlaceOrder(Order order) {

    String requestId = System.currentTimeMillis().toString() +
                java.util.UUID.randomUUID().toString();

    order.setIdentifier(requestId);

    // Assume this submits to a queue
    (new FulfillmentGateway(order)).submit();

    return BaseURL + requestId;
  }

  @GET
  @Path("/{requestId}")
  @ProduceMime("application/xml")
  public Order GetOrder(
    @UriParam("requestId")
        String requestId){

    return (new FulfillmentGateway(requestId)).getOrderStatus();
  }
}
```

Example: *Leveraging WS-Addressing for Request/Acknowledge/Relay*

The OrderProcessor class below, written in C#, is an example of a request processor and *Command* [GoF] that can be instantiated from within a web service
method. This class processes requests and relays callback messages to callback
services. It gets the callback list from the WS-Addressing ReplyTo header. You
may assume that this object is enqueued by the web service to a background
process, dequeued by the background process, and executed there rather than
on the web server.

```csharp
public interface IRequestProcessor
{
  void Execute();

public class OrderProcessor:IRequestProcessor
{
  OrderMessage request;
  string replyto=null, from=null, msgId=null;

  public OrderProcessor (OrderMessage request)
  {
    this.request = // perform deep copy of request
    replyTo = OperationContext.Current.IncomingMessageHeaders.ReplyTo;
    from = OperationContext.Current.IncomingMessageHeaders.From;
    msgId = OperationContext.Current.IncomingMessageHeaders.MessageId;
  }

  public void Execute()
  {
    // Logic to process order would go here

    // Now, let's relay information to a shipper

    ShipperMessage shipperMsg = new ShipperMessage(
        request.OrderId, request.ShipToInfo);

    ShipperDispatcher shipper = new ShipperDispatcher(replyTo,from);

    shipper.Notify(shipperMsg, msgId);
  }
}
```

The ShipperDispatcher class encapsulates the logic for relaying messages. It
dynamically constructs the appropriate connection to a shipper service given a
destination URI. The target service must implement the IShipperService interface.

```csharp
[ServiceContract]
public interface IShipperService
{
```

```
  [OperationContract]
  ShipperMessage PickupOrder(ShipperMessage request);
}

public class ShipperDispatcher{

  private EndpointAddress destination;
  private EndpointAddress initialSender;

  public ShipperDispatcher( EndpointAddress dest,
                    EndpointAddress sender)
  {
    destination = dest;
    initialSender = sender;
  }

  public void Notify(ShipperMessage shipperOrder,
                    UniqueId correlationId)
  {
    ChannelFactory<IShipperService> factory =
      new ChannelFactory<IShipperService>(
                        new WSHttpBinding(),
                        destination);

    IShipperService shipper = factory.CreateChannel();

    using(new OperationContextScope((IContextChannel)shipper))
    {
      SetMessageHeaders(correlationId);

      using (shipper as IDisposable)
      {
        shipper.PickupOrder(shipperOrder);
      }
    }
  }

  private void SetMessageHeaders(UniqueId correlationId)
  {
    OperationContext.Current.OutgoingMessageHeaders.MessageId =
      new UniqueId(Guid.NewGuid().ToString());

    OperationContext.Current.OutgoingMessageHeaders.RelatesTo =
      correlationId;

    OperationContext.Current.OutgoingMessageHeaders.To =
      destination.Uri ;

    OperationContext.Current.OutgoingMessageHeaders.From =
      initialSender;
  }
}
```

Media Type Negotiation

Clients that use services with *Resource APIs* (38) often have preferences for different media types.

Media Type
Negotiation

How can a web service provide multiple representations of the same logical resource while minimizing the number of distinct URIs for that resource?

Web services that are used by large and diverse client populations must often accommodate different media type preferences. Some clients may, for example, prefer XML while others favor JSON. The service owner must therefore devise a means by which clients' preferences can be indicated. Each service must then detect these preferences, format an appropriate response, and serialize the response accordingly. There are many ways for a client to convey its preferences. Some use URIs for this purpose. With this approach, the preferred type appears as the final segment of the URI, as a file extension, or as a query parameter in the URI. Examples are shown below.

```
http://acme.org/product/123/json
```

```
http://acme.org/product/123.html
```

```
http://acme.org/product/123.pdf
```

```
http://acme.org/product/123?fmt=json
```

This common approach does have a few advantages. It's intuitive, easy to read, and often works well with browsers. Since the URI encapsulates both resource identification and the preferred representation type, it's also easy to test the service, save its address, and forward the address to interested parties. However, this approach has several disadvantages as well. URIs should be used to identify distinct resources. In this example, there really is only one resource (i.e., information on product 123) that can be represented in four ways. The use of multiple URIs in this example is misleading because it implies that there are four different resources. Furthermore, if the client has a prioritized list of media type preferences, then it must know how to formulate the correct URI for each type, and must contact each service, one after the other. This has the unfortunate side effect of increasing client-service coupling and overall latency. If the request uses query strings to indicate client preferences, then intermediary cache providers may consider each response to be unique whether or not the parameters are the same across multiple requests (re: RFC 2616, section 13.9). This strategy can also be tedious for service developers to implement because the desired type must be parsed and separated from other URI segments that identify the business entity (e.g., product). A better approach is to leverage standard HTTP protocols for content negotiation.

Allow clients to indicate one or more media type preferences in HTTP request headers. Send requests to services capable of producing responses in the desired format.

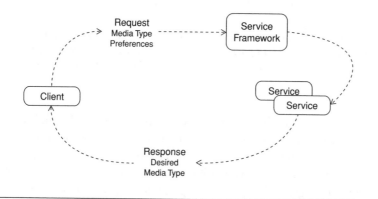

Content negotiation (a.k.a. Conneg) is described in RFC 2616, section 12. This specification describes how HTTP servers and clients can collaborate on selecting a response that matches the client's preferred language, character set, and media type. While the original intent of the specification was to address the needs of people sitting at browsers, the protocol can also be used to facilitate polymorphic data exchange with automated clients. *Media Type Negotiation* leverages this protocol in a way that enables services to provide multiple representations of the same logical resource. This pattern is primarily used with *Request/Response* (54).

The specification for content negotiation describes three basic approaches. The most common of these is server-driven negotiation. In this approach, the client provides its media type preferences through the Accept Request header. The client can provide multiple preferences and can also indicate which media types are most preferred. When a request is received, web service frameworks that enable the *Service Controller* pattern (85) will route or select a Request Handler (i.e., Web Method) based in part on how well the client's preferences match up to the handler's Media Type Annotations (see Figure 3.3). Developers use these annotations to indicate the media types consumed or produced (i.e., serialized)

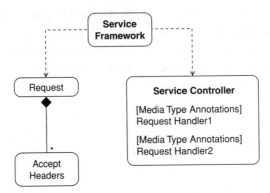

Media Type Negotiation

Figure 3.3 *In server-driven negotiation, the service framework selects a request handler (i.e., web method) based, in part, on how well the client's preferences, as indicated through HTTP Accept headers, match up to the handler's Media Type Annotations.*

by a given handler. This also eliminates the need to create additional web service logic that parses and directs requests to an appropriate routine. A given handler annotation usually only identifies one media type, but developers may include more if the framework supports it. All popular frameworks automatically serialize and deserialize generic types (e.g., `application/xml`, `application/json`, `text/plain`, `text/html`). If you want to receive or return custom types, then you'll have to write custom serializers.

The logic used to select a handler varies per platform. However, they all follow a few general rules. If the client doesn't supply preferences, the web service provides a default response. When the client provides a single type preference, the framework will try to find an annotation that matches the client's preference exactly. If the client provides multiple preferences, or a handler is annotated to produce multiple types, then the selection process becomes a bit more complex. In short, the framework will try to find a best match between the client's types and the handler annotations. If the client provides multiple type preferences, the framework will consider the client's ranking of these preferences. The framework will also select more specific types like `application/vnd.acme.custSummary` over generic types like `application/xml` when possible.

A second negotiation style is client-driven negotiation. Here again, the client sends a request containing its media type preferences through an HTTP Accept Request header. A web service receives the request and responds by providing a list of URIs the client may consider. For example, a client could send a request asking for the technical specifications on a particular product. The service may then provide a response containing *Linked Services* (77) that point to services capable of producing acceptable media types. The client must then review the list, select the service that best meets its needs, and send the "real" request.

Considerations

Developers considering *Media Type Negotiation* should consider the following.

- **Server versus client-driven negotiation:** Server-driven negotiation may be appropriate when the service owner wishes to provide the client with options while maintaining control over the media type selection process. This variation on the pattern helps to simplify client logic, and also tends to minimize network round-trips. The downside is that, when the client does not provide explicit preferences, the server's response might not be recognized by the client, or it might be inappropriate for the intended use.

  Client-driven negotiation may be appropriate when you want the client to have more control over the types it receives. The drawback is that the client must initiate two *Request/Response* (54) exchanges, one to query for a list of service addresses and a second to obtain the ultimate response.

  Server-driven negotiation can make it harder to leverage cached data. As the number of types returned from a specific URI increases, the chances of satisfying a request from an intermediary cache (i.e., Proxy Server) tend to decrease. Clients using client-driven negotiation often have a better chance of being served data from cache because a one-to-one ratio exists between URIs and media types.

- **Use with Service Controllers:** Server-driven negotiation is most easily implemented with frameworks that enable the *Service Controller* pattern (85), as was described in the preceding paragraphs. One may achieve server-driven negotiation without Service Controllers and Media Type Annotation, but it can be a lot of work. In this case, custom service logic must be created to extract the Accept Request header, interpret the client's preferences, and then select and create a response structure that meets the client's needs. Once the structure has been populated, the service must serialize the response accordingly.

- **Client-driven negotiation versus WS-Discovery:** Client-driven negotiation has similarities to WS-Discovery in that both provide a means for clients to discover services while attempting to minimize coupling to service locations. WS-Discovery is a protocol in which clients send SOAP messages to a multicast group in order to receive the addresses of services that meet their requirements. This specification has exacting requirements for the structure of client "probe messages," and is equally rigid regarding the structure of responses. Client-driven negotiation, on the other hand, is a flexible pattern whose implementation is left to the service owner.

- **Possibility of code duplication:** There is a possibility that the code in request handlers may be duplicated. This risk can be mitigated if each request handler delegates all processing to a common *Command* [GoF].

- **Use of Service Connectors:** *Service Connectors* (168) can assist with *Media Type Negotiation* by encapsulating knowledge of the client's preferred types and by creating the necessary request headers. This information may be hardcoded, but may also be read from a configuration file.

Media Type
Negotiation

Example: *Using HTTP Accept Headers to Indicate Preferred Types*

Clients can indicate the priority of their preferences by using the q parameter in an HTTP Accept header. The scale for this parameter ranges from 0 to 1, with the most preferred type having a rank of 1. The example below shows how a client has requested information on customer 123. The most preferred type is the second version of a customer summary, followed by the first version of that same type. The client will also accept any other representation that uses the MIME type of application; the assumption is that the subtypes will most likely be XML or JSON.

```
GET http://acmeCorp.org/customers/123
Accept: application/vnd.acme.custSummary.v2;q=1.0,
        application/vnd.acme.custSummary.v1;q=0.9,
        application/*;q=0.8
```

Example: *Server-Driven Negotiation*

The following HTTP GET shows a client request where the most preferred type is JSON, followed by any text format (e.g., HTML, rich text, plain text, etc.).

```
GET http://acmeCorp.org/stores
Accept: application/json;q=1.0,
        text/*;q=0.9
```

The first request handler named getStores is capable of returning both XML and JSON media types. Since the client has indicated that JSON is the preferred type, the service framework will automatically serialize the response as that media type. A second request handler named getStoresAsText performs the same query, but returns the response as plain text.

```
@Path("/stores")
public class StoreService {

  @GET
  @Produces("application/xml")
  @Produces("application/json")
  public JAXBElement<Stores> getStores()
  {
    Stores stores = Stores.getStores();

    return new JAXBElement<Stores>(
      new QName("Stores"), Stores.class, stores);
  }

  @GET
  @Produces("text/plain")
  public String getStoresAsText()
  {
    return Stores.getStores().toString();
  }

}
```

Media Type
Negotiation

Example: *Client-Driven Negotiation*

The following HTTP response fragment shows how a web service can provide a list of URIs the client may consider. The client must parse ProductData in order to find a link relation that contains the media type it's most interested in. Once a link relation has been selected, the client may submit a request to the URI identified in the corresponding href attribute.

```
<ProductData>
  <link rel="self"
    href ="http://acmeCorp.org/products/123" />

  <link rel="http://acmeCorp.org/products/getImage"
    type="image/jpg"
    href="http://images.acmeCorp.org/products/123" />

  <link rel="http://acmeCorp.org/products/getJson"
    type="application/json"
    href= "http://data.acmeCorp.org/products/123" />
```

```
<link rel="http://acmeCorp.org/products/getXML"
  type="application/xml"
  href= "http://data.acmeCorp.org/products/123" />

<link rel="http://acmeCorp.org/products/getPDF"
  type="application/pdf"
  href= "http://docs.acmeCorp.org/products/123" />
</ProductData>
```

Media Type Negotiation

Here we can see that subdomains (e.g., images, data, docs) are created for different media types. These domains may be deployed to different server clusters, and scaled according to the anticipated workload.

Linked Service

A set of related software functions is exposed as web services. These services are frequently called in specific sequences. For example, a client that calls an "Order Creation" service will frequently call "Order Update", "Order Cancel", and "Order Status" services thereafter.

▼

Once a service has processed a request, how can a client discover the related services that may be called, and also be insulated from changing service locations and URI patterns?

▲

Linked Service

Clients must, of course, have a way to acquire service URIs. One approach is to store this information in configuration files on the client. If a service location changes, the developer need only edit the configuration file and redeploy it. However, service owners must give adequate notice, and client developers must deploy the updated files at just the right time. If the configuration file is deployed too early or too late, the client will probably break. The implication is that client and service changes must be carefully coordinated. This may be feasible in "small" environments, but it becomes untenable when many client applications are affected. One can avoid this issue by leveraging sophisticated software infrastructures. Client applications could, for example, query a central *Service Registry* (220) to acquire current service addresses. Requests could also be submitted to a "broker service" that finds and executes services on behalf of clients. While these approaches insulate clients from changing service locations, the client must know how to find and use these infrastructures. Response times may also increase due to the overhead incurred by these intermediaries. Additionally, infrastructures like these often entail steep learning curves, significant cash outlays, and vendor lock-in.

Web services are frequently called in specific sequences. For example, a client that calls an "Order Creation" service will frequently call "Order Update", "Order Cancel", and "Order Status" services thereafter. None of the aforementioned techniques helps the client to understand what they can do after any given service call. Fortunately, service developers can leverage hyperlinks to provide clients with properly formatted URIs that are both current and relevant to the most recent request.

Only publish the addresses of a few root web services. Include the addresses of related services in each response. Let clients parse responses to discover subsequent service URIs.

Linked Service

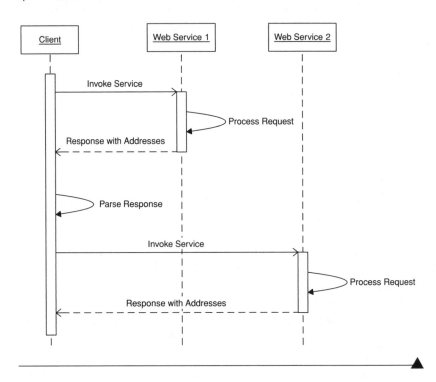

The *Linked Service* pattern is fairly easy to understand. The service owner publishes one or a few "root services" that provide the initial "entry points" for a set of related functions. When a service prepares a response, it includes addresses of related services. If the client invokes an "Order Creation" service, the response might, for example, contain addresses for "Order Update", "Order Cancel", and "Order Status" services. Clients must parse each response to acquire subsequent service addresses. All addresses included in the response are supposed to be current and correctly formatted.

This pattern offers other significant benefits.

- **Provides relevant addresses for each request:** Responses may be constrained to only provide service addresses that make sense given the context of the most recent request. Continuing with the current example, if the client calls an "Order Creation" service and the order could not be shipped immediately, then the response might contain addresses for "Order Update", "Order Cancel", and "Order Status" services. On the other hand, if the order was shipped, the response might only contain the URI of a "Shipment Tracking" service. This pattern therefore provides an effective mechanism to guide clients through valid workflow state transitions.

- **Ensures correctly formatted addresses:** *Resource APIs* (38) are frequently accompanied by specifications that explain the URI patterns (i.e., URI templates) clients must understand. It is the responsibility of each client to invoke services in accordance with these specifications. Unfortunately, it's all too easy for clients to construct invalid addresses. Clients may leave out a URI path segment, put segments in the wrong order, or fail to encode addresses properly (re: URL encoding). The *Linked Service* pattern can abate these issues because each response contains preconstructed addresses clients may use.

- **Protects clients from changing URI patterns and service locations:** *Linked Services* provide an effective way to decouple clients from service locations and even URI patterns. Clients can trust that each response contains only the most current URIs for a set of related services. This makes it easy for service owners to change their URI patterns, or even move a service to an entirely different domain without breaking clients.

- **Makes it easy to add or remove services:** Service owners can introduce new services with ease by adding information about them into the relevant responses. Clients must, of course, be updated to recognize new links and interact with the services referenced by these links. Service owners can also exclude links to services they wish to discontinue. If a client attempts to use a deprecated service, even though a link to that service has not been provided in a response, the server can notify the client that the service has been removed by returning an HTTP status of 410.

Considerations

Developers should consider the following when using the *Linked Service* pattern.

- **Use with Resource APIs:** This pattern is primarily used with services that have *Resource APIs* (38). Nonetheless, services that have *RPC APIs* (18) and *Message APIs* (27) are not barred from using this pattern. These services may, for example, use WS-Addressing for this purpose.

  Clients must know how to parse each response. Services with *Resource APIs* (38) typically create responses containing one or more link relation elements. Each link relation has a link relation type that identifies the semantics or meaning of the link, a link relation media type that identifies the media types consumed or produced by the service, and a hyperlink reference that identifies the URI or address of the service.

Clients search link relations for specific relation types. If the client wants to invoke an "Order Update" service, it might search for a relation type of "OrderUpdate". The client would then extract the corresponding hyperlink reference to acquire the service URI, and prepare a request using the media type identified in the link relation. Clients must have forehand knowledge of what HTTP methods (i.e., GET, PUT, POST, DELETE) to use for each *Linked Service*, and must also be familiar with the requisite media types.

Linked Service

- **Security:** Service owners should take precautions against man-in-the-middle (MITM) attacks when responses are sent over public networks. The problem is that an intermediary can intercept the response and change it so that it refers to a malicious service. While such risks cannot be completely eradicated, they can be mitigated to a large extent by conducting all client-service interactions over secure channels (e.g., TLS). One could also use digital signing to protect the message from tampering, and encrypt the service hyperlinks so that they can't be read by unauthorized parties.

- **Generation of hyperlinks:** This pattern assumes that each service is capable of generating the correct hyperlinks. Service developers might therefore create classes that encapsulate these algorithms. These classes could be used by all services, and would ensure that hyperlinks are generated in a consistent manner.

  Service owners must also consider how links to external services should be acquired for use in responses. Ironically, the services that provide hyperlinks could become tightly coupled to external service locations just as clients had been. Web services must therefore have access to a shared data store that provides consistent information regarding external services. One could, for example, create a hashtable containing service lookup information and cache it on each web server.

Example: *Atom Publishing Protocol, Service Documents, and Link Relations*

Atom Publishing Protocol (APP) provides a generic protocol that may be used to convey information about related web services. Clients usually start by retrieving a service document from a "root service." This document provides basic information clients may parse to discover subsequent services. The service document accomplishes this by grouping one or more Atom collections into a workspace. Each collection can be used to signify an application domain. Clients may search these collections and acquire the address of the "root web service" for a given application domain by parsing for a particular title. The following service document shows two resource collections named Customers and Loans. The href attribute provides clients the URI of the root service for each application domain.

```
<?xml version="1.0" encoding='utf-8'?>
<service xml:base="http://acmeCorp.org/"
  xmlns:atom="http://www.w3.org/2005/Atom"
  xmlns:app="http://www.w3.org/2007/app"
  xmlns="http://www.w3.org/2007/app" >

  <workspace>
    <atom:title>Acme Corp</atom:title>
      <collection href="http://customers.acmeCorp.org" >
        <atom:title>Customers</atom:title>
        <accept>application/vnd.acme.cust+xml</accept>
      </collection>

      <collection href="http://loans.acmeCorp.org/" >
        <atom:title>Loans</atom:title>
        <accept>application/vnd.acme.LoanApplication+xml</accept>
      </collection>
  </workspace>
</service>
```

A client might then submit an HTTP POST to http://loans.acmeCorp.org in order to create a new loan application. The service could respond with a response that contains more link relations. The listing below shows a response that contains links to services that enable the client to modify loan terms, cancel the loan, or submit a new loan application. These are identified with the relation type values modifyTerms, cancelApplication, and submitApplication, respectively.

```
<Loan>
  <id>105</id>
  <status>Created</status>
  <updated>2010-06-10T14:45:32z</updated>

  <link rel="self"
        type="application/vnd.acme.LoanApplication+xml"
        href="http://loans.acmeCorp.org/105" />

  <link rel="http://loans.acmeCorp.org/modifyTerms"
        type="application/vnd.acme.LoanApplication+xml"
        href="http://loans.acmeCorp.org/105" />
```

```
<link rel="http://loans.acmeCorp.org/cancelApplication"
      type="application/vnd.acme.LoanApplication+xml"
      href="http://loans.acmeCorp.org/105" />

<link rel="http://loans.acmeCorp.org/submitApplication"
      type="application/vnd.acme.LoanApplication+xml"
      href="http://loans.acmeCorp.org/" />
</Loan>
```

Linked Service

This example assumes that the client knows that they should issue an HTTP GET to retrieve the current version of the loan, a PUT to modifyTerms, and a POST to submitApplication. What's not so evident is that the client should probably issue an HTTP DELETE to invoke the cancelApplication operation.

Chapter 4

Request and Response Management

Introduction

Software applications are frequently organized into layers that contain logically related entities. Since layers consolidate and isolate the logic for a particular concern, developers can often standardize behaviors, make isolated changes, or swap out significant functionality without affecting other parts of a system. Layering can also help to facilitate understanding of large and complex systems since you can often focus on the purpose and design patterns used in individual layers rather than trying to comprehend the entirety of a system at once.

Consider the layers that have become common in many applications. The Presentation Layer contains logic that displays information and receives user input. This layer uses business logic found in the *Domain Layer* [DDD] to fulfill user requests. The Domain Layer, in turn, calls upon the entities in the Data Source Layer, to read and write information to databases or other data stores (e.g., files, messaging systems, etc.). From this, we can see that higher layers depend on lower layers, but lower layers know nothing of the upper layers.

A *Service Layer* [POEAA] can be used to create a distinct API for multiple client types. This API establishes a clear boundary between client applications and the logic for a specific domain. The Service Layer is actually a part of the Domain Layer. Services within this layer often fulfill client requests by coordinating the actions of objects that are members of the *Domain Model* [POEAA]. They may also provide access to application workflows, code libraries, commercial packages, and legacy applications. This chapter reviews a few patterns that belong to the Service Layer. These patterns are used to manage web requests and responses, and are outlined in Table 4.1.

83

Table 4.1 *Request and Response Management Patterns*

Pattern Name	Problem	Description
Service Controller (85)	How can the correct web service be executed without having to maintain complex parsing and routing logic?	Create a class that identifies a set of related services. Annotate each class method with routing expressions that can be interpreted by a Front Controller.
Data Transfer Object (94)	How can one simplify manipulation of request and response data, enable domain layer entities, requests, and responses to vary independently, and insulate services from wire-level message formats?	Create distinct classes to represent request and response data structures. Consolidate the mapping logic that reads and writes these structures.
Request Mapper (109)	How can a service process data from requests that are structurally different yet semantically equivalent?	Create specialized classes that leverage structure-specific APIs to target and move select portions of requests directly to domain layer entities or to a common set of intermediate objects that can be used as input arguments to such entities. Load a particular mapper based on key content found in the request.
Response Mapper (122)	How can the logic required to construct a response be reused by multiple services?	Create a class that consolidates the data mapping and transformation logic used to create a response.

Service Controller

A web service uses an *RPC API* (18), *Message API* (27), or *Resource API* (38). The service owner would like to use similar mechanisms to invoke web service logic regardless of the API style.

▼
———

How can the correct web service be executed without having to maintain complex parsing and routing logic?

———
▲

All web services require a mechanism to receive requests, evaluate the request's meaning, and route requests to procedures (i.e., class methods, request handlers), which implement the desired service behaviors. Service designers may adapt the *Front Controller* pattern [POEAA] for this purpose. This pattern centralizes request processing by funneling all requests through a single handler that evaluates information from the request to determine how it should be processed. Java developers have traditionally used Java servlets for this purpose, while .NET developers have used .NET HTTP handlers. Handlers for services with *Resource APIs* (38) simply parse information from the URI. For example, an HTTP GET issued to http://acmeCorp.org/customers/123 would normally indicate that the client wants to retrieve information on customer 123. Handlers for services with *RPC APIs* (18) and *Message APIs* (27) work a little differently. These often look for information in SOAP headers. Therefore, an HTTP POST issued to http://acmeCorp.org might be interpreted as a request to retrieve customer data if the SOAPAction header contains GetCustomer. Once the handler has evaluated the request, it selects and instantiates a *Command* [GoF] object, which encapsulates the web service logic.

Several web-oriented frameworks (e.g., Apache Struts, Ruby on Rails, ASP.NET MVC) strive to insulate the developer from the internal complexities of Front Controllers. The Rails framework, for example, lets developers maintain the rules that correlate requests with subcontrollers (i.e., commands) in a separate routing file. In a similar fashion, the ASP.NET MVC framework enables developers to define these rules in configuration files. These practices let developers centralize the routing rules for large and complex applications.

Front Controllers that use these techniques work quite well for services with *Resource APIs* (38) since Commands can usually be selected by simply parsing the requested URI. However, the routing logic becomes more complex if different *Commands* [GoF] must be selected based on the client's preferred media types. In this case, the developer may need to write a *Service Interceptor* (195) that parses message headers and overrides the default Command associated with the requested URI. This same pattern may be required for services with *RPC APIs* (18) and *Message APIs* (27) since the client's intent is typically provided in a message header or body. Unfortunately, these interceptors can be rather complex to write. Some frameworks let developers configure the Commands that should be triggered when specific message headers are found. This, however, can be quite tedious. Developers could benefit from a simpler declarative approach that can be interpreted by a *Front Controller* [POEAA].

Service Controller

Create a class that identifies a set of related services. Annotate each class method with routing expressions that can be interpreted by a Front Controller.

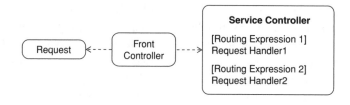

Service Controllers are created in programming languages like Java and C# with ordinary classes. Each class contains one or more public methods that control the execution of business tasks and coordinate access to resources (e.g., documents, images, etc.). This pattern refers to these methods as Request Handlers or Web Methods. The rules that define which handlers should be invoked for different requests are provided through annotations known collectively as Routing Expressions. These expressions precede each web method in the *Service Controller,* and are used by the *Front Controller* [POEAA] of frameworks like JAX-WS, JAX-RS, Axis2, and WCF. When a web server receives a request, the framework selects and invokes handlers by evaluating various aspects of the request against these expressions.

This pattern also makes it easy to leverage data-binding technologies that automatically deserialize requests and serialize responses. This eliminates the need to create custom logic that parses, extracts, and copies data to and from objects that are used in the service. The underlying frameworks use various technologies to accomplish this. The methods on *Service Controllers* can be annotated with binding instructions to tell the framework how requests and responses should be handled. The default options include XML and JSON, but developers may also tell the framework to use a custom approach.

The types of routing expressions used in *Service Controllers* depend on the service API style. Frameworks that support *Resource APIs* (38) employ URI Templates, Request Method Designators, and Media Type Annotations (see Figure 4.1).

URI Templates are expressions that define how requested URIs should be parsed. In frameworks like JAX-RS and WCF, these appear as annotations that precede the handler's signature. Templates divide URIs into multiple URI segments and query strings. A segment is an alphanumeric value that occurs between delimiters such as forward slashes and semicolons. Consider the following URI:

`http://www.acmeCorp.org/products/123`

This address contains three segments: `www.acmeCorp.org`, `products`, and `123`. URI templates can also indicate if a segment has fixed or variable content. The latter is recognized when a sequence of characters is enclosed in curly braces. Consider the following template:

`http://www.acmeCorp.org/products/{ProductId}`

This template contains two fixed segments and one segment with variable content. Web service frameworks substitute variable segments at runtime with the data sent in the request. This information is usually mapped to an input parameter of a request handler. Therefore, a handler annotated with the template shown above would receive requests that matched this pattern, and would also map the value `123` into a variable named `ProductId`.

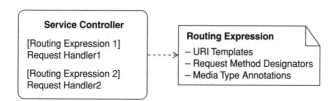

Figure 4.1 *Frameworks like JAX-RS and WCF employ routing expressions, which include URI Templates, Request Method Designators, and Media Type Annotations. This information establishes the criterion that must be met in order to execute methods on the* Service Controller.

Request Method Designators are a second type of routing expression used by frameworks that support *Resource APIs* (38). Given the template shown above, we might determine that distinct handlers should be created to support read, update, and delete operations for a product resource. These handlers could use the same URI template, but we would also need to indicate which server methods (e.g., GET, PUT, DELETE) should trigger each handler. In the current example, a single "Product Controller" might have three handlers named ReadProduct, UpdateProduct, and DeleteProduct that share the same URI template. The request method designator provides the information that lets the framework decide which handler should be executed.

Services that use *Resource APIs* (38) often provide clients the ability to indicate their data type preferences through *Media Type Negotiation* (70). *Service Controllers* that respond to these requests may contain multiple handlers that invoke the same logic and share the same URI templates and Request Method Designators. The only difference may be the data formats received and returned. One handler might use XML, while another might use JSON. Frameworks like JAX-RS and WCF therefore use Media Type Annotations to indicate the media types consumed and produced by the service. When a request is received, the framework selects the handler whose URI templates, method designators, and media type annotations best match the client's criterion. The framework may also optionally leverage data-binding technologies to automatically serialize and deserialize input and output data according to the annotations.

Several frameworks that support *RPC APIs* (18) and *Message APIs* (27) also use routing expressions in *Service Controllers,* but their syntax is a little different. These annotations (see Figure 4.2) are used by services that exchange SOAP messages and use WSDL *Service Descriptors* (175).

These frameworks parse SOAP messages in order to find a "best match" against the expressions in the *Service Controller.* The expressions may include explicit values for SOAPAction or WS-Addressing Action headers. Developers

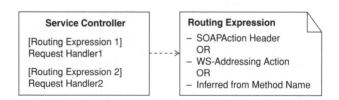

Figure 4.2 *Frameworks that support* RPC APIs *(18) and* Message APIs *(27) use Routing Expressions that examine headers in order to route SOAP messages to appropriate handlers.*

can also omit values for these items, in which case the framework will usually infer the matching criteria from the name of the annotated method. For example, if an annotated method is named GetCustomer and no other expressions are provided, then the framework may route messages to that method if the SOAP-Action header contains a URI with the value of GetCustomer. Of course, the specific rules regarding how the framework makes these decisions vary per platform. As of this writing, most frameworks have relied on the SOAPAction header because it is recommended in the WS-I Basic Profile 1.1. However, more and more SOAP frameworks are supporting and encouraging adoption of WS-Addressing mechanisms because these can be used with other transports aside from HTTP. Client developers must therefore understand what information the target platform uses to dispatch requests to handlers in order to construct requests that will be properly routed.

Service
Controller

Considerations

Developers should consider the following issues when using the *Service Controller* pattern.

- **Use of interface classes:** Developers often create Service Interface Classes that define request handlers and routing expressions, but don't have any implementation (note: JAX-WS refers to these as Service Endpoint Interfaces). *Service Controllers* that use these interfaces must implement methods that have the same signatures as the methods found in the interface class. The controllers can omit routing expressions since they are defined in the interface.

  Interface classes have traditionally been used to provide a standard contract for a family of related objects that exhibit different behaviors. Client developers are encouraged to code to the interface rather than to the class implementation. This makes it easier to alter a class's logic without affecting clients because coupling to internal classes is prevented. Service interface classes aren't used for quite the same reasons.

  Service Interface Classes provide two key benefits. Routing expressions are usually easier to manage because one doesn't have to look through a lot of service implementation code. One need only look at an interface class, which is usually much smaller than the controller. Service interface classes are also instrumental when using a practice known as Contract-First, a subject that is introduced in the following paragraph.

- **Contract-First versus Code-First:** Contract-First is most closely associated with services that use SOAP and WSDL, but the concept can also be partially applied to services that don't use either. With Contract-First, the developer first creates WSDL and XSDs and then feeds this information through a binding compiler, which generates a Service Interface Class. The compiler may also create *Data Transfer Objects* (94) if the interface leverages data-binding technologies; *Resource API* (38) developers can leverage this technique as well.

  The Code-First approach can be used with *RPC APIs* (18), *Message APIs* (27), and *Resource APIs* (38). In this approach, the developer creates a *Service Controller*, and possibly *Data Transfer Objects* (94). If service clients expect WSDL, then the framework will automatically generate WSDL and XSDs when clients query the base URI of the service.

  For a detailed discussion of these topics, see the *Service Descriptor* pattern (175).

Service
Controller

- **Enumeration of Service Controllers:** Developers must determine how many *Service Controllers* should be created for a given problem domain. Developers often create one controller for each logical resource in the problem domain when designing a *Resource API* (38). A domain that involves customers, orders, and products might therefore have three controllers. Each controller would typically contain the handlers for CRUD operations (i.e., Create, Read, Update, and Delete) or nonstandard operations (i.e., POST) that should be allowed for the resource. Resource controllers often include handlers that provide access to related resource collections as well. A customer resource controller might therefore have a handler for a collection of orders that would refer to a separate order controller.

  The controllers for *RPC APIs* (18) and *Message APIs* (27) are often identified by enumerating the use cases in a given problem domain. These use cases are then typically grouped into related sets (i.e., use-case packages). One controller may be created for each use-case package (e.g., customer account management, order management, etc.), and each use case within the package is implemented as a distinct request handler in the *Service Controller*. The challenge is to determine how many use cases should be implemented on a single controller since controllers that contain large numbers of handlers can become quite difficult to manage.

Example: *A Resource Controller*

The StoreService controller shown below defines a *Resource API* (38) that uses JAX-RS. Clients can retrieve a collection of all Stores by issuing an HTTP GET to http://someBaseURI/stores. Information on a specific store may be acquired by sending a GET to a URI like this: http://someBaseURI/stores/123. Stores may be created by issuing a POST to http://someBaseURI/stores and updated by sending a PUT to a URI like http://someBaseURI/stores/123.

```
@Path("/stores")
public class StoreService {

  @GET
  @Produces("application/xml")
  public JAXBElement<Stores> getStoresAsXML()
  {
    Stores stores = Stores.getStores();

    return new JAXBElement<Stores>(
      new QName("Stores"), Stores.class, stores);
  }

  @Path("/{id}")
  @GET
  @Produces("application/xml")
  public Store getStoreAsXML(@PathParam("id") String id)
  {
    // implementation here
  }

  @POST
  @Consumes("application/xml")
  @Produces("application/xml")
  public Store createStore(JAXBElement<Store> store)
  {
    // implementation here
  }

  @Path("/{id}")
  @PUT
  @Produces("application/xml")
  public Store updateStore(@PathParam("id") String id)
  {
    // implementation here
  }

}
```

Service
Controller

The definition for the Stores resource is shown below. This class encapsulates access to a collection of stores.

```java
@XmlRootElement(name = "Stores")
public class Stores {
    private static Collection<Store> stores = null;

    public static Collection<Store> getStores() {
        if(null == stores){
            // instantiate stores collection and
            //  populate from database
        }

        return stores;
    }
}
```

Service Controller

The definition for the Store resource is shown below.

```java
@XmlRootElement(name = "Store")
@XmlType(name = "", propOrder = {"id", "address" })
public class Store {
    private long id;
    private String address;
    // other fields here

    public Store() {;}

    public void setId(long storeId){
        id = storeId;
    }

    public long getId(){
        return id;
    }

    public void setAddress(String addr){
        address = addr;
    }

    public String getAddress(){
        return address;
    }

    // other getters and setters here
}
```

Example: *An RPC Controller*

This example shows the controller for an *RPC API* (18) that uses WCF. The interface class IBargainAirService defines a single handler (i.e., operation) denoted by the OperationContract annotation. This routing expression indicates that the framework should invoke this method when a SOAPAction header contains GetFlightSchedules. The GetFlightSchedules handler includes a message of the type TravelOptions, which is used in requests and responses. These are automatically deserialized and serialized by the framework.

```
[ServiceContract]
public interface IBargainAirService
{
  [OperationContract(Action="urn:GetFlightSchedules")]
  TravelOptions GetFlightSchedules(TravelOptions request);

  // other operations might appear here
}
```

Service
Controller

The definition for the TravelOptions message is shown below.

```
[DataContract]
public partial class TravelOptions
{
  [DataMember]
  public TravelConstraints DepartConstraints{get;set;}

  [DataMember]
  public TravelConstraints ReturnConstraints{get;set;}

  [DataMember]
  public Flights MatchingFlights{get; set;}
}
```

The concrete implementation of BargainAirService is shown below.

```
public class BargainAirService : IBargainAirService
{
  public TravelOptions GetFlightSchedules(TravelOptions request)
  {
    // implementation here
  }
}
```

Data Transfer Object

A web service uses JSON or XML structures in requests or responses.

How can one simplify manipulation of request and response data, enable domain layer entities, requests, and responses to vary independently, and insulate services from wire-level message formats?

One allure of web services is that data can be exchanged with clients by leveraging open standards like XML and JSON. However, when a service receives a request, the data is often extracted and copied from the XML or JSON structures to meaningful domain objects (e.g., customers, products, etc.) because these tend to be easier to work with. This process can be rather involved. The developer must first deserialize or convert the request stream to the required data format (e.g., XML, JSON). Data in these structures can then be parsed and copied to the target domain objects by using an API specific to the data format being read. The same process happens in reverse when responses are returned. Regardless of the data formats or parsers that are used, developers must write a fair amount of code to navigate through these structures and extract, convert, and copy data to target domain objects (see Figure 4.3).

In an attempt to simplify this process, developers often modify domain objects to leverage data-binding technologies like JAXB and .NET's DataContractSerializer. With this approach, developers annotate the properties (i.e., getter/setter methods, attributes) of domain objects to define how their data should be used in requests or responses. When a request is received, the underlying

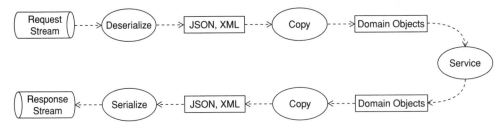

Figure 4.3 *Developers must write a fair amount of code to navigate through request structures in order to extract, convert, and copy data to meaningful domain objects that can be used by the service. Similar code must be written for the response.*

technologies automatically deserialize the request stream, instantiate the required objects, and shuttle data from the request to these objects. This process happens in reverse when responses are returned. These technologies are supposed to facilitate productivity since developers don't have to work with low-level streams, parse data, or use APIs specifically geared to a particular format like XML or JSON.

Unfortunately, several problems arise when domain objects are used in requests and responses. Object graphs often have circular references, and when these structures are serialized, a stack overflow exception may be thrown if the serializer is unable to find a terminating node. One way to deal with this problem is to instruct the serializer to ignore certain properties when the object graph is serialized. For example, if a graph of Company objects contains references to Employee objects, and each Employee also refers to a Company object, the service owner could alter the annotation to instruct the serializer to ignore the Employee.Company relationship. He could also deliberately opt out of serialization by not marking the Company property on the Employee object for serialization. This, however, assumes that all services will retrieve the object graph in the same way. If a different service retrieves an Employee object first, then the data for the Company will be missing. Rather than instructing the serializer to ignore parent references, developers can deal with the circular reference problem by leveraging XML's ID and IDREF constructs. The former functions like a primary key on a database table row, while the latter is like a foreign key to a table. When an object is prepared for serialization, it may be assigned a unique ID attribute, and related elements in the same document can refer to that item through their IDREF attribute. Unfortunately, this approach requires the XSDs to be modified to support these attributes.

Data Transfer Object

Developers who choose to annotate domain objects with data-binding instructions must therefore contend with circular references. Of greater concern are the dependencies that result between domain layer entities and the request or response structures. The problem is that whenever domain objects are annotated with XML or JSON serialization attributes, and these objects are used in requests or responses, their structures are, in effect, projected out to clients. This means that any change made to the object model will ripple out to clients, forcing them to change as well. Likewise, a change to a request or response data structure may require the *Domain Model* [POEAA] to change. Developers need a way to define request and response structures that can vary independently from domain layer entities.

Developers may therefore revert to using structure-specific APIs to parse data from requests and to build responses rather than annotating domain objects with data-binding instructions. While this provides a level of indirection between domain entities and service messages, developers must still decide where this logic should be located. They may be tempted to include it directly within the service, but this tends to make the service harder to read and maintain. This also causes the service to become too familiar with the wire-level formats and structures used in messages. If the structures or formats change, then the service must change as well. This problem is further exacerbated if the parsing logic must be used by a number of services and is duplicated. How, then, can developers enable requests, domain layer entities, and responses to evolve independently, provide a convenient means to manipulate message payloads, and ensure that services are ignorant of wire-level formats?

Data Transfer Object

Create distinct classes to represent request and response data structures. Consolidate the mapping logic that reads and writes these structures.

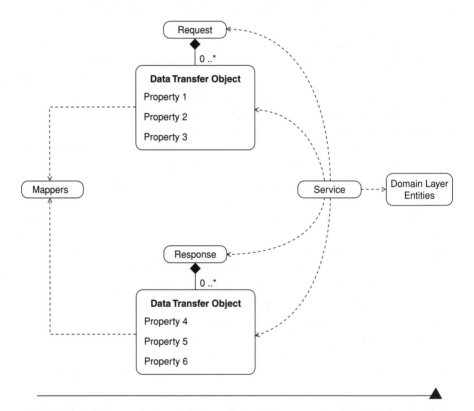

Data Transfer Objects [POEAA] (a.k.a. DTOs) are reusable classes that contain related data and no business logic. They may be defined on the service side, client side, or both sides of the communication channel. Their properties (i.e., getters/setters) may wrap primitive data types (e.g., integers, strings, etc.) or other DTOs. *Data Transfer Objects* were first described as a means to reduce the number of method calls in distributed object systems (e.g., CORBA, DCOM). However, this same pattern can also be used by web services to simplify manipulation of request and response data and to decouple message structures from domain layer entities. Services have an easier time manipulating request and response data because they don't have to use APIs for JSON, XML, or other formats. Domain layer entities are decoupled from request and response structures because DTOs are created as separate entities whose sole purpose is to define how data is received and returned from a service.

Data may be mapped into and out of DTOs through custom code or data binding. With the former approach, DTOs can be populated from requests through statements that use any number of APIs and frameworks for a given format. The most common way to extract XML data is through DOM and SAX parsers. DOM parsers load entire XML documents into memory and permit random access to any node in the document. SAX parsers read forward through documents and trigger events in a designated object whenever elements, attributes, or other content is found. The former approach is more flexible, while the latter is more efficient on memory. Similar frameworks are available for services that exchange JSON structures. Developers must also create logic to convert DTO content to the necessary wire-level formats (i.e., XML, JSON, etc.) for responses, serialize these structures to byte streams, and transmit the data back to the client. Regardless of the message format or framework that is used, the logic required to move data into and out of *Data Transfer Objects* should be centralized. As a first step, it is usually a good idea to consolidate this logic within the DTO itself. If the code becomes sufficiently complex, it may be better to extract it into separate *Request Mappers* (109) and *Response Mappers* (122).

Developers may also use an approach known as Data Binding. This eliminates the need to create custom code that reads and writes message structures. Data binding can be realized in two ways. Both approaches enable developers to create "mapping rules" that define how request items (i.e., elements, attributes, objects, etc.) are written into DTOs, and how DTO properties (i.e., attributes, getters) should populate responses. Some frameworks store mapping rules in external configuration files. These rules are usually loaded into memory before the service receives a request. When a message is received, the service must explicitly invoke the framework's deserialization process to convert the stream to a target DTO type. Likewise, the service must explicitly invoke framework operations to serialize and transmit responses. Castor, a data binding framework that lets developers map XML messages to and from Java objects, is an example of a binding framework that stores mapping rules in external files.

Data Transfer
Object

The second approach to data binding enables developers to annotate a class's properties (i.e., getters/setters) with keywords that are interpreted by the service framework at runtime. This eliminates the need to explicitly load mapping rules or invoke serialization processes. Given these annotations, the framework is able to instantiate and populate the appropriate DTOs with request data. These frameworks can also read, populate, and serialize response messages from DTOs in the required format (i.e., JSON, XML). JAX-WS, JAX-RS, and WCF are examples of frameworks that offer data binding through class annotations.

While data binding can eliminate a lot of custom parsing logic, it has some significant trade-offs. Several of these issues are discussed in the following section.

Data-Binding Considerations

Data Transfer Object

Developers who use *Data Transfer Objects* with data binding should consider the following issues.

- **Strong coupling to messages:** Whether the mapping rules are defined in external files or occur as annotations on class properties, data binding causes *Data Transfer Objects* to become tightly coupled to request and response structures. In other words, you'll usually have to regenerate and redeploy the related DTOs whenever the structures change. This being said, coupling can be reduced when the annotations let items occur in any sequence, and when items are marked as optional rather than required.

    Service developers can eliminate coupling to message parts they don't care about by employing a hybrid solution that uses a *Tolerant Reader* (243). In this approach, the reader extracts specific message fragments (e.g., customer address, account information, order information, etc.) while ignoring the rest. These fragments can then be automatically deserialized into corresponding DTOs that leverage data binding. Nevertheless, these DTOs are still tightly bound to the structure of the corresponding message fragments.

- **Contract-First versus Code-First:** These terms are commonly used by developers who employ data binding technologies. With the former approach, a developer defines service artifacts through meta-languages first and then sends this information through a binding compiler to generate code. In the latter approach, the developer creates annotated classes that are interpreted by a framework at runtime in order to produce metadata that can be consumed by client developer tools.

    Contract-First is most closely associated with services that use SOAP and WSDL, but the concept can also be applied to services that use neither. With Contract-First, the developer creates WSDL and XSDs first, then feeds this information through a binding compiler that generates a *service interface class* [see *Service Controller* (85)]. These compilers also typically create *Data Transfer Objects* from XSDs. Note that *Resource API* (38) developers can leverage binding compilers as well to create DTOs from XSD or even JSON schema.

The Code-First approach can be used with *RPC APIs* (18), *Message APIs* (27), and *Resource APIs* (38). In this approach, the developer creates a *Service Controller*, and possibly *Data Transfer Objects*. If the service uses WSDL, the framework will automatically generate WSDL and XSDs when clients query the base URI of the service. For a detailed discussion of these topics, see the *Service Descriptor* pattern (175).

- **Proprietary formats:** While this book emphasizes open message formats like XML and JSON, developers can use proprietary formats with HTTP as well. Some teams, for example, use technologies like Google's Protocol Buffers to encode messages in an extremely compact and efficient binary format. The client and service must, of course, use binding compilers created specifically for the format. It should go without saying, but platform-specific data types and proprietary serialization mechanisms can hinder interoperability.

- **Schema validation:** Since schema validation can consume significant memory and CPU cycles, most popular frameworks (that support data binding) disable automatic request validation. This means that the framework will not throw exceptions when it is unable to map a part of the message. In situations like these, the DTO content that could not be mapped is often preserved in a special construct (e.g., WCF's `ExtensionDataObject`).

General Considerations

This section provides an overview of several issues that developers should consider, regardless of whether DTOs use custom code or data binding.

- **Convenience:** DTOs make it easy for services and other domain layer entities to manipulate message content without having to know anything about wire-level formats.

- **Naming:** DTOs are often hard to distinguish from *Domain Model* [POEAA] objects. Some developers prefix or suffix DTO classes with the acronym `Dto` to facilitate identification (e.g., `CustomerDto`). These classes can also be grouped into namespaces that indicate they're DTOs (e.g., `SomeCompany.AccountMgt.DTOs`). When the classes are instantiated, it's often helpful to use similar techniques (e.g., `CustomerDTO customerDTO = new CustomerDTO();`).

- **Additional work effort:** *Data Transfer Objects* require developers to create additional code to move data from DTOs to domain layer entities, and vice versa. This logic can be fairly simple when request and response structures are shallow. In more complex cases, developers may want to create distinct *Request Mappers* (109) and *Response Mappers* (122).

- **Client-specific Data Transfer Objects:** Service developers should consider whether or not custom *Data Transfer Objects* should be created for each client when their structures vary yet are semantically equivalent. This strategy could lead to a proliferation of services and *Data Transfer Objects*. One could instead create *Request Mappers* (109) that translate disparate requests into common objects used by a web service.

- **DTO size:** As the breadth or depth of a *Data Transfer Object* increases, it becomes harder to understand, maintain, and use. The size of a DTO can also affect server performance and network utilization.

  Service developers should consider how much of the content conveyed in the request is actually relevant to the service. Consider a service that receives a large and complex XML document designed by an industry trade group. If a single *Data Transfer Object* is created to process the entire document, then the framework will probably expend undue time deserializing irrelevant content, thus incurring unnecessary server load. For scenarios like these, it may be better to create smaller *Data Transfer Objects* that correspond to smaller sections within the message (e.g., address information, product data, etc.). These message fragments can then be surgically extracted by a *Tolerant Reader* (243) or *Request Mapper* (109). Once the fragments have been extracted, the reader or mapper can leverage the platform's serialization APIs (e.g., JAXB, .NET DataContractSerializer) to instantiate and populate DTOs.

- **Message formats and serialization:** Developers should consider what message formats will be used. XML tends to be quite bulky, while JSON is more compact. The implication is that, for equivalent messages, JSON will have lower network latency. The manner in which messages are serialized makes a big difference too. The default approach is to serialize XML and JSON as plain text. Some frameworks enable developers to serialize these formats in binary form as well. This can help to reduce network latency. Of course, the message sender and receiver must use the same serialization algorithms (e.g., MTOM, BSON, WCF, Google Protocol Buffers, etc.).

- **Promoting chunky data transfers:** Services can encourage better network utilization by using *Data Transfer Object Collections*. This pattern suggests that *Data Transfer Objects* should be designed to use collections when possible so that like data can be conveyed in a single request or response. Consider the case where a client has to update information on five customers. When *Data Transfer Object Collections* are not used, a client might call a service five times, once for each customer update. This would incur five network round-trips, which in turn would increase overall latency. The parties may also be tempted to use distributed transactions to ensure data integrity. Unfortunately, this strategy tends to inhibit scalability because locks on underlying (table) resources are often held for inordinate periods of time. In contrast to this approach, when *Data Transfer Object Collections* are used, the client bundles all of the customer data into a *Data Transfer Object* that is sent in a single request. This minimizes network traffic and reduces overall latency. The size of the request payload increases, but this is generally offset by the performance gains achieved through fewer network transitions. By leveraging *Data Transfer Object Collections,* the service can process multiple items within a single local transaction that it controls. This simplifies client logic and ensures consistent error handling. If the service encounters a problem, it can easily roll back its transaction, and return a response providing detailed error information on each item in the collection.

Data Transfer Object

- **Use with Tolerant Readers:** The *Tolerant Reader* pattern (243) enables a client or service to function properly even when some of the message content received is unknown or when the data structures vary. Tolerant Readers often populate *Data Transfer Objects*. Developers can ensure loose coupling to message structures when custom code, rather than data binding, is used to populate DTOs.

Example: *A Data Transfer Object That Uses Custom Code*

The DTO shown below, written in Java, uses custom code to acquire message content while tolerating structural changes and missing items. Note that XPath-Parser encapsulates the XPath processing logic used to fetch data from the request stream; the implementation for this class has been omitted since it is tangential to this example. You should assume that getNodeValueAsString does not throw an XPathExpressionException when an item can't be found, but instead returns an empty string.

```java
public class BillingAddress extends Address {
  public static BillingAddress Get(XPathParser parser)
  {
    BillingAddress address = new BillingAddress();
```

```
try{

  address.setId(
    parser.getNodeValueAsString(
      "//BillingAddress/@id"));

  address.setStreet(
    parser.getNodeValueAsString(
      "//BillingAddress/@street"));

  address.setCity(
    parser.getNodeValueAsString(
      "//BillingAddress/@city"));

  address.setState(
    parser.getNodeValueAsString(
      "//BillingAddress/@state"));

  address.setZip(
    parser.getNodeValueAsString(
      "//BillingAddress/@zip"));
  }
  catch(Exception ex){
    // handle error here
  }

  return address;
  }
}
```

The base class for BillingAddress is shown below.

```
public abstract class Address {
  private String id;
  private String street;
  private String city;
  private String state;
  private String zip;

  public String getId() {
    return id;
  }

  public void setId(String value) {
    this.id = value;
  }

  public String getStreet() {
    return street;
  }
}
```

Data Transfer
Object

```
  public void setStreet(String value) {
    this.street = value;
  }

  public String getCity() {
    return city;
  }

  public void setCity(String city) {
    this.city = city;
  }

  public String getState() {
    return state;
  }

  public void setState(String state) {
    this.state = state;
  }

  public String getZip() {
    return zip;
  }

  public void setZip(String zip) {
    this.zip = zip;
  }
}
```

Example: *A Resource API That Receives and Returns JSON with Data Binding*

In this example, a C# service receives a JSON request containing information required to create quotes on a home loan. The response returns a series of tables showing quotes for various types of loans. The first code fragment shows the interface definition for the service.

```
[ServiceContract]
public interface ILoanService
{
  [OperationContract]
  [WebInvoke(Method="POST",
             BodyStyle = WebMessageBodyStyle.Bare,
             RequestFormat = WebMessageFormat.Json,
             ResponseFormat = WebMessageFormat.Json,
             UriTemplate = "/Quotes")]
  LoanQuotes CreateLoanQuotes(LoanInfo request);
}
```

Here you can see how the request is received by a request handler that automatically deserializes the request to a LoanInfo *Data Transfer Object*. This provides an intuitive way to extract information from the request and pass it into a domain layer object. A *Response Mapper* (122) is used to convert the structure returned from LoanCalculator.GetQuotes to a *Data Transfer Object*.

```
public class AcmeLoanService : ILoanService
{
  public LoanQuotes CreateLoanQuotes (LoanInfo request)
  {
    Quotes quotes = (new LoanCalculator()).GetQuotes(
                                    request.Purpose,
                                    request.Terms,
                                    request.LoanTypes,
                                    request.FinancingType,
                                    request.LoanAmount,
                                    request.HomeValue,
                                    request.State);

    return (new QuotesMapper()).Execute(quotes);
  }
}
```

Data Transfer Object

The *Data Transfer Object* used in the request appears below. The binding annotations eliminate the need to write code that parses the request and populates the target object.

```
[DataContract]
public class LoanInfo
{
  [DataMember]
  Public string Email{get; set;}

  [DataMember]
  public string Purpose { get; set; }

  [DataMember]
  public string FinancingType { get; set; }

  [DataMember]
  public int LoanAmount { get; set; }

  [DataMember]
  public int HomeValue { get; set; }

  [DataMember]
  public string State { get; set; }

  [DataMember]
  public string LoanTypes { get; set; }
```

```
  [DataMember]
  public string Terms { get; set; }
}
```

The *Data Transfer Objects* used in the response follow.

```
[DataContract]
public class LoanQuotes
{
  [DataMember]
  public List<RatesForLoanType> Quotes { get; set; }
}

[DataContract]
public class RatesForLoanType
{
  [DataMember]
  public string LoanType { get; set; }

  [DataMember]
  public List<RateTable> Rates;
}

[DataContract]
public class RateTable
{
  [DataMember]
  public decimal Rate { get; set; }

  [DataMember]
  public decimal Points { get; set; }

  [DataMember]
  public decimal APR { get; set; }

  [DataMember]
  public decimal ClosingFees { get; set; }

  [DataMember]
  public decimal Payment { get; set; }
}
```

Data Transfer Object

Example: *Abstract Data Transfer Objects*

Abstract *Data Transfer Objects* can be used to define "base types" for a family of structures used in requests or responses. Whenever an XSD contains a reference to an abstract type, the sender may insert a type derived from that abstract type. This creates an effect similar to polymorphism. New types can be added over time without requiring the client to be updated, unless they need or want to use these new types.

In the following Java web service, the BuyProduct operation is defined on an interface named MediaSvc. The message wrappers, BuyProduct and BuyProductResponse, are auto-generated. Both of these messages contain a *Data Transfer Object* of the type Order, which contains a reference to an abstract element named MediaType. The MediaSvc interface definition has been annotated with the XmlSeeAlso keyword so that the service can determine the specific subtype that was sent. This annotation also provides the framework the necessary information to generate the XSDs for the subtypes at runtime. Public fields are used rather than getters and setters in order to keep the code listing shorter.

Data Transfer Object

```
@WebService()
@XmlSeeAlso({DSE.Movie.class, DSE.MusicAlbum.class} )
public interface MediaSvc {
  @WebMethod(operationName = "BuyProduct")
  public Order BuyProduct(@WebParam(name = "request")
                                      Order request );
}

@XmlAccessorType(XmlAccessType.FIELD)
@XmlType(name = "Order",
  propOrder = {"CustomerAccountNumber", "Media"})
@XmlRootElement(name = "Order")
public class Order {

  @XmlElement(name="CustomerAccountNumber",required=true)
  public String CustomerAccountNumber;

  @XmlElement(name="Media",required=true)
  public MediaType Media;
}

@XmlAccessorType(XmlAccessType.FIELD)
@XmlType(name = "MediaType",
  propOrder = {"SKU", "Name"})
@XmlRootElement(name = "MediaType")
public abstract class MediaType {

  @XmlElement(name="SKU",required=true)
  public String SKU;

  @XmlElement(name="Name",required=true)
  public String Name;
   // etcetera
}

@XmlAccessorType(XmlAccessType.FIELD)
@XmlType(name = "Movie",
  propOrder = {"Description", "Director"})
@XmlRootElement(name = "Movie")
public class Movie extends MediaType {
```

```
    @XmlElement(name="Description",required=true)
    public String Description;

    @XmlElement(name="Director",required=true)
    public String Director;

    // etcetera
}

@XmlAccessorType(XmlAccessType.FIELD)
@XmlType(name = "MusicAlbum",
  propOrder = {"ArtistName", "RecordingLabel"})
@XmlRootElement(name = "MusicAlbum")
public class MusicAlbum extends MediaType {

    @XmlElement(name="ArtistName",required=true)
    public String ArtistName;

    @XmlElement(name="RecordingLabel",required=true)
    public String RecordingLabel;
}

@WebService(endpointInterface="ServiceContracts.MediaSvc")
public class MediaService {

  public Order BuyProduct(Order request) {

  // common business logic for Data Transfer Objects would appear here
  }
}
```

Data Transfer Object

The following listing shows key portions of the WSDL and XSD generated from the preceding code.

```
<portType name="MediaService">
  <operation name="BuyProduct">
    <input message="tns:BuyProduct" />
    <output message="tns:BuyProductResponse" />
  </operation>
</portType>

<message name="BuyProduct">
  <part name="parameters" element="tns:BuyProduct" />
</message>

<xs:complexType name="BuyProduct">
  <xs:sequence>
    <xs:element name="request" type="tns:Order" minOccurs="0" />
  </xs:sequence>
</xs:complexType>
```

```
<xs:complexType name="Order">
  <xs:sequence>
    <xs:element name="CustomerAccountNumber" type="xs:string" />
    <xs:element name="Media" type="tns:MediaType" />
  </xs:sequence>
</xs:complexType>


<xs:complexType name="MediaType" abstract="true">
  <xs:sequence>
    <xs:element name="SKU" type="xs:string" />
    <xs:element name="Name" type="xs:string" />
  </xs:sequence>
</xs:complexType>


<xs:complexType name="Movie">
  <xs:complexContent>
    <xs:extension base="tns:MediaType">
      <xs:sequence>
        <xs:element name="Description" type="xs:string" />
        <xs:element name="Director" type="xs:string" />
      </xs:sequence>
    </xs:extension>
  </xs:complexContent>
</xs:complexType>


<xs:complexType name="MusicAlbum">
  <xs:complexContent>
    <xs:extension base="tns:MediaType">
      <xs:sequence>
        <xs:element name="ArtistName" type="xs:string" />
        <xs:element name="RecordingLabel" type="xs:string" />
      </xs:sequence>
    </xs:extension>
  </xs:complexContent>
</xs:complexType>
```

Data Transfer Object

It should be noted that abstract types use the extension construct, which, as of this writing, is not addressed by the WS-I Basic Profile, nor does the WS-I compliance test suite include a test for it [Brown 2]. Regardless, popular service frameworks have done a pretty good job of supporting this feature, and developers can effectively use this technique if they understand how it works.

Request Mapper

A web service receives XML. The service owner has little to no control over the design of request structures.

How can a service process data from requests that are structurally different yet semantically equivalent?

In an ideal scenario, one organization controls the design of all message structures that are exchanged. However, in the real world this doesn't always happen. In many cases, the service developer must collaborate with external departments or businesses to design messages. Unfortunately, these groups may not agree on what should be included or excluded, or how data should be organized. Each organization may lobby for structures that reflect their understanding of the data. Others may insist that their structures be used. If these entities are external customers that are important to the business, it is usually wise to accommodate them. The net result is that the service developer may have to accept multiple requests that are structurally different yet are used for the same purpose. One could write distinct services for each client's variation on a request, but this would inevitably become a maintenance nightmare since the logic that moves data from requests to domain layer entities (i.e., *Table Modules, Domain Objects* [POEAA]), not to mention the service's control logic, would have to be rewritten for each client. Depending on the chosen language and platform, the service might also have to be recompiled and redeployed each time a client's structures changed.

Another way to process disparate request structures that are semantically equivalent is to create a service that simply validates and enqueues each request to a background process. This process would transform each request to a common structure that can be processed, and would also invoke the logic to process those structures. This approach scales quite well because the rate at which requests are processed can be easily controlled by the background process. However, it is more difficult for clients to acquire responses because the service that receives the request only returns a simple acknowledgment. If the client needs a response, it must either poll for it or deploy a service that receives callbacks.

Services that receive and process variant requests often revert to using lower-level APIs rather than data-binding technologies (e.g., JAXB, .NET's XmlSerializer)

Request
Mapper

in order to attain higher degrees of control and flexibility. These services may implement the logic to parse each request directly, but this tends to bloat the service code, making it hard to read and maintain. Service developers should instead separate the logic used to translate messages from the core service logic.

Create specialized classes that leverage structure-specific APIs to target and move select portions of requests directly to domain layer entities or to a common set of intermediate objects that can be used as input arguments to such entities. Load a particular mapper based on key content found in the request.

Request Mapper

Services typically have to process disparate yet semantically equivalent requests when the service owner has little to no control over request structure definitions. *Request Mappers* can be useful in this context because they eliminate the need to create a service for each variant request. *Request Mappers* are a specialization of the *Mapper* pattern [POEAA]. They are used to isolate request structures from domain layer entities and enable each to evolve independently. *Request Mappers* are responsible for parsing data from requests and moving this data into domain entities like *Table Modules* or *Domain Models* [POEAA], or into intermediate structures that can be used as inputs to these entities.

Mappers may be explicitly selected by the service implementation code. Alternatively, the service may delegate this responsibility to a *Factory Method* [GoF] or an *Inversion of Control* (IoC) container (for more information, see *Dependency Injection*). These approaches return a generic interface after selecting an appropriate mapper. The logic used to select a mapper can vary greatly. For instance, a factory method might parse the request for client credentials and instantiate a specific mapper based on the client's identity. Another common approach is to select a mapper based on the qualified name of the root element in the request. Regardless, once the service acquires an interface to a mapper, it invokes one or more methods on the mapper's interface in order to initiate parsing and to acquire the resultant domain entities or intermediate objects.

Request Mappers often parse entire requests by loading the request into an XML DOM. The advantage with this approach is that it enables the data to be randomly accessed many times over. However, if a document is very large, it can consume a significant amount of memory, which could exhaust heap space if the request load is high. Mappers may be hardcoded to programmatically select data from the DOM. The desired domain entities or intermediate structures are created as the mapper reads this data. This hardcoded approach, however, requires the mapper and service to be updated and redeployed whenever request structures change. A better approach is to leverage XSLT scripts to surgically extract and transform XML fragments. XSLT scripts maintained in files can often be altered and redeployed without forcing a full redeploy of the services. The output from the XSLT can even be deserialized directly to common *Data Transfer Objects* (94) by leveraging the platform's data-binding APIs (e.g., JAXB); an example of this is provided in the following code examples. A lighter-weight alternative to the XML DOM involves a streaming parser like SAX. This type of parser doesn't load entire documents into memory, which makes it more appropriate for high-load scenarios. Streaming parsers read through documents in a forward-only fashion, triggering events in the mapper as they go along. Each event that is fired in the mapper acquires some portion of the data from the request. Once the entire document has been read, the desired domain entities or intermediate structures will have been created. There exists yet another approach service designers may use to map requests. Dynamic languages like JavaScript can be leveraged by the host service to parse data. These mini scripts are typically maintained in separate files, so they too can be altered and redeployed without forcing a full redeploy of the services.

Request
Mapper

Considerations

The *Request Mapper* pattern should only be used after thoughtful consideration of the following.

- **Minimum criteria for adoption:** The true value of *Request Mappers* is realized when data must be extracted from requests that are semantically equivalent yet structurally different. If all you need to do is map data from a single request structure, then it may be better to encapsulate this logic in *Data Transfer Objects* (94).

Request Mappers are also useful when the service only needs a small portion of the data in a request. This often occurs when requests are designed by industry standards groups. Such requests usually carry information that is extraneous to the service's purpose. In cases like these, the mapper can parse out and validate only what it needs and ignore the rest.

- **Relation to different service API styles:** *Request Mappers* are most often used with *Message APIs* (27), but may also be used with *Resource APIs* (38). They generally aren't used with *RPC APIs* (18) because their message structures are derived from the signatures of class methods. The *Request Mapper* pattern implies that the developers must consider the design of the XML message structures first, irrespective of any service implementation. It should be noted that XML schemas aren't always used. In fact, some implementers only provide documentation depicting sample XML structures.

Request Mapper

- **Use in reducing client dependencies:** *Request Mappers* can help to insulate clients from domain layer entities (e.g., objects, record sets, etc.). This means that a change to a domain layer entity won't necessarily force clients to change and vice versa.

- **JSON:** *Request Mappers* aren't used as much with JSON since their structures are usually driven by the service owner.

- **Mapper specialization:** *Request Mappers* are frequently responsible for translating entire requests. However, specialized mappers that process smaller XML fragments can also be created if the request structure is particularly complex. For example, an order request that contains customer and product information may be processed by mappers designated for each logical data type. This approach can help to simplify maintenance quite a bit.

- **Code complexity:** *Request Mappers* can become quite complex. Developers may have to write a nontrivial amount of code to navigate through XML, and extract, convert, and copy data to target objects. Specialized mappers are often required to process data for specific clients. While XPath and XSLT can be an effective tool to parse and convert requests, developers can't always just change XPath and XSLT when request structures change. Sometimes they must also alter the code for the mappers or services, which may require the service to be recompiled and redeployed. Additionally, XSLT isn't very easy to read and maintain. Fortunately, graphical tools capable of generating XSLT can be leveraged.

- **Utilization of web server resources:** *Request Mappers* can be CPU- and memory-intensive, depending on the complexity of the work performed, the size of the requests, and the technologies used to parse the request.

- **Response time:** Request mapping logic can increase latency. If average response times become unacceptable, one should consider using the *Request/Acknowledge* pattern (59) wherein the service forwards the request to an asynchronous background process, usually by way of a queue, and sends the client an acknowledgment. This background process could invoke a *Command* [GoF] that uses a *Request Mapper* to transform the request to a common structure. Clients that require a response would have to use *Request/Acknowledge/Poll* or *Request/Acknowledge/Callback*.

- **Relation to integration patterns:** The *Request Mapper* pattern is quite similar to the *Normalizer* pattern [EIP]. The key difference is that normalizers use a *Message Router* [EIP] to forward the request to a *Message Translator* [EIP] over a *Message Channel* [EIP]. Queues are typically used as the channel between the router and translator, and this implies an asynchronous paradigm. The request is also passed through several process boundaries.

  Request Mappers are conceptually similar, but are quite a bit simpler. They often select and transform the request within the process space of the web service, and can be easily used in synchronous *Request/Response* (54) exchanges and in asynchronous interchanges like *Request/Acknowledge* (59). Another difference between the *Request Mapper* and *Normalizer* patterns is that the former can be used to create target domain objects, while the latter only converts between message types.

Request
Mapper

Example: *A Request Mapper That Transforms a Request with XSL*

In this example, a *Resource API* (38) receives invoices from a variety of trading partners. Each of these partners has its own way of formatting invoices. The following represents a simple invoice from the fictional Acme Corporation.

```
<AcmeInvoice>
  <InvId>123</InvId>
  <WO>456</WO>
  <Services>
    <svc id="678" time="3" />
    <svc id="876" time="2" />
  </Services>
</AcmeInvoice>
```

Since all partners have their own format for invoices, the service must convert each to a standard format. This target structure is shown below.

```
<Invoice>
  <InvoiceId>Acme.123</InvoiceId>
  <WorkOrder>Acme.456</WorkOrder>
  <BilledHours>
    <Billed><BillCode>678</BillCode><Time>3</Time></Billed>
    <Billed><BillCode>876</BillCode><Time>2</Time></Billed>
  </BilledHours>
</Invoice>
```

The service uses XSL to transform Acme's invoice to the standard format. By creating XSLT scripts for each partner, the service owner avoids having to maintain programmatic XML navigation and conversion logic.

Request Mapper

```
<?xml version="1.0" encoding="ISO-8859-1"?>
<xsl:stylesheet version="1.0"
    xmlns:xsl="http://www.w3.org/1999/XSL/Transform">


  <xsl:template match="/">
    <Invoice>
      <xsl:apply-templates />
    </Invoice>
  </xsl:template>

  <xsl:template match="AcmeInvoice/InvId">
    <InvoiceId>Acme.<xsl:value-of select="."/></InvoiceId>
  </xsl:template>

  <xsl:template match="AcmeInvoice/WO">
    <WorkOrder>Acme.<xsl:value-of select="."/></WorkOrder>
  </xsl:template>

  <xsl:template match="AcmeInvoice/Services">
    <BilledHours>
      <xsl:apply-templates />
    </BilledHours>
  </xsl:template>

  <xsl:template match="//svc">
    <Billed>
      <BillCode><xsl:value-of select="./@id"/></BillCode>
      <Time><xsl:value-of select="./@time"/></Time>
    </Billed>
  </xsl:template>
</xsl:stylesheet>
```

The request handler for the web service is shown below. Trading partners may issue an HTTP POST to the service and provide a media type of application/xml. The service sends the request stream to a MapperFactory responsible for creating a *Request Mapper* that knows how to handle the specific request. Once the service has acquired a mapper, it invokes its Deserialize method in order to acquire a fully populated *Data Transfer Object* (94) of type Invoice. The data from this object may then be fed into domain entities such as *Table Modules* or *Domain Objects* [POEAA].

```
@Path("/invoices")
public class InvoiceHandler {

    @POST
    @Consumes("application/xml")
    public void ProcessAllInvoices(InputStream stream) {

        BaseRequestMapper mapper = MapperFactory.getMapper(stream);
        Invoice invoice = (Invoice)mapper.Deserialize();

        // Pass data from standard Invoice into domain entities,
        //    set HTTP return code
    }
}
```

Request
Mapper

The getMapper *Factory Method* [GoF] of the MapperFactory class calls another factory method in order to instantiate a DocWrapper class. This class instantiates an XML DOM and populates it with data from the request stream. Once the DocWrapper has been created, the name of the root node is retrieved and passed to the getMapper method of the MapperList class. This information is used to determine which concrete mapper should be used to handle the request. The DocWrapper is then passed into the mapper, and all are returned to ProcessAllInvoices.

```
public class MapperFactory {

    public static BaseRequestMapper getMapper(InputStream stream)
        throws ParserConfigurationException,
               SAXException,
               IOException,
               CloneNotSupportedException
    {
        DocWrapper doc = DocWrapper.getDocWrapper(stream);
        String rootNodeValue = doc.getRootNodeName();
        BaseRequestMapper mapper = MapperList.getMapper(rootNodeValue);
        mapper.setDocWrapper(doc);
        return mapper;
    }
}
```

The code for DocWrapper is shown below. This class contains an XML DOM and provides a few convenience methods.

```java
public class DocWrapper {

  private Document doc=null;

  public static DocWrapper getDocWrapper(InputStream stream)
    throws ParserConfigurationException,
           SAXException,
           IOException
  {
    DocWrapper wrapper = new DocWrapper();
    wrapper.loadXMLDocument(stream);
    return wrapper;
  }

  private void loadXMLDocument(InputStream stream)
    throws ParserConfigurationException,
           SAXException,
           IOException
  {
    DocumentBuilderFactory factory =
        DocumentBuilderFactory.newInstance();

    factory.setNamespaceAware(true);
    DocumentBuilder builder = factory.newDocumentBuilder();
    doc = builder.parse(stream);
  }

  public String getRootNodeName(){
    return getDocument().getFirstChild().getLocalName();
  }

  public Document getDocument() {
    return doc;
  }
}
```

The code for MapperList is shown below. This class contains a Hashtable that holds *Prototypical* instances [GoF] of all possible *Request Mappers* that might be used. These prototypes are loaded into the Hashtable through the Initialize method. When MapperFactory calls this class's getMapper method, the value retrieved from the root node of the message is used as a key to find a prototypical instance in the hashtable. MapperList then clones the prototype and returns it to MapperFactory.

```java
public class MapperList {

  private static Hashtable<MessageTypes,BaseRequestMapper>
      msgTypes = null;
```

```
  public static BaseRequestMapper getMapper(String msgName)
    throws CloneNotSupportedException
  {
    MessageTypes currentMsg =
      MessageTypes.valueOf(msgName.toUpperCase());

    return (BaseRequestMapper)getInstance().get(currentMsg).clone();
  }

  public static Hashtable<MessageTypes,BaseRequestMapper>
          getInstance(){

    if(null== msgTypes) Initialize();
    return msgTypes;
  }

  private static void Initialize(){

    // logic to lock the shared object has been omitted.

    msgTypes = new Hashtable<MessageTypes,BaseRequestMapper>();

    msgTypes.put(MessageTypes.AcmeInvoice,
            new AcmeRequestMapper());

    // other mappers would appear here
  }
}

public enum MessageTypes {
    AcmeInvoice

    // other message types would appear here
}
```

The code for a concrete *Request Mapper* named AcmeRequestMapper is shown below. This is a child class of BaseRequestMapper, which is shown later in this example. The AcmeRequestMapper class uses generics to indicate that all incoming requests should be converted to a target object of type Invoice. Each concrete mapper class also provides the name of the XSLT file that should be used to transform request content.

```
public class AcmeRequestMapper extends BaseRequestMapper<Invoice>{
  public String getXslFileName() {
    return // name of file could be retrieved from config file
          // or a memory cache
  }
  public String getPackageName(){
    return // name of Java package containing the Invoice object
  }
}
```

The BaseRequestMapper class contains the core logic for the *Request Mapper* pattern. This class invokes the retrieved XSLT script by calling the Transform method of xslTransformer. The results of this transformation are returned to a string buffer named resultsBuffer. The mapper then instantiates JaxBUnmarshaller for the target object type. Recall that this type was defined by the child mapper class. The mapper uses the JaxBUnmarshaller class to unmarshal the transformed request.

Request
Mapper

```
public abstract class BaseRequestMapper<TargetType>
  implements Cloneable{

  public abstract String getXslFileName();
  public abstract String getPackageName();

  private DocWrapper docWrapper;

  @Override
  public Object clone() throws CloneNotSupportedException{
    return super.clone();
  }

  public TargetType Deserialize()
    throws ParserConfigurationException,
           SAXException, IOException,
           TransformerConfigurationException,
           TransformerException,JAXBException
  {
    Document doc = docWrapper.getDocument();

    String resultsBuffer =
        xslTransformer.Transform(doc, getXslFileName());

    JaxBUnmarshaller<TargetType> unMarshaller =
        new JaxBUnmarshaller<TargetType>();

    TargetType returnObj =
        unMarshaller.unMarshall(resultsBuffer, getPackageName());

    return returnObj;
  }

  public void setDocWrapper(DocWrapper wrapper) {
    docWrapper = wrapper;
  }
}
```

The xslTransformer class uses JAXP APIs to transform Acme's request to the standard XML invoice structure shown earlier. The source data is passed in as an XML DOM, and the name of the file containing the XSLT script is also provided. The result of the transform is returned as a string.

```
public class xslTransformer {

  public static String Transform(Document src,String xslFileName)
    throws ParserConfigurationException, SAXException,
           IOException,TransformerConfigurationException,
           TransformerException
  {
    DOMSource xmlSource =new DOMSource(src);
    Transformer xform = initTransformer(xslFileName);

    Writer resultBuffer = new StringWriter();
    StreamResult streamResult = new StreamResult(resultBuffer);

    xform.transform( xmlSource, streamResult);

    return resultBuffer.toString();
  }

  private static Transformer initTransformer(String xslFile)
    throws TransformerConfigurationException
  {
    TransformerFactory factory =
        TransformerFactory.newInstance();

    StreamSource xslStream = new StreamSource(xslFile);

    return factory.newTransformer(xslStream);
  }
}
```

Request Mapper

JaxBUnmarshaller deserializes the transformed request to the desired target type object originally identified by the concrete mapper class AcmeRequestMapper.

```
public class JaxBUnmarshaller<TargetType> {

  public JaxBUnmarshaller(){}

  public TargetType unMarshall(String xmlString,
                              String srcPackage)
    throws JAXBException
  {
    TargetType returnObj = null;
```

```
    JAXBContext jc = JAXBContext.newInstance(srcPackage);
    Unmarshaller unmarshaller = jc.createUnmarshaller();

    StringBuffer buffer = new StringBuffer(xmlString);

    StreamSource src =
      new StreamSource( new StringReader( buffer.toString() ));

    return (TargetType)unmarshaller.unmarshal( src );
  }
}
```

The *Data Transfer Objects* (94) used in this example are provided below.
XML schemas were created first, and the xjc binding compiler was used to generate the code.

```
@XmlAccessorType(XmlAccessType.FIELD)
@XmlType(name = "", propOrder =
                   {"invoiceId", "workOrder","billedHours"})
@XmlRootElement(name = "Invoice")
public class Invoice {

  @XmlElement(name = "InvoiceId", required = true)
  protected String invoiceId;

  @XmlElement(name = "WorkOrder", required = true)
  protected String workOrder;

  @XmlElement(name = "BilledHours", required = true)
  protected BilledHours billedHours;

  public String getInvoiceId() { return invoiceId;}
  public void setInvoiceId(String value) {invoiceId = value;}

  public String getWorkOrder() {return workOrder;}
  public void setWorkOrder(String value) {workOrder = value;}

  public BilledHours getBilledHours() {return billedHours;}
  public void setBilledHours(BilledHours value)
                                    {billedHours = value;}
}

@XmlAccessorType(XmlAccessType.FIELD)
@XmlType(name = "BilledHours", propOrder = {"billed"})
public class BilledHours {

  @XmlElement(name = "Billed") protected List<Billed> billed;
```

```
    public List<Billed> getBilled() {
      if (billed == null) {
        billed = new ArrayList<Billed>();
      }
        return this.billed;
    }
}

@XmlAccessorType(XmlAccessType.FIELD)
@XmlType(name = "Billed", propOrder = {"billCode","time"})
public class Billed {

    @XmlElement(name = "BillCode", required = true)
    protected String billCode;

    @XmlElement(name = "Time", required = true)
    protected BigDecimal time;

    public String getBillCode() {return billCode;}
    public void setBillCode(String value) {billCode = value;}

    public BigDecimal getTime() {return time;}
    public void setTime(BigDecimal value) {time = value;}
}
```

Response Mapper

A web service returns a text-based response.

How can the logic required to construct a response be reused by multiple services?

Services should generally provide a layer of indirection that insulates clients from the means used to fulfill requests. The client should not know if, for example, the service accesses a database directly or delegates work to object models, workflows, software packages, or legacy applications. Even when the internal mechanisms used to fulfill requests are well hidden, clients can still become invisibly coupled to domain layer entities. If, for example, domain objects are annotated with XML or JSON serialization attributes (e.g., JAXB, WCF), and these objects are used directly in responses, then their structures are, in effect, projected out to clients. This means that any change made to the object model will also ripple out to clients, forcing them to change as well. This is why it's generally a good idea to create distinct data structures (i.e., messages or media types) whose sole purpose is to carry request and response data in the form required by the client. This enables the domain layer entities to vary independently from the structures used by clients.

While such data structures can decouple clients from domain layer entities, additional logic is required to move data to and from these structures. This logic may be straightforward if there is a one-to-one relation between domain entities and the response structures. However, the data used in responses is often pulled from multiple sources. Additionally, there can be a significant disparity between domain layer structures and response structures. This disparity happens quite frequently when responses are defined by business partners, industry consortiums, or trade groups. In situations like these, the service may need to convert data types, merge or split data, aggregate data, and eliminate duplicate data. The logic to transform and move data to these response structures could be included directly in the service, but this makes the service that much harder to maintain and may also result in duplicate code if the logic is used by many services.

One could mitigate this risk and promote reuse by moving this logic to the domain layer entities. This, however, would create a dependency between the source domain entities and the response structures. How can the logic that creates complex responses be reused while encouraging the independent evolution of domain layer entities and the response structures used by clients?

Create a class that consolidates the data mapping and transformation logic used to create a response.

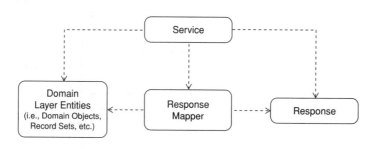

Response Mappers are a specialization of the *Mapper* pattern [POEAA]. They consolidate the data transformation, mapping, and serialization logic used to create a specific response or family of responses. *Response Mappers* are often selected and instantiated directly by services, but other techniques may be used (e.g., IoC) to create these mappers as well. Once a mapper has been instantiated, the service calls methods on the mapper as it iterates over data it retrieves from domain layer entities. This causes the mapper to assemble the data for the response in small increments. The service might also process the request in its entirety and send the final results to the mapper in a single method call. Regardless of whether the mapper receives data little by little or all at once, the service usually calls the mapper at the end to acquire the final response (see Figure 4.4).

Services may pass domain objects, *Record Sets* [POEAA], structs, and primitive data to mappers. This data is typically copied to internal data structures that compile the data in a form that roughly resembles the response format. These may be implemented in many ways. An XML DOM may, for example, be used if the output format is XML and the developer wishes to maintain complete control over the shape of the response. This, however, can entail a significant amount of custom coding. This code can be eliminated by copying response data to *Data Transfer Objects* (94) that use data binding.

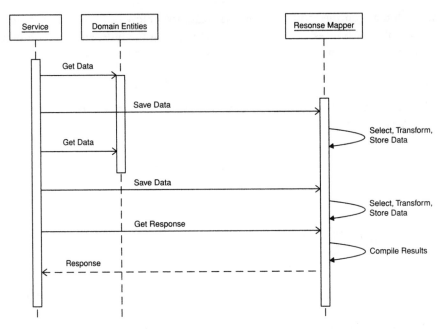

Figure 4.4 *A service may call mapper methods from within a loop as it iterates over data it retrieves from the domain layer. This causes the mapper to compile the data for the response in small increments. The service might also send the final results to the mapper in a single method call. Regardless, the handler usually calls the mapper at the end to acquire the response.*

Considerations

Developers should consider the following issues when contemplating use of the *Response Mapper* pattern.

- **Minimum criteria for adoption:** *Response Mappers* may be used to consolidate the logic that constructs complex responses. This makes it easier to share this logic across multiple web services.

   While the *Response Mapper* can be considered a relative of the classic *Builder* pattern [GoF], the manner in which it is implemented and the motivations for using it are somewhat different. The goal of the *Builder* pattern is to separate the process used to create complex data structures from those structures. This motivation holds true for response mappers because the logic used to create responses is separated from the response structures themselves. However, the more important goal is to remove this construction logic from web services.

The *Builder* pattern suggests that it may be used when the representation of a complex object (in this case, a response) varies. Individual *Response Mappers* should generally be designed to produce specific responses. These mappers, however, may inherit from a base class that represents a family of mappers. After the service retrieves the data to be used in a response, it could call a *Factory Method* [GoF], which returns the appropriate mapper for a particular client. The service would then call methods on the common mapper interface, and wouldn't have to know anything about the specific response message being returned.

- **Use in reducing client dependencies:** *Response Mappers* can help to insulate clients from domain layer entities (e.g., objects, record sets, etc.). This means that a change to a domain layer entity won't necessarily force clients to change and vice versa.

- **Additional work effort:** The effort expended to create and maintain *Response Mappers* may not be worth it if the response is relatively simple or isn't returned from multiple services. If a single service returns a given response, one might instead consider extracting the mapping logic to a separate routine in the *Service Controller* (85).

- **Scope of responsibility:** Sometimes it can be difficult to determine what logic should remain in the web service and what should go into the *Response Mapper*. In most cases, the service should generally perform the bulk of the work, and should coordinate interactions with specific domain layer entities. If the service uses a rich *Domain Model* [POEAA], it would call methods on the model and give the mapper selected objects containing information to be used in the response. In a similar fashion, if the service uses *Table Modules* [POEAA], it would pass individual *Record Sets* [POEAA] to the mapper. While it may be tempting to include business logic within the mapper, this type of logic should remain in the *Domain Model* [POEAA] or service.

- **Use with linked services:** *Response Mappers* that are used by *Resource APIs* (38) often construct URIs to related services and include these addresses in the response. However, it may not be a good idea to put this logic directly in the mappers if a common approach for URI construction is required across several mappers. Instead, a consistent and reusable approach for URI construction can often be ensured when the logic is

Response
Mapper

extracted and encapsulated within separate classes that are called by *Response Mappers.*

- **Relation to integration patterns:** Similarities exist between the *Response Mapper* and *Message Translator* patterns [EIP]. Both patterns provide a solution to convert data structures and types, and to alter data formats as well. *Message Translators,* however, are frequently used as filters that are deployed between clients and services or between services. Multiple translators can be arranged into a chain of filters between services. In contrast, *Response Mappers* are used within a service.

Response Mapper

Example: *A Service with a Resource API That Uses a Response Mapper*

In this example, a service with a *Resource API* (38) returns an invoice for a particular year/month period. This invoice has a list of work orders that contains summaries of the hours billed for the period and the total cost of that work. Each work order also contains a link to a URI where the client may obtain detailed information on the work order. This first code fragment shows the interface of the service. The client may request an invoice by submitting a GET to a URI that looks like http://www.acmeCorp.org/123/invoices/?yyyy=2010&mm=3.

```
[ServiceContract]
[XmlSerializerFormat]
public interface IInvoiceService
{
  [WebGet(BodyStyle = WebMessageBodyStyle.Bare,
   RequestFormat = WebMessageFormat.Xml,
   ResponseFormat = WebMessageFormat.Xml,
   UriTemplate = "/{clientId}/invoices/?yyyy={year}&mm={month}")]
  [OperationContract]
  Invoice GetInvoice(string clientId, string year, string month);
}
```

The following code shows how the service might be implemented. The request handler calls an object in a *Domain Model* [POEAA] to retrieve a list of BilledHours. Each of these objects contains the hours a particular contractor has billed to a given work order along with the contractor's rate. The service then instantiates a *Response Mapper,* iterates through the collection of BilledHours, and passes each instance to the mapper. For each instance of BilledHours, the service also updates the total work order hours and cost. The service then calls the mapper's GetResponse method. The response is automatically serialized as XML since the Invoice and its contained objects use *Data Transfer Objects* (94) with data-binding annotations.

```
public class InvoiceService : IInvoiceService
{
  public Invoice GetInvoice(string clientId, string year,
                             string month)
  {
    IList<BilledHours> hoursBilled =
      BillableHoursManager.GetBillableHoursForPeriod(
        clientId, int.Parse(year), int.Parse(month));

    InvoiceResponseMapper mapper = new InvoiceResponseMapper();
    mapper.Initialize(clientId, year, month);

    foreach(BilledHours contractorHours in hoursBilled){

      WorkOrder wo = mapper.AddData(contractorHours);

      wo.Hours += contractorHours.Hours;
      wo.Cost += contractorHours.Hours * contractorHours.Rate;
    }
    return mapper.GetResponse();
  }
}
```

The abstract class ResponseMapper and the concrete class InvoiceResponseMapper are shown below. The latter maintains a list of WorkOrder objects. Whenever the AddData method on InvoiceResponseMapper is called, the mapper determines if it already has the work order identified in the BilledHours object. If it doesn't, it creates a new WorkOrder. It also provides *Linked Services* (77) the client may use to see the details of the work order. If the work order is found in the mapper's collection, it is updated to reflect the contractor's data. Keep in mind that the mapper should not contain any domain logic; it is only responsible for mapping data. That's why the service updates the work order's hours and cost.

```
public abstract class ResponseMapper<InputType, ContainedType, ReturnType>
{
  public abstract ContainedType AddData(InputType inputData);
  public abstract ReturnType GetResponse();
}

public class InvoiceResponseMapper :
               ResponseMapper<BilledHours, WorkOrder, Invoice>
{
  private const string BaseURI = "http://www.acmeCorp.org/";

  string clientId, month, year;
  private IList<WorkOrder> workOrders = new List<WorkOrder>();
```

```
public InvoiceResponseMapper() { }

public void Initialize(string clientId, string year,
                       string month)
{
  //skipped validation
  this.clientId = clientId;
  this.year = year;
  this.month = month;
}

public override WorkOrder AddData(BilledHours billedHours)
{
  string workOrderId = billedHours.WorkOrderId;

  WorkOrder workOrder =
    workOrders.Find(
      delegate(WorkOrder wo){return wo.Id == workOrderId;});

  if(null== workOrder)
    workOrder = CreateNewWorkOrderElement(workOrderId);

  return workOrder;
}

private WorkOrder CreateNewWorkOrderElement(string workOrderId)
{
  WorkOrder workOrder = new WorkOrder();

  workOrder.Id = workOrderId;
  workOrder.UriLink = CreateLinkToWorkOrderDetail(workOrder);

  workOrders.Add(workOrder);

  return workOrder;
}

private UriLink CreateLinkToWorkOrderDetail(WorkOrder wo)
{
  UriLink link = new UriLink();

  link.Relation = RelationTypes.GetWODetails;
  link.MediaType = MediaTypes.WorkOrder;

  link.URI = String.Format("{0}{1}/workOrders/{2}",
             BaseURI, clientId, wo.Id);

  return link;
}
```

Response Mapper

```
public override Invoice GetResponse()
{
  Invoice invoice = new Invoice();

  invoice.Id = String.Format("{0}.{1}.{2}",
              clientId, year, month);

  invoice.WorkOrders = this.workOrders;

  return invoice;
}
}
```

The domain entity BilledHours is shown in the following code listing.

```
public class BilledHours
{
  public string WorkOrderId{get; set;}
  public string ContractorId{get; set;}
  public decimal Hours{get; set;}
  public decimal Rate{get; set;}
}
```

Here are the *Data Transfer Objects* (94) used in this example.

```
[XmlRoot]
public class Invoice
{
  [XmlAttribute]
  public string Id{get; set;}

  [XmlElement]
  public List<WorkOrder> WorkOrders{get; set;}
}

[XmlRoot]
public class WorkOrder
{
  [XmlAttribute]
  public string Id{ get; set; }

  [XmlAttribute]
  public decimal Hours{ get; set; }

  [XmlAttribute]
  public decimal Cost { get; set; }

  [XmlElement(ElementName = "link")]
  public UriLink UriLink{ get; set; }
}
```

```
[XmlRoot]
public class UriLink
{
  public UriLink() { }

  [XmlAttribute(AttributeName = "rel")]
  public string Relation { get; set; }

  [XmlAttribute(AttributeName = "type")]
  public string MediaType { get; set; }

  [XmlAttribute(AttributeName = "href")]
  public string URI { get; set; }
}
```

Response
Mapper

Chapter 5

Web Service Implementation Styles

Introduction

Web services can be used for a variety of purposes. Some make it easier for developers from different departments to use internal resources like databases or domain objects. Others provide a standardized means to invoke common business logic. Regardless of the purpose, developers must decide how much logic should be included within each web service. This chapter looks at a few common ways to implement web services. These patterns are listed in Table 5.1.

Table 5.1 *Web Service Implementation Styles*

Pattern Name	Problem	Description
Transaction Script (134)	How can developers quickly implement web service logic?	Write custom logic for database access, file manipulation, or other purposes directly within the web service method.
Datasource Adapter (137)	How can a web service provide access to internal resources like database tables, stored procedures, domain objects, or files with a minimum amount of custom code?	Create a web service that uses a specialized Datasource Provider. Leverage developer tools that generate datasource metadata and produce controllers that not only encapsulate and interpret the rules for request processing, but also direct the actions of Datasource Providers and Message Formatters.
Operation Script (144)	How can web services reuse common domain logic without duplicating code?	Encapsulate common business logic in domain layer entities that exist outside of the web service. Limit the logic within web services to algorithms that direct the activities of these entities.

Continues

Table 5.1 *Web Service Implementation Styles (continued)*

Pattern Name	Problem	Description
Command Invoker (149)	How can web services with different APIs reuse common domain logic while enabling both synchronous and asynchronous request processing?	Create command objects that fully encapsulate common request processing logic. Instantiate and invoke these commands from within the web service, or forward them to an asynchronous background process.
Workflow Connector (156)	How can web services be used to support complex and long-running business processes?	Use a Workflow Engine to manage the life cycle and execution of tasks within complex or long-running business processes. Identify a web service that will trigger each logical business process. Use Callback Services to receive additional data for these long-running processes, and forward messages from these Callback Services to the Workflow Engine.

Design Considerations for Web Service Implementation

The following factors should be considered when writing web service code.

- **Atomicity:** Web services should be atomic and adhere to an "All-or-Nothing" philosophy. In other words, they should guarantee that all tasks they direct complete successfully or are entirely reversed. Database transactions may be managed by the service itself or by lower-level domain layer entities (e.g., domain objects). If the service coordinates the work of these entities, it should always ensure that data is left in a valid state by instructing the entities to commit or abort at the appropriate times.

- **State management:** Stateful web services allocate server memory for each client session. These services save information from individual client requests to session variables that can be accessed in subsequent requests. This enables clients to use web services as if they were stateful local objects, and can also help to reduce database load if the data kept in the session variables would have normally been retrieved from a database. Unfortunately, as the web server load increases, the memory needed to support stateful web services usually increases as well. If too much memory is consumed, then data may be swapped from memory to disk, thereby hurting server performance. In the worst-case scenario, a server fault may occur.

The use of stateful web services can cause other scalability problems as well. Client requests may have to be sent back to the server where the client's session was established unless an alternative mechanism for state management is used. Client state could, for example, be stored in a distributed memory cache that is accessible to all web servers. It could also be written to a file system or database. Both approaches, however, require additional out-of-process calls which may add to the overall response time. Access of information held in distributed memory caches can be very fast, but data may be lost upon a crash. Information stored in a file system or database can usually survive a server crash, but the data retrieval time may lag.

These are just a few of the reasons why many create stateless web services. With this approach, any server memory allocated for clients is released at the end of each request. Since requests may be sent to any web server, and temporary client data is rarely held in distributed state management infrastructures, it becomes much easier to balance client load across a clustered web server tier and scale the overall system. However, since the server does not store data from previous requests, the size of each request tends to increase, and this may cause network utilization to increase as well. The web service may also have to retrieve more data from the database on each request since nothing is saved in memory from prior requests.

For a more in-depth discussion of session state, I recommend *Patterns of Enterprise Application Architecture* [POEAA] and *Architectural Styles and the Design of Network-based Software Architectures* [Fielding].

- **Service composition:** Consistent and reliable outcomes are more likely when the web service controls its own execution and has few dependencies on outside forces. One may certainly create complex web services that call other web services, but the ramifications must be carefully considered. First is the problem of network latency. The overall response time of a web service that calls other web services may be unacceptable for certain situations. The service designer must also think about network and server failures. If a subordinate service is unavailable, then what should the parent service do? Should the parent make multiple attempts to connect to the service? Should the parent fail if a subordinate fails? If the parent decides to fail, it may need to instruct its subordinates to undo any work that they completed prior to the failure. How should it do this? The service designer must also consider whether or not the client should be kept waiting as all of this transpires. These are just a few of the questions that must be answered when building composite services.

Transaction Script

The logic for a web service is relatively simple and is not reused in other web services.

How can developers quickly implement web service logic?

Web services can be used to provide access to databases or to text or binary files, offer a simplified API for a packaged application, make legacy applications available to new clients, or provide domain-specific business logic. A decision must be made regarding where the logic to manipulate these targets should be located. In many cases, the most practical approach is to create this logic directly within the web service method.

Write custom logic for database access, file manipulation, or other purposes directly within the web service method.

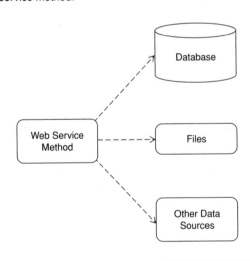

Web services can be implemented as Transaction Scripts [POEAA] that have intimate knowledge of databases, file systems, file types, or the APIs of third-party packages and legacy applications. If the service performs a business function, it contains all of the validation logic, calculations, conditional statements, and other logic required to implement the function. The most common type of *Transaction Script* involves databases. In this scenario, the web method (a.k.a. request handler) contains all of the code required to interact with a database. This typically includes code to manage database connections and transactions, execute SQL, and retrieve *Record Sets* [POEAA].

Considerations

Service developers should consider the following when thinking about using the *Transaction Script* pattern.

- **Simplicity:** *Transaction Scripts* are easy to understand and are a natural starting point for many. Implementation of service logic is straightforward because the developer simply writes all of the code required to manipulate databases, files, and other data sources (e.g., legacy applications and commercial packages) directly within the web service method. This is often the fastest approach in the face of looming deadlines because one doesn't have to spend the time creating *Domain Models* [POEAA], application *Gateways* [POEAA], or common file-access libraries intended for reuse. This is often a pragmatic approach when the logic is relatively simple and will not be duplicated in other web services.

- **Potential for long methods and code duplication:** The code in *Transaction Scripts* often becomes increasingly complex over time, which, of course, makes it difficult to maintain. Since short methods are easier to understand and manage, some may decide to extract portions of the web method out into smaller specialized methods located within the same class as the web method itself [i.e., the *Service Controller* (85)]. This can make the web method easier to read and maintain, but tends to make the controller less maintainable because it now contains a mix of web service methods and supporting functions.

  Developers who use this pattern are most concerned with speed of implementation. The consequence is that the service's logic may be duplicated. Developers may decide to refactor the web service to use the *Operation Script* (144), *Command Invoker* (149), or *Workflow Connector* (156) pattern if it becomes apparent that the service's logic must be reused. In most cases, this can be done with minimal impact to clients.

- **Tight coupling to data sources and APIs:** *Transaction Scripts* have intimate knowledge of and are tightly coupled to the underlying resources (i.e., file systems, file types, databases, application APIs, etc.) that they use. When these sources change, the service's code usually has to be altered as well.

Transaction
Script

Example: *A Service That Has an Intimate Understanding of a Database*

This example in C# shows a *Transaction Script* that has an intimate understanding of a database table. In the first code snippet we see the interface definition for a *Service Controller* (85). Note that a *Data Transfer Object* (94) is used to produce results as JSON.

```
[ServiceContract]
public interface IEditorialService
{
  [OperationContract]
  [WebGet(ResponseFormat=WebMessageFormat.Json,
        UriTemplate = "stories/{authorId}")]

  List<Story> GetStoriesToReview(int authorId);

  // other operations here
}
```

Transaction
Script

This code fragment shows the actual web service implementation. The code for CommonDBLogic has been omitted.

```
public class EditorialService : IEditorialService
  public List<Story> GetStoriesToReview(int authorId)
  {
    using(IDbConnection conn = CommonDBLogic.GetDBConnection() )
    {
      IDbCommand cmd = CommonDBLogic.GetCommand(conn);

      cmd.CommandText =
        @"SELECT Id, Headline
          FROM NewsStories
          WHERE State = 1
          AND WorkerId = @AuthorId
          ORDER BY RowTimestamp DESC";

      CommonDBLogic.AddParameter(cmd, "AuthorId", authorId);

      List<Story> stories = new List<Story>();

      using (IDataReader rdr = cmd.ExecuteReader())
      {
        while (rdr.Read())
          stories.Add(
            new Story( rdr.GetInt32(0), rdr.GetString(1)  );
      }
    }

    return stories;
  }
}
```

Datasource Adapter

Several clients would like to use internal system resources, but access to these entities must be controlled. The clients might be running on different computing platforms.

> How can a web service provide access to internal resources like database tables, stored procedures, domain objects, or files with a minimum amount of custom code?

Database tables, stored procedures, domain object models, and files must often be shared with clients that run on different computing platforms. The organization could migrate all clients to a homogeneous platform. This, however, could be an impractical move. Rather than trying to create a uniform environment, one could provide access to these resources through web services. However, this too can cause a significant amount of work. Consider the following C# web service that provides access to a database table.

Datasource Adapter

```csharp
public List<Story> GetStoriesToReview(int authorId)
{
  using(IDbConnection conn = CommonDBLogic.GetDBConnection())
  {
    IDbCommand cmd = CommonDBLogic.GetCommand(conn);

    cmd.CommandText =
      @"SELECT Id, Headline FROM NewsStories
        WHERE State = 1 AND WorkerId = @AuthorId";

    CommonDBLogic.AddParameter(cmd, "AuthorId", authorId);

    List<Story> stories = new List<Story>();

    using (IDataReader rdr = cmd.ExecuteReader())
    {
      while (rdr.Read())
        stories.Add(
          new Story( rdr.GetInt32(0), rdr.GetString(1));
    }
  }
  return stories;
}
```

While this code is relatively simple, it takes time to create and will require periodic maintenance. How can a service developer provide access to data resources without having to write so much code?

▼

Create a web service that uses a specialized Datasource Provider. Leverage developer tools that generate datasource metadata and produce controllers that not only encapsulate and interpret the rules for request processing, but also direct the actions of Datasource Providers and Message.Formatters.

Datasource Adapter

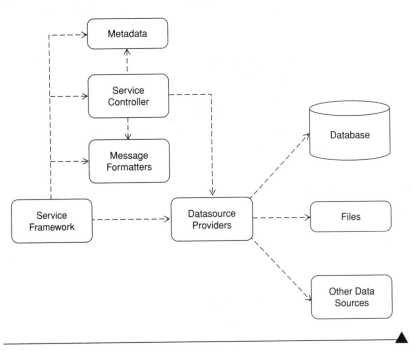

The *Datasource Adapter* is a variation on the *Adapter* pattern [GoF]. Adapters are used to convert one class interface to another interface, thereby making it possible for classes that were previously incompatible to interact. A metaphor can help to explain this. Americans who use laptop computers in Europe must often use an adapter to convert the power cable's interface (i.e., the plugs) to one that is compatible with the wall socket. Services that function as Adapters work much like this. They make internal resources like database tables, stored procedures, domain objects, or files accessible to clients that normally couldn't use them. *Datasource Adapters* accomplish this objective with a minimum amount of code. Several vendors (e.g., Microsoft, IBM, Oracle) use the term "data service" when speaking of web services that use this pattern.

Service frameworks that support the *Datasource Adapter* pattern intercept requests for specific web services. Requests are automatically translated into one or more actions against a specialized Datasource Provider, which encapsulates the logic required to manipulate a target resource. Typical providers include Object Relational Mappers (ORMs) and components that manage specific file types. Once the provider has processed the request, the service framework uses a Message Formatter to produce an appropriate response.

Datasource Adapters are usually created with graphical design tools. Developers begin the design process by selecting a target resource that should be "web-enabled." Some tools also provide the means to select the logical operations (e.g., Create, Read, Update, Delete) or specific SQL statements that should be allowed. The tool may automatically select a Datasource Provider or enable developers to select their own. The structure of request and response messages must also be determined at design time. Some tools let developers design their own message structures, while others impose a format derived from the target resource. The information collected by the tool is saved at the end of the design session. Some tools save this information as metadata in XML files while others generate the code for *Service Controllers* (85). The information stored in metadata files is used by the service framework at runtime to interpret and translate requests into actions against datasource providers. Controllers typically contain pregenerated logic used to achieve a similar end. As the name implies, they control or coordinate actions against the providers.

Clients can often discover the contracts for these services. Services with *RPC APIs* (18) or *Message APIs* (27) frequently use *Service Descriptors* (175) like WSDL that support design-time generation of *Service Proxies* (168). Services with *Resource APIs* (38) often let client developers query a root service to retrieve Atom Publishing Protocol's (APP's) Service Document. Some client tools can also generate *Service Connector* (168) code given this information.

Datasource Adapter

Considerations

Service developers should consider the following when thinking about using the *Datasource Adapter* pattern.

- **Assumptions regarding providers:** This pattern assumes developers use a Datasource Provider that is compatible with the selected service framework and developer tools. Even then, developers may have to spend time creating custom code for the providers. Some ORMs, for example, require developers to create the *Domain Model* [POEAA] entirely by hand. Other ORM design tools are able to generate Domain Models from the database.

- **Ease of use:** This pattern makes it easy for clients to access resources they normally wouldn't be able to use. The tools promote rapid application development, which makes them particularly useful in proof-of-concept projects.

- **Coupling:** This pattern implies a "bottom-up" design approach. The risk is that clients may become tightly coupled to the underlying resources exposed by the web service. When changes are applied to the backing data source, clients frequently have to change as well. This is a special problem when database tables are the backing source. Consider, for example, what might happen when tables are partitioned vertically (i.e., split into two tables), or when columns are added or removed. Client developers must be notified and may also have to re-create their *Service Connectors* (168).

- **Custom code:** While this pattern reduces the amount of code required to manipulate backing data sources, one may have to create custom code to handle such matters as client authentication, data encryption, data validation, and data transformation. This can usually be accomplished with *Service Interceptors* (195).

- **Service API styles:** Service developers should consider what API style "works best" for the target resource. A *Resource API* (38) can be appropriate for database tables and some files, while *RPC APIs* (18) may work better for stored procedures or object methods. Some tools impose a specific API style while others give you a choice.

- **Access privileges:** Service owners should consider who should be able to access internal resources exposed in this manner. Should developers in different departments of the same company be able to use the service? It depends. Service owners should carefully consider whether or not these resources should be exposed to groups outside of the company. Common risks include mining for confidential information and denial-of-service attacks.

- **Latency:** Developers should carefully consider the performance implications of calling several table-backed web services to complete a single use case. The problem is that each call to a web service entails multiple network traversals from the client, to the web service, to the database, and back again, and each network hop has a significant impact on overall latency. Therefore, a use case that involves several database tables could result in a very chatty conversation with high latency. For cases like these, performance can usually be improved if the use-case logic that manipu-

Datasource Adapter

lates these tables is moved into a single web service. The end result is that clients need only call one web service rather than multiple services in order to achieve the desired goal. This approach also helps to mitigate the problems associated with partial failures (i.e., when the client, server, or network independently fails for some reason).

- **Use with Domain Models:** The *Domain Façade* pattern [POEAA] provides a thin façade over a *Domain Model* [POEAA]. The service doesn't implement any business logic of its own, but instead delegates all requests to the underlying objects. The *Datasource Adapter* can be used for this purpose. However, one must be careful about circular references. For more information on this topic, see the *Data Transfer Object* pattern (94).

Example: *WCF Data Services*

This example uses a *Domain Model* [POEAA] that was automatically generated from a database. This model includes several entities, but we'll focus on Company and Person objects. A many-to-many relationship exists between these entities. Therefore, a Company may have a relationship with multiple Person(s), and vice versa.

Datasource Adapter

.NET developers can use the Visual Studio development environment to create a service that binds to this domain model. The following code is all that is required to get this service up and running. Notice that the name of the domain model is provided to the DataService class from which CRMService inherits.

```
public class CRMService : DataService<DomainModel.AcmeCorp>
{
  public static void InitializeService(
                          DataServiceConfiguration config)
  {
    config.SetEntitySetAccessRule("*", EntitySetRights.All);
    config.UseVerboseErrors = true;
  }
}
```

Once the code is deployed, clients can query the base URI of the service to acquire an APP Service Document that looks like this:

```
<?xml version="1.0" encoding="utf-8" standalone="yes" ?>
  <service:base=
    "http://acmeCorp.org/PeopleService/"
      xmlns:atom="http://www.w3.org/2005/Atom"
      xmlns:app="http://www.w3.org/2007/app"
      xmlns="http://www.w3.org/2007/app">
```

```
<workspace>
  <atom:title>People Service</atom:title>
  <collection href="Companies">
    <atom:title>Companies</atom:title>
  </collection>
  <collection href="People">
    <atom:title>People</atom:title>
  </collection>
</workspace>
```

```
</service>
```

This describes the services that clients may use to access Companies and People. Clients can issue an HTTP GET to http://acmeCorp.org/PeopleService/Companies in order to retrieve data for all companies. The response appears below.

```
<?xml version="1.0" encoding="utf-8" standalone="yes" ?>
<feed xml:base="http://acmeCorp.org/PeopleService"
  xmlns:d="http://schemas.microsoft.com/ado/2007/08/dataservices"
  xmlns:m="http://schemas.microsoft.com/ado/2007/08/dataservices/metadata"
  xmlns="http://www.w3.org/2005/Atom">

  <title type="text">Companies</title>
  <id>http://acmeCorp.org/PeopleService/Companies</id>
  <updated>2010-10-06T19:57:56Z</updated>
  <link rel="self" title="Companies" href="Companies" />

  <entry>
    <id>http://acmeCorp.org/PeopleService/Companies(1)</id>
    <title type="text" />
    <updated>2010-10-06T19:57:56Z</updated>
    <author>
      <name />
    </author>

    <link rel="edit" title="Company" href="Companies(1)" />

    <link
rel="http://schemas.microsoft.com/ado/2007/08/dataservices/related/People"
type="application/atom+xml;type=feed"
title="People" href="Companies(1)/People" />

    <category term="LabDbModel.Company"
scheme="http://schemas.microsoft.com/ado/2007/08/dataservices/scheme" />

    <content type="application/xml">
      <m:properties>
        <d:Id m:type="Edm.Int32">1</d:Id>
        <d:Name>Acme</d:Name>
      </m:properties>
    </content>
  </entry>
```

```
<entry>
  <id>http://acmeCorp.org/PeopleService/Companies(2)</id>
  <title type="text" />
  <updated>2010-10-06T19:57:56Z</updated>
  <author>
    <name />
  </author>

  <link rel="edit" title="Company" href="Companies(2)" />

  <link
rel="http://schemas.microsoft.com/ado/2007/08/dataservices/related/People"
type="application/atom+xml;type=feed"
title="People" href="Companies(2)/People" />

  <category term="LabDbModel.Company"
scheme="http://schemas.microsoft.com/ado/2007/08/dataservices/scheme" />

  <content type="application/xml">
    <m:properties>
      <d:Id m:type="Edm.Int32">2</d:Id>
      <d:Name>Dunder Mifflin</d:Name>
    </m:properties>
  </content>
 </entry>
</feed>
```

Datasource
Adapter

The format of this response is an extension to APP called Open Data Protocol (OData). Client developers can parse the link relations in this response and submit additional requests to create, read, update, and delete related resources. For example, a client may issue an HTTP PUT to http://acmeCorp.org/PeopleService/ Companies(2) to update information on "Dunder Mifflin". When the framework receives the request, it automatically translates it into an action against the domain model.

Operation Script

Common domain logic must be shared across a number of web services that may have different API styles (see Chapter 2).

How can web services reuse common domain logic without duplicating code?

Web services often contain all of the business or data access logic required to process a client's request. The service may validate input data, perform calculations, select the tables, rows, or files that should be accessed, and execute SQL. The service may also manage database transactions. Web services implemented in this manner are called *Transaction Scripts* [POEAA], which effectively organize business logic into individual procedures. This pattern is relatively easy to implement and may work well when the amount of logic in each service is small. However, the code can also become quite complex, lengthy, and challenging to maintain over time, and portions may be replicated across a number of web services. The risk, of course, is that duplicated code tends to be difficult to synchronize, and inconsistencies are likely to arise.

To combat these problems the service developer can extract certain code fragments out into smaller methods. This can help to make the web service easier to read and maintain. However, the developer must now determine where the extracted methods should be located. The code could be placed in the same class as the web service method, but this often does little to minimize duplicate code. When a web service's logic is particularly complex, it often makes sense to push that logic to a separate layer and make the service as thin as possible.

Encapsulate common business logic in domain layer entities that exist outside of the web service. Limit the logic within web services to algorithms that direct the activities of these entities.

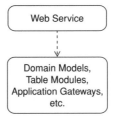

Web Service

↓

Domain Models,
Table Modules,
Application Gateways,
etc.

Web services that implement the *Operation Script* pattern [POEAA] may contain some application logic consisting of conditional (e.g., if, switch), iteration (i.e., looping), and sequencing statements. However, the bulk of the domain logic resides in external domain layer entities (e.g., *Domain Models, Table Modules* [POEAA]). The service inspects the request and uses this information to determine which domain layer entities should be used. The service may pass request data through without alteration, or may transform it in a way that can be consumed by the target entities. If a response is to be returned, the service constructs and populates the appropriate message with data from these entities.

Operation Scripts often function as the topmost transaction manager for the entities that are used to fulfill the client's request. They frequently start transactions after requests are received but before target objects are instantiated. If everything goes well, they commit the transaction, which causes the enlisted entities to commit their work as well. If an exception is thrown before the end of the transaction, the service will abort the transaction, causing the entities to roll back all changes.

Operation
Script

Considerations

Use of this pattern should be preceded by consideration of the following factors.

- **Local versus distributed transactions:** The transactions managed by *Operation Scripts* are usually local. In other words, the service typically manages transactions that operate against a single data source (e.g., database, queue, etc.). Distributed transactions that enlist multiple data sources may be used; however, developers should carefully consider the ramifications. Distributed transactions can be problematic when used in web services because of their tendency to increase latency and contribute to lock contention on database tables.

- **Inversion of Control:** *Operation Scripts* often use Inversion of Control (IoC) containers to decouple web service logic from the actual objects used to process requests (see Dependency Injection). IoC containers like Spring enable developers to avoid direct instantiation of target objects. Instead, the service asks the IoC framework to dynamically create and return an instance of an object that implements a particular interface. The IoC framework typically looks at a configuration file to see what type of concrete class should be loaded. IoC containers make it relatively easy to plug in new implementations of domain objects without affecting the service logic.

- **Potential for duplication of application logic:** Since the domain layer entities called by the web service encapsulate most of the common business logic, code duplication can largely be avoided. However, the validation, control-flow, and exception-handling logic that is left over in the web service might still be replicated across services. To avoid code duplication, the developer may decide to move this logic to a *Command* object [GoF] that can be called from multiple services. For more information see the *Command Invoker* pattern (149).

• **Application gateways:** Web services sometimes provide access to proprietary APIs offered by commercial applications or legacy systems. Developers could direct activities against these APIs from directly within web service methods. However, this creates a very strong coupling between the web services and the backing API. Developers may, instead, encapsulate the logic that manipulates these APIs in distinct *Gateways* [POEAA] that provide a simplified interface or *Façade* [GoF] over the API. The web service can then call the gateway methods and be completely ignorant of the APIs used by the commercial or legacy application. This makes it much easier to swap out the provider (in this case, the system providing the API) for a new one while maintaining a common web service API and the control-flow logic within the web service.

Operation Script

Example: *A Service That Delegates Work to Domain Layer Entities*

This example in C# shows how an *Operation Script* with a *Resource API* (38) can delegate most of its work to domain layer entities. In this listing, you can see that a service named GetAlbums instantiates an AlbumFinder object and executes the method GetByArtistName in order to retrieve a list of albums for the artistName extracted from the URI path. If results are found, the handler maps these results onto a *Data Transfer Object* (94), which serializes the data as JSON. The implementations of AlbumFinder and MusicAlbum have been omitted to keep this example brief.

```
[ServiceContract]
public interface IMediaService
{
  [OperationContract]
  [WebGet(ResponseFormat=WebMessageFormat.Json,
          UriTemplate = "music/albums/{artistName}")]
  List<MusicAlbum> GetAlbums(string artistName);
}
```

```
public class MediaService: IMediaService
{
  public List<MusicAlbum> GetAlbums(string artistName)
  {
    DomainLayer.AlbumFinder finder = new DomainLayer.AlbumFinder();

    List<DomainLayer.Album> albums =
        finder.GetByArtistName(artistName);


    if (null == albums)
    {
      WebOperationContext.Current.OutgoingResponse.SetStatusAsNotFound();

      return null;
    }

    List<MusicAlbum> results = new List<MusicAlbum>();

    // Map results to a Data Transfer Object
    foreach (DomainLayer.Album album in albums)
      results.Add( new MusicAlbum(album.Name,
                                  artist.Name,
                                  album.Genre));

    return results;
  }
}
```

Operation
Script

Example: *A Service with Complex Application Logic*

This Java example shows a web service that interacts with several domain objects. As you can see, data is first extracted from the request. If the date range is not valid, a fault message is thrown and the service terminates. Otherwise, the service attempts to retrieve the customer's unique identifier from the request. If the customer provided a valid identifier, information about the customer is retrieved from a database, and a Customer object is populated. Otherwise, an object of this same type is initialized for new customers. A pricing list is then retrieved given the class of vehicle the customer would like to rent. Next we see that the rental cost is computed, the customer's account is charged, and a rental request is submitted to the pickup location. This last act also generates an acknowledgment that is returned to the client.

The implementations of the domain objects and *Data Transfer Objects* (i.e., RentalCriteria, RentalAck) have been omitted because they are somewhat tangential to this sample. This example demonstrates how an ORM might be used to initiate a database transaction. The specifics of this have been left out as well.

```
@WebMethod(operationName = "ReserveAuto")
public RentalAck ReserveAuto(RentalCriteria request){

  DateRange dateRange = new DateRange( request.getFromDate(),
                                        request.getToDate() );

  if( ! dateRange.isValid() )
    throw new InputDataValidationFault(
                                dateRange.getErrorMessage());

  String customerId = request.getCustomer().getCustomerId();
  Customer customer;

  RentalAck response = null;

  // start transaction
  SessionManager session = SessionFactory.CreateSession();

  if(null != customerId){
    customer = Customer.getById(customerId);
  } else {
    customer = Customer.initForNewAccount(request.getCustomer());
  }

  PriceList pricing = new PriceList(request.getVehicleClass());

  Money cost = pricing.getRentalCost(request.getPickupLocation(),
                                      request.getDropOffLocation(),
                                      dateRange);

  customer.chargeAccount(cost);

  RentalLocation rentalLocation =
  RentalLocation.getRentalLocation(request.getPickupLocation());

  ReservationRequest rentalRequest = new ReservationRequest(
                                customer,
                                request.getVehicleClass(),
                                pricing.getListId(),
                                dateRange);

  response = rentalLocation.submitReservation(rentalRequest);

  session.commit();

  return response;
}
```

Command Invoker

Equivalent requests may be received through multiple web services with different API styles (see Chapter 2). The service owner would like to have the option of processing the request synchronously or asynchronously.

▼

How can web services with different APIs reuse common domain logic while enabling both synchronous and asynchronous request processing?

▲

Web services often contain application logic that directs how *Domain Models* [POEAA] and database tables are used to process requests. While the bulk of the domain logic can be found in domain layer entities, the service might still contain intricate conditional, looping, and sequencing statements that direct these entities. There are times when even this logic may be duplicated across web services. Consider a case in which the service owner must implement two service APIs for different clients. Perhaps the first service has a *Message API* (27) while the second uses a *Resource API* (38). Developers may be tempted to copy and paste code between equivalent services, but it would probably become quite difficult to ensure consistent and reliable behaviors for these services over time.

When web services contain application logic, a high degree of temporal coupling usually exists because it is assumed that requests will be processed immediately. Unfortunately, a spike in request load could overwhelm the web and database servers. Service architects must consider other issues that might hinder scalability as well. Consider a web service that occasionally receives requests that take a "long time" (e.g., minutes or longer) to process. A product update service might, for example, enable clients to update their entire catalogue or a small portion of it. If the client uploads their entire inventory, then web server capacity could be diminished to the point where other requests are rejected. Web services that execute application logic as soon as requests are received can therefore be hard to scale.

Developers often need a way to consolidate and reuse common application logic that can be invoked from multiple web services. This shared logic could also be encapsulated in a way that enables the request to be forwarded to a background process for deferred processing.

Create command objects that fully encapsulate common request processing logic.
Instantiate and invoke these commands from within the web service, or forward
them to an asynchronous background process.

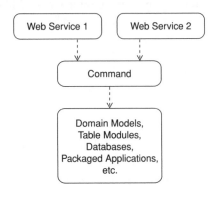

**Command
Invoker**

When a web service is implemented as a *Command Invoker,* all domain and
exception-handling logic is removed from the web service and moved to *Command* objects [GoF]. The code that is left over in the web service does very little.
In its simplest form, the service selects a Command, provides request data to the
Command, and calls a method that causes it to begin processing the request.

Command Invokers offer several benefits. All recurring control-flow and
exception-handling logic for a given domain is consolidated within a single
entity. This enables the web service to remain ignorant of the *Domain Models*
[POEAA], *Table Modules* [POEAA], databases, or packaged applications used
to fulfill a client's request. By encapsulating all of this logic within a separate
class, one enables it to be shared across a number of services. One could, for
example, create a *Resource API* (38) for one set of clients and a *Message API*
(27) for another and have each call the same Command. This ensures that
duplicate logic is avoided. Additionally, clients that don't need to use web services can invoke the Command directly.

Considerations

Service developers should consider the following issues.

- **Invoking Commands from within the web service:** Commands may be
  invoked in a few ways. The simplest approach is to have the web service
  instantiate the *Command* [GoF] on receipt of the request and direct it to
  execute immediately (see Figure 5.1). This option may be considered if the

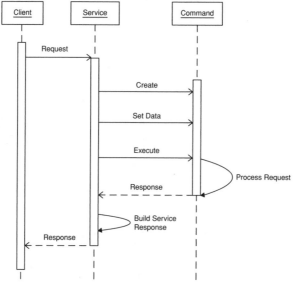

Figure 5.1 Commands *[GoF] may be instantiated and executed directly by the web service if the average request processing time is relatively short (i.e., less than a few seconds) and there is sufficient server capacity to handle spikes in request load.*

Command Invoker

average request processing time is relatively short (i.e., less than a few seconds) and there is sufficient server capacity to handle spikes in request load.

- **Forwarding requests to background processes:** The web service could also use *Request/Acknowledge* (59) and forward the request to an asynchronous worker (e.g., daemon, Windows service), which processes the request in the background. This approach should be considered if the time required to process a request might exceed a few seconds, or when spikes in request load occur from time to time. There are two ways that *Command Invokers* can be used to support asynchrony. The service could instantiate the *Command* [GoF] first, and then forward it to a background request processor by way of a queue or database (see Figure 5.2). This approach may be used for a number of reasons. The web service may, for example, need to collect information that enables the Command to be routed to the correct background request processor. Rather than adding this information to the original request, it's usually better to leave the request alone and add this information to the Command object.

  The web service might also forward the request directly to the background process and let it instantiate the Command (see Figure 5.3). This

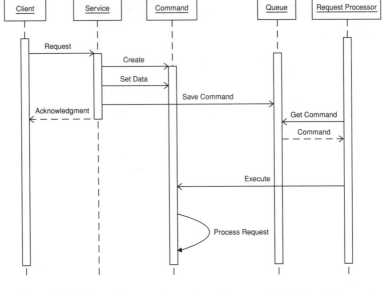

Figure 5.2 *Web services can instantiate Commands [GoF] and forward them to asynchronous background processes (i.e., Request Processors) by way of a queue or a database.*

Command Invoker

option may be considered when additional data isn't required to route the request. This approach also tends to minimize the amount of work performed by the web service, and this helps to reduce web server memory and CPU consumption, thereby promoting availability.

- **Use with Request Mappers:** *Request Mappers* (109) may be used to translate request data to domain layer entities upon which the *Command* [GoF] operates. This enables the Command to be unaware of the format and structure of data received or returned from the web service which, in turn, enables the domain layer entities and message structures to vary independently.

- **Command implementation patterns:** Commands themselves can be implemented in many ways. They may be implemented as *Transaction Scripts* [POEAA] that have complete knowledge of the data sources (e.g., databases) they interact with. They might also be designed to function as *Operation Scripts* [POEAA] that contain a minimum amount of domain logic and instead delegate most of their work to a *Domain Model* [POEAA].

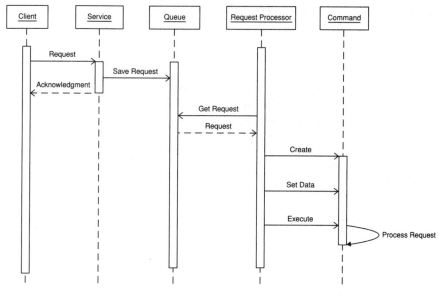

Figure 5.3 *Web services can forward requests directly to asynchronous background processes (i.e., Request Processors) by way of queues or databases. These processors retrieve requests, instantiate the required Commands [GoF], and execute the commands.*

Command Invoker

Example: *Command Processing in Asynchronous Background Processes*

This example shows how a *Command Invoker* can be used in conjunction with the *Request/Acknowledge* pattern (59). In this first code listing the request is forwarded to an asynchronous worker for processing. A unique "Request Identifier" (a.k.a. *Correlation Identifier* [EIP]) is generated and injected into the request. RentalSystemGateway forwards the request to an asynchronous background process, the details of which have been excluded. Once the request has been forwarded, the request identifier is returned to the client for future reference.

```
@WebMethod(operationName = "ReserveAuto")
public String ReserveAuto(RentalCriteria request){

  String requestId = System.currentTimeMillis().toString() +
                     java.util.UUID.randomUUID().toString();

  request.setRequestId(requestId);
```

```
// Send to async background process by way of a queue
RentalSystemGateway.SendRequest( request );

return requestId;
}
```

The following code shows a simple asynchronous worker which polls for incoming messages that are forwarded from the web service. This object exemplifies the *Polling Consumer* [EIP] pattern, and runs on a dedicated thread within a background process. Again, most of this logic (e.g., exception handling, logic to start/stop the thread, etc.) has been omitted to keep the sample brief. AsyncWorker instantiates a specific *Command* [GoF] for each request retrieved from the queue.

```
public class AsyncWorker:BaseWorker
{
  public void start()
  {
    while( isRunning )
    {
      // read request from a queue
      RentalCriteria request = RentalSystemGateway.GetRequest();

      RentalCommand command = new RentalCommand();

      command.setRequest(request);

      command.execute();
    }
  }
}
```

Command Invoker

This final listing shows the actual *Command* [GoF] that fulfills the client's request. You may assume that RequestMsg is the base class for RentalCriteria.

```
public interface Command{
  void setRequest(RequestMsg req);
  void execute();
}
public class RentalCommand implements Command
{
  RentalCriteria request;

  public RentalCommand(){ }

  public void setRequest(RentalCriteria req)
  {
    request = req;
  }
```

```
public void execute()
{
  DateRange dateRange = new DateRange(
                            request.getFromDate(),
                            request.getToDate());
  if( ! dateRange.isValid() )
  {
    // enqueue error message to be emailed out
    return;
  }

  String customerId = request.getCustomerId();

  Customer customer;

  // start a transaction
  SessionManager session = SessionFactory.CreateSession();

  if(null != customerId){
    customer = Customer.getById(customerId);
  } else{
    customer = Customer.initForNewAccount(
                          request.getCustomer());
  }

  PriceList pricing = new PriceList(
                        request.getVehicleClass());

  Money cost = pricing.getRentalCost(
                      request.getPickupLocation(),
                      request.getDropOffLocation(),
                      dateRange);

  customer.chargeAccount(cost);

  RentalLocation rentalLocation =
   RentalLocation.getRentalLocation(
                      request.getPickupLocation());

  RentalHold rentalHold = new RentalHold(
                      request.getRequestId(),
                      customer,
                      request.getVehicleClass(),
                      pricing.getListId(),
                      dateRange,
                      rentalLocation);

  rentalHold.submit(rentalHold);

  session.commit();
}
}
```

Command
Invoker

Workflow Connector

Web services are to be used by a complex business process that runs for minutes, hours, days, or weeks.

> How can web services be used to support complex and long-running business processes?

Web services are often used to launch complex business processes that run for extended periods of time. A web service may, for example, trigger tasks that reserve flights, hotels, and car rentals for a vacation package. Processes like these can take several minutes, hours, or even days to complete. A web service that contained all of the code for a process like this would undoubtedly become quite difficult to read and maintain. One could increase readability by extracting portions of this logic out to specialized classes. The service would then merely direct how and when these classes are used to conduct the business process. However, web server scalability would still be compromised since the web service instance remains in memory until the request has been fully processed. As the load on the web server increases, the probability that new requests would be rejected increases as well. Additionally, if the web server crashes, then the client's request may be lost. Most client connections would also time out on a long-running process like this.

You could instead establish a *Pipes and Filters* [EIP] style of architecture. In this approach, a web service would receive the request, save it to a database table or queue, and return a response acknowledging the client's request. A background process (e.g., daemon or Windows service) would then poll the database or queue and execute a single command (e.g., reserve flight) for each retrieved request. Once a task has completed, the request would be forwarded to the next background process to perform the next task (e.g., reserve hotel), and so on. The request is therefore processed much like a baton is passed from one runner to the next in a relay race. Web server scalability is promoted because the work is off-loaded from the web servers. This pattern also provides a relatively fault-tolerant way to conduct long-running business processes. However, it can be challenging to understand the entire business process at a macro level, and it can also be difficult to change or debug control-flow logic since these rules are typically buried within individual services, configuration files, routing tables, and messages in transit. Furthermore, the status of a client's request can be difficult to ascertain for similar reasons.

The complexity of the software infrastructures required to support a Pipes and Filters architecture should not be underestimated. Infrastructures that direct the flow of control through a strict sequence of tasks are the simplest to implement. However, most business processes aren't that simple. The vacation booking process could, for example, be designed to run the flight, hotel, and car reservation tasks simultaneously. This raises several technical questions. Should these tasks be created as separate threads of execution in a single "machine process," or should they run in separate processes? If the tasks are distributed across threads or computer processes, how can the results of each task be synchronized and come together to produce a final result?

Several business questions must be answered as well. In the current example, what should happen if a hotel is sold out for the requested date range? Should the flight reservations and automobile rentals be cancelled? With short-running processes that operate on a single data source (e.g., database), the web service could easily roll back all database changes made within the scope of a single transaction. Unfortunately, transactions cannot be used in the same way for long-running business processes. Web services that are exposed to external business partners generally don't support distributed transactions for reasons relating to security and scalability. This means that another technique must be employed to reverse the results of individual tasks. The common solution is **compensation.** In the current example, let's say that flight, hotel, and car reservation tasks are distributed to different business partners and executed in parallel. If the requested hotel is sold out, then the business process might dictate that the car rental should be cancelled. Compensation would occur by calling a web service that cancels the car rental and reverses any associated charges. However, this isn't always so easy. One may not be able to connect to a compensating service due to network or server problems, and retry logic may be required to ensure that the compensating requests are eventually delivered. The bottom line is that these processes can become quite complex.

Time could be spent developing custom software infrastructures that manage complex business processes like these. The infrastructure must know how and when to instantiate a logical business process and what conditions cause the process to terminate. Issues like task execution, exception handling, retries, task compensation, failover, load balancing, and resource optimization must be addressed. Most businesses would be wise to refrain from building these infrastructures because of the related development and maintenance costs. Fortunately, business developers can leverage powerful workflow technologies.

Workflow Connector

Use a Workflow Engine to manage the life cycle and execution of tasks within complex or long-running business processes. Identify a web service that will trigger each logical business process. Use Callback Services to receive additional data for these long-running processes, and forward messages from these Callback Services to the Workflow Engine.

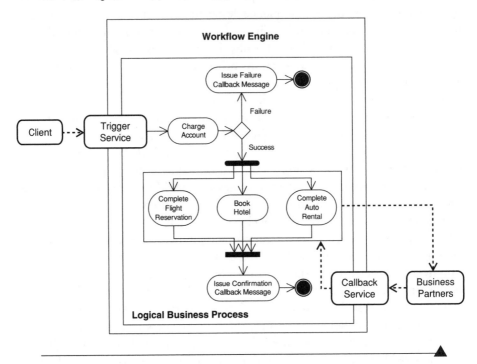

Workflow Connector

In the broadest use of the term, **workflow** describes how tasks performed by humans or computers can be arranged to fulfill a specific business objective. The *Workflow Connector* pattern uses this term to refer to business automation. Workflow technologies automate business processes by arranging tasks (a.k.a. activities) into executable sequences. These tasks may execute code written in a particular programming language, send data to a queue, read from and write to databases, or invoke web services. Tasks that compensate (i.e., reverse or undo) work performed in prior tasks may be included as well.

A sizable pattern language has been compiled for workflow. One notable catalogue organizes workflow concepts into Control-Flow, Data, Resource, and Exception-Handling patterns [van der Aalst, et al.]. The Control-Flow category includes more than 40 patterns that describe how workflow tasks can be ordered and executed. The most basic of these include Sequence (i.e., serial execution of tasks), Exclusive Choice (e.g., if-else statements), and Structured Loops (e.g., while, repeat-until loops). Advanced concepts like parallel task execution, thread synchronization (i.e., joins), task cancellation, and process termination are also discussed.

The rules for control flow are frequently saved in a Process Definition artifact created with graphical design tools (see Figure 5.4). These tools typically let developers depict control flow through UML activity diagrams and flowcharts. Process Variables may be defined to store the input or output from individual tasks. The information collected from these tools is often used to generate declarative meta-languages like BPEL or XAML. Process definitions can often be created manually and saved in XML files as well. In the end, these definitions identify a sequence of activities that are executed by a Workflow Engine. Some process definitions are precompiled for fast runtime execution while others are interpreted. It all depends on the chosen tools and selected infrastructure.

Workflow (engine) technologies make it possible for developers to create *Process Managers* [EIP] that govern entire workflow life cycles from process instantiation to termination. These technologies trigger task execution, and keep track of which tasks are executing, which are waiting or suspended, and which must be resumed or restarted. The Workflow Engine also keeps track of the values stored in process variables throughout the process lifetime. Many workflow engines save the state of tasks and variables to a database before and after tasks are executed. These Process Snapshots provide several benefits. One may query the database to determine the status of any process instance. If a process instance crashes, the database may be queried to determine the last task that completed successfully, and the process may be restarted from that step. This is one way Workflow Engines help to ensure fault tolerance.

Workflow Connector

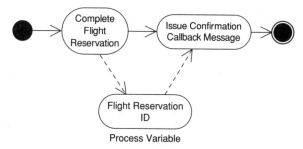

Figure 5.4 *Graphical workflow design tools let developers depict control flow through UML activity diagrams and flowcharts. Information may be mapped from one task to another through Process Variables.*

The *Workflow Connector* pattern uses web services as a means to launch the business processes managed by workflow engines. Developers designate a Trigger Service that creates new process instances for a given process definition. So, while a single "order fulfillment process" may be defined, one Process Instance is created each time a client calls a trigger service. When a process is instantiated, the workflow engine typically creates a unique Process Identifier. The engine then executes the tasks according to the process definition. Once the workflow has started, it often returns an acknowledgment and continues to execute. The acknowledgment may be a SOAP message containing the process identifier or a URI that uniquely identifies the process instance. Either approach may be used by the client to refer to the process in the future.

Workflow Engines facilitate service composition by enabling services to be assembled into complex processes (see Figure 5.5). The engine acts like a *Mediator* [GoF], which uses web services to fulfill individual tasks within a workflow while keeping each service independent of the others. Process definitions may use one of several client-service interaction styles to call these services. *Request/ Response* (54) may be used if a quick response is needed and the target service is relatively fast. The *Request/Acknowledge* pattern (59) may be used if the target service initiates a long-running process of its own. The developer may designate a Callback Service to receive responses from these services. Since multiple

Workflow Connector

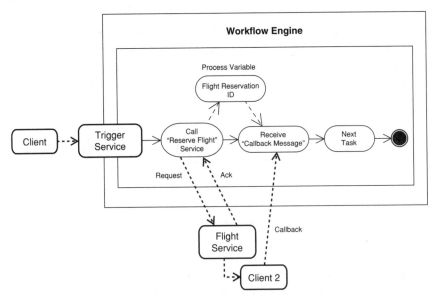

Figure 5.5 *Workflow Engines enable services to be composed into complex processes.*

process instances of the same type may be running concurrently, the engine must extract information from each callback message to determine which process instance should be contacted. This practice is known as **correlation.** The engine may look for a Process Identifier or use other message content. Once the correct instance has been identified, the Workflow Engine routes the Callback Message to the task designated to receive the callback. If the time spent waiting for the callback exceeds a threshold defined in the Process Definition, the engine may remove the process from memory and persist its state (i.e., process variables, information on executing tasks, etc.) to a file system or database. When the callback does arrive, the engine restores the proper instance into server memory, and the task that was waiting for the callback will execute. This helps to conserve server memory and also promotes scalability.

Workflow clients may or may not receive final responses; it all depends on what type of business process is being automated. Some clients choose to periodically poll a service in order to acquire final results. This enables the client to pick up results at its leisure. Polling, however, can be inefficient, and the client may not get its response as soon as it is ready. Client developers might therefore choose to set up a Callback Service that can be invoked by the workflow when it has completed (see Figure 5.6). The implication is that either the client must provide callback information to the trigger service, or the workflow owner

Workflow
Connector

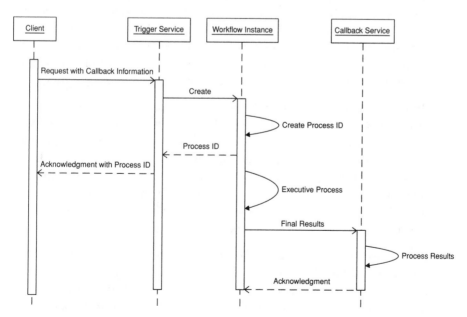

Figure 5.6 *Workflows may provide final results through Callback Services.*

must have this information on record for each client. For more information on this topic, see *Request/Acknowledge/Callback* (63).

Considerations

Service designers would be wise to consider the following factors before using the *Workflow Connector* pattern.

- **Process complexity:** Workflow technology may be overkill for simple control flows or for processes that are short-running. These technologies are best reserved for complex and long-running business processes. Such processes often include parallel task execution and asynchronous interactions with external providers.

- **A variety of choices:** A wide variety of commercial and open source workflow engines have become available in recent years, and their capabilities vary greatly. Some must be hosted on specialized application servers, while others run on web servers or even on desktops. Some workflow frameworks are lightweight software infrastructures that can be integrated directly into the execution environment of the web server. *Orchestration Engines* (224), on the other hand, are advanced computing platforms that exist apart from the web server tier as separate servers in their own right. These servers offer such features as load balancing and mechanisms to control resource (i.e., CPU, memory) allocation. Unfortunately, the most sophisticated workflow engines can be quite expensive and often contribute to vendor lock-in. Developers and IT support personnel must also possess specialized skills to effectively use them and keep them operational.

- **Business Activity Monitoring:** Some workflow engines can be used in conjunction with a specialized type of software classified as Business Activity Monitoring (BAM) software. Since workflow engines often send process-state information to "event sinks" (i.e., web services) or databases, BAM software can leverage this information to produce reports and "dashboards" showing business metrics and Key Performance Indicators (KPIs) in real time. One could, for example, show the rate at which orders are fulfilled, or monitor which tasks for a given process instance are being executed.

- **Ease of use and maintenance:** Workflow design tools generally make it easy to define and alter process definitions. However, their ease of use frequently masks the impact of these changes. These tools typically require a high level of technical training, and usually aren't meant for business analysts. In many cases, the promised productivity gains are often overstated because the logic invoked in each task can still be quite complex and may

Workflow Connector

require significant development time. Indeed, these tools often do more to hide complexity rather than to reduce it. Testing can be a challenge too, since the workflow engine is often tightly coupled to the service and cannot be easily stubbed out.

Example: *Microsoft Workflow Foundation*

A plethora of workflow products are available, especially for the Java platform. Microsoft has a high-end orchestration and integration product called BizTalk, and a more modest engine that is a part of its .NET framework.

Figure 5.7 shows a workflow designer used to create Process Definitions. On the left you can see the toolbox with an array of messaging, control-flow, and other activity options. In the center is the designer itself. The behavior of each activity (i.e., task) is set, in part, by selecting the activity and providing values in the Properties window on the right. Process Variables are defined in the window shown at the bottom.

Workflow Connector

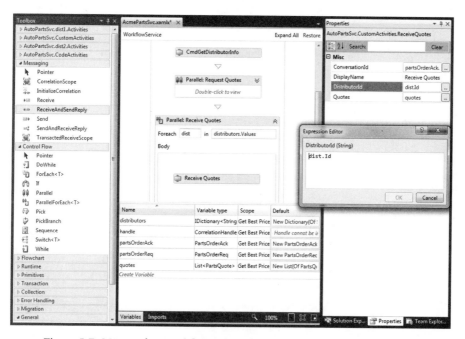

Figure 5.7 *Microsoft's Workflow Designer enables developers to construct complex workflows by selecting activities from a toolbox that includes messaging, control-flow, and a number of other activity options. Developers may constrain workflow behaviors by setting the values for activity properties, and shared variables may be defined for each workflow or child activity.*

Chapter 6

Web Service Infrastructures

Introduction

Certain software functions are so generic that they can be used over and over again by different web services and their clients. These functions are collectively referred to as **software infrastructure.** Frameworks like Java Enterprise Edition (Java EE) and .NET provide the most basic infrastructures for things like web application hosting, database connectivity, and security. Software developers frequently build their own infrastructures on top of these frameworks. Examples include frameworks for Object Relational Mapping (ORM) and workflow management. Software infrastructures like these are the foundation, low-level plumbing and glue used to build modern software. They also help to enforce consistent behaviors.

Technology vendors and open source communities have created many infrastructures to address the common needs of web services. The code examples in this book have featured the JAX-WS, JAX-RS, and WCF frameworks. These infrastructures are either a part of the "base framework" or can be easily incorporated to extend the capabilities of that framework. One of the most basic infrastructural requirements provided by frameworks like these is web service hosting (see Figure 6.1). This type of infrastructure provides the mechanisms to receive client requests, dispatch requests to web services, manage the lifetime of each service, and return responses to clients. When a client submits a request, it must first acquire a connection from a connection pool managed by the web server infrastructure. Once a connection has been established, the web server infrastructure forwards the request to the service framework which invokes the appropriate web service. However, before the service is activated, the infrastructure must consider the service's rules for instantiation; these are usually configured by the service developer. The most common approach is to process the client's request by allocating one worker thread from a common thread pool. The web service framework might also take advantage of data-binding

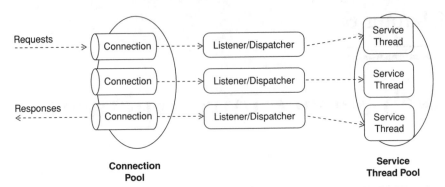

Figure 6.1 *Web service frameworks like JAX-WS, JAX-RS, and WCF are built to run on top of web server infrastructures. All together, they provide the mechanisms to receive client requests, dispatch requests to web services, manage the lifetime of each service, and return responses.*

technologies (e.g., JAXB, .NET's XmlSerializer) in order to provide automatic deserialization of the request. When the web service has finished processing the client's request, the framework may optionally serialize the response. The response stream is then transmitted back over the client's connection, and the service thread and connection are released back to their respective pools so that they can be reused for other requests.

Unless you work for a company like IBM, Oracle, or Microsoft, or are a committer to an open source organization like the Apache Software Foundation, you probably won't need to develop low-level service frameworks like these. Still, there are many infrastructure concerns that web service developers must address. This chapter discusses a few of the most common and basic web service infrastructure patterns, which are listed in Table 6.1.

Table 6.1 *Web Service Infrastructure Patterns*

Pattern Name	Problem	Description
Service Connector (168)	How can clients avoid duplicating the code required to use a specific service, and also be insulated from the intricacies of communications logic?	Create a library or set of classes that encapsulates the logic a client must implement in order to use a group of related services. Create a high-level interface that abstracts the details of this logic, thereby making the classes easier to use.

Table 6.1 *Web Service Infrastructure Patterns (continued)*

Pattern Name	Problem	Description
Service Descriptor (175)	How can development tools acquire the information necessary to use a web service, and how can the code for Service Connectors be generated?	Produce a standardized and machine-readable description of related services that identifies URIs, logical operations, messages, server methods, and usage policies.
Asynchronous Response Handler (184)	How can a client avoid blocking when sending a request?	Dispatch requests on a separate thread of execution apart from the main client thread. Wait for the response on this thread while attending to other matters on the main thread.
Service Interceptor (195)	How can common behaviors like authentication, caching, logging, exception handling, and validation be executed without having to modify the client or service code?	Encapsulate cross-cutting behaviors within individual classes. Load these classes into pipelines that are managed by client or service frameworks.
Idempotent Retry (206)	How can a client ensure that requests are delivered to a web service despite temporary network or server failures?	Design the client such that common connectivity exceptions are caught. When a connection error occurs, reconnect to the service and resend the request. Limit the number of times such attempts are made. Include a unique identifier in each request so that the service can identify duplicate requests. Alternatively, send the request to a unique URI designated for the specific request.

Web Service Infrastructures

While web services also use security and caching infrastructures, these concerns are far beyond the scope of this book.

This chapter will close with a quick review of a few infrastructure patterns that are frequently used in corporate SOA infrastructures.

Service Connector

A client wishes to interact with a service that has an *RPC API* (18), *Message API* (27), or *Resource API* (38).

> How can clients avoid duplicating the code required to use a specific service, and also be insulated from the intricacies of communications logic?

Clients must know a lot about services in order to use them. A lot depends on the service design style. *Resource APIs* (38) require clients to use certain media types, set HTTP headers for various purposes, and issue specific server methods in order to achieve a desired outcome. *RPC APIs* (18) and *Message APIs* (27) often require the request to be formatted as XML. They may also require the formatted request to be wrapped in a SOAP message that uses certain SOAP headers. Regardless of the service design style, the client must know what URI to send the request to. The request must then be serialized into a stream of bytes that can be transmitted over the network and deserialized by the service. The client must perform a similar process when responses are received from the service.

Service Connector

As a first step, one could create a simple utility class that encapsulates the most basic APIs necessary to communicate with the target service. The following listing provides an example of just such a class written in C#.

```csharp
public class WebClient
{
  public WebClient(){ ; }

  public string Get(string uri)
  {
    return GetResponse(InitWebRequest("GET", uri));
  }
  public string CreateOrUpdate(string uri,string requestAsXML)
  {
    HttpWebRequest request = InitWebRequest("PUT", uri);

    if (requestAsXML != null){
      WriteXMLToRequestStream(request, requestAsXML);
    }

    return GetResponse(request);
  }
```

```
private HttpWebRequest InitWebRequest(string method,
                                      string uriString)
{
  Uri uri = new Uri(uriString);

  HttpWebRequest request=
                    (HttpWebRequest)WebRequest.Create(uri);

  request.Method = method;
  request.Timeout = DEFAULT_TIMEOUT;
  return request;
}
private void WriteXMLToRequestStream(HttpWebRequest request,
                         string requestAsXML)
{
  UTF8Encoding encoding = new UTF8Encoding();
  byte[] byteArray = encoding.GetBytes(requestAsXML);
  request.ContentType = "text/xml";
  request.ContentLength = byteArray.Length;
  Stream requestStream = request.GetRequestStream();
  requestStream.Write(byteArray, 0, byteArray.Length);
  requestStream.Close();
}
private string GetResponse(HttpWebRequest request)
{
  WebResponse response = request.GetResponse();
  Stream stream = response.GetResponseStream();
  UTF8Encoding encoding = new UTF8Encoding();
  StreamReader reader = new StreamReader(stream, encoding);
  return reader.ReadToEnd();
}
}
```

Service Connector

Utilities like these free client developers from having to worry about the communications-related APIs required to use a service. Since they are generic and aren't designed to be used with specific services, they don't have to be rebuilt when a service changes. However, clients must still implement additional logic specific to each service. Certain services may require data to be encrypted or demand that clients submit security claims (e.g., username/password tokens, X.509 certificates, SAML tokens, etc.). The client must always know how to acquire or construct the service's address, select the appropriate server method, format requests, and decode responses.

Each client application could develop a custom solution to meet the specific requirements of the service. Of course, if the service is called by many client applications, this would result in duplicate code that would be difficult to synchronize and maintain. It would be much better to consolidate this logic so that it can be reused by multiple clients.

Create a library or set of classes that encapsulates the logic a client must implement in order to use a group of related services. Create a high-level interface that abstracts the details of this logic, thereby making the classes easier to use.

Service Connectors make services easier to use by hiding the specifics of communications-related APIs. Connectors encapsulate many generic functions, and also include additional logic that is quite specific to given services. Some of the generic functions typically handled by connectors include the following.

- **Service location and connection management:** Connectors are responsible for discovering service addresses, establishing connections to the service, and capturing all connection-related exceptions. Connectors use the APIs of the client's computing platform to accomplish this. When the client has finished communicating with the service, the connector disconnects from the service and releases client-side resources.

- **Request dispatch:** Once a connection has been established, the connector can send requests to the service on behalf of the client application. Web service connectors must first serialize requests into a stream of bytes before transmitting the stream over the network. The connector must also dispatch the request using the appropriate HTTP server method.

- **Response receipt:** Connectors are responsible for receiving response streams as well. They may provide functions that help client applications deserialize these streams into data types they can understand. Connectors often capture all HTTP status codes returned from services as well. Once a request is dispatched, the connector may block and return a response directly to the next statement in the calling routine of the client application. Alternatively, it may provide an *Asynchronous Response Handler* (184) that enables the client to do other useful work while waiting for the response.

Service connectors provide additional value beyond that of simple web utility classes. Their purpose is to encapsulate the logic clients must use in order to interact with a specific group of related services. To this end, service connectors often provide operations (i.e., class methods) that correspond to specific use

Service Connector

cases in a given problem domain. These operations provide a high-level interface that simplifies the client's interaction with the service. Here are a few functions these operations often provide:

- Constructing, retrieving, or acquiring the URI for the service

- Selecting and issuing the appropriate HTTP server method

- Converting input data from connector operations into the format (e.g., SOAP, XML, JSON, Atom Publishing Protocol, binary, etc.) required by the service

- Deserializing and converting response streams into specific data structures or types that can be easily consumed by the client application

- Implementing an *Idempotent Retry* (206) strategy specific to the needs of the client

There are two types of *Service Connectors*. The first is the *Service Proxy* (a.k.a. Proxy). This type of connector is a specialization of the *Remote Proxy* [GoF] and is used with *RPC APIs* (18) and *Message APIs* (27). Web service proxies are classes whose interfaces are typically derived from the metadata contained in a service's WSDL. These classes typically have methods whose names match the operation names listed in the WSDL port or interface (note: Port types are used in WSDL 1.x, while interfaces are used in WSDL 2.0). Clients are able to call services by executing methods on the proxy's interface. These methods usually have names indicating the use cases they fulfill (e.g., CreateOrder, CheckAvailability, PostResume). Once a method is called, the proxy connects to the service, dispatches the request, and usually waits for a response.

Proxies hide the service's URIs from clients. These URIs are frequently retrieved from a configuration file. This makes it possible to change a service address on the client without having to regenerate the proxy or recompile the client application. However, the client must ensure that the configuration file is always updated whenever service addresses change. Since this is usually a manual effort, which is time-consuming and prone to error, some proxies query a *Service Registry* (220) at runtime in order to resolve service locations. This ensures that the proxy always uses the correct address. Another approach is to have the proxy send requests to a *Virtual Service* (222). These services behave as brokers and are responsible for forwarding messages to the actual services that fulfill requests.

Proxies are typically created with code generation tools (e.g., wsimport for Java, svcutil for WCF). Given the URI of a service's WSDL, these tools will

Service Connector

output one or more class files that can be imported into the client code. While the early WSDL-oriented code generation tools often formatted messages in ways that were incompatible across disparate platforms, most of the newer tools have adopted the standards of organizations like the Web Services Interoperability Organization. This has helped to alleviate many interoperability problems. The biggest problem here is that whenever a breaking change occurs in the *Service Descriptor* (175), the proxy must be regenerated, and the client may have to be rebuilt and deployed as well. (For more on breaking changes, refer to the section What Causes Breaking Changes? in Chapter 7.)

The second type of *Service Connector* is the *Service Gateway*. This variation on the connector is actually a specialization of the *Gateway* [POEAA], a pattern used to encapsulate access to a remote system. Service gateways are used with *Resource APIs* (38). Unlike service proxies, they usually aren't generated by tools. Instead, *Service Gateways* are manually created by the service owner, the client, or a "developer community." The method names on these classes generally correspond to common use cases in the problem domain. Clients are able to call services by executing methods on the gateway. Much like service proxies, the method uses the native APIs of the local computing platform to connect to the service, send requests, and wait for responses.

Service Gateways often hide many things in order to simplify client-service interaction. They may, for example, hide service URIs and the processes used to format inbound and outbound data structures. They may encapsulate the logic which sets HTTP headers used for security credentials, *Media Type Negotiation* (70), language selection, caching, or "Conditional Gets" [for more information, see *Resource API* (38)]. Gateways may parse response content in order to retrieve the addresses of related services [see the *Linked Service* pattern (77)] or construct URIs for services they want to call. They may also convert raw HTTP status codes into domain-specific data which makes sense in the client application.

Unlike the *Gateway* pattern, the *Service Gateway* pattern doesn't always make it easy to swap out one service (resource) for another. In fact, *Service Gateways* are usually designed for use with specific services.

Considerations

Developers who use *Service Connectors* should consider the following issues.

- **Use in unit testing:** *Service Connectors* can be used to facilitate unit testing. One can usually modify the connector to prevent it from calling the web service and have it instantiate an object that "stands in" for the ser-

---

Service Connector

vice. These *Test Doubles* [Meszaros, Gerard] provide client developers the ability to test integration with services that are in development or are unavailable.

- **A convenient place to inject generic client-side behaviors:** *Service Connectors* provide a place where generic "cross-cutting" logic can be inserted with ease. This type of logic is usually executed before requests are sent or after responses are received. A few examples include the *Idempotent Retry* pattern (206), request logging, request validation, exception handling, and insertion of user credentials into the request. *Service Connectors* can also reference local caches that can be checked to see if the client has received recent data that would fulfill a new request. This can help to avoid duplicate service calls. Connectors can also be configured to route requests through a Proxy Server, which checks client credentials before allowing access into certain subnets. The possibilities are endless. All of these capabilities can be encapsulated by *Service Interceptors* (195) and inserted into a pipeline (i.e., handler chain) of the connector's web service framework.

- **Connectors and client-service coupling:** All connectors are coupled to the services they are built for whether or not a *Service Descriptor* (175) is used. In the case of *RPC APIs* (18), if a breaking change occurs in the WSDL, the client's *Proxy* must be regenerated. (For more on breaking changes, refer to the section What Causes Breaking Changes? in Chapter 7.) While *Resource APIs* (38) don't typically use descriptors, the client's *Service Gateway* is coupled to the service nonetheless. All connectors must have intimate knowledge of the service's messages, media types, and related protocols (e.g., when to issue a PUT, POST, etc.). If the service owner changes these structures or protocols, the connector must be updated.

  Most tools that generate Proxies enable client developers to configure such things as service addresses, client authentication policies, and data encryption policies. This enables the behavior of the client application to change without having to recode and, in many cases, redeploy the entire client. The problem is that the client developer must be notified of these changes in advance so that the configurations can be made. If this is not done, the proxy may throw an exception when the altered service is called.

- **Location transparency:** *Service Connectors* are often criticized because they often try to hide the fact that cross-machine calls are taking place. Because of this, clients may not be aware of the potential latencies involved, and may not always implement the necessary logic to handle

Service Connector

network-related failures like lost connections, server crashes, and busy services. However, many developers have learned that use of a *Service Connector* typically implies distributed communications, and that one must create exception-handling logic around the connector to handle communication errors.

Example: *Examples of Popular Service Connectors*

A number of Software-as-a-Service (SaaS) providers and their developer communities have produced robust *Service Connectors*. Two notable examples include

Amazon Web Services: http://aws.amazon.com/

Twitter: https://dev.twitter.com/docs/twitter-libraries

Example: *A Typical Client-Service Interaction through a Service Proxy*

The following Java code demonstrates how a client might interact with an *RPC API* (18). This *Service Proxy* was generated from the service's WSDL.

Service Connector

```
BargainAirService proxy = new BargainAirService();

BargainAir port = proxy.getBargainAirPort();

TravelOptionsRequest request = new TravelOptionsRequest();

// populate request here

TravelOptionsRequest response = port.getFlightSchedules(request);

// do something with the response request
```

Service Descriptor

A client application uses a web service that has an *RPC API* (18), *Message API* (27), or *Resource API* (38). Client developers may use *Service Connectors* (168) or development tools that are able to incorporate services into workflows.

▼

How can development tools acquire the information necessary to use a web service, and how can the code for Service Connectors be generated?

▲

Client applications must know the required URIs, media types, messages, and server methods to use when invoking specific web services. Client developers could study the service documentation and manually create their own *Service Connectors* (168) to encapsulate the required logic. Unfortunately, this documentation may not be kept up-to-date or be very helpful. Even when the documentation is well written, there's no guarantee that developers will interpret it correctly.

Rather than relying on traditional documentation, service owners could describe services through unit tests, and client developers could consult these tests when creating connectors. Such tests are primarily used as regression tests to ensure that changes made to the service won't cause breaks or alter expected service behaviors. However, they can also be used to help client developers understand how a service can be used. Unfortunately, this approach suffers from the same drawbacks as traditional documentation. Service owners must create and maintain up-to-date tests that are complete and easy to understand. Client developers must also interpret these tests correctly in order to create the necessary client code.

Traditional documentation and unit tests typically can't be used as input to code generation tools that produce *Service Connectors* (168) or by workflow development tools, nor can this information be read by automated agents at runtime. Service owners could supplement these approaches by providing machine-readable service metadata.

Service
Descriptor

Produce a standardized and machine-readable description of related services that identifies URIs, logical operations, messages, server methods, and usage policies.

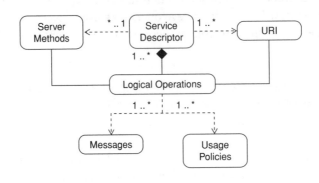

Service Descriptors provide a consolidated, machine-readable listing that identifies a set of logical operations or resources that are managed by a single organization. One might, for example, create one descriptor for customer management services and another for loan application services. The metadata for each logical operation (or resource) identifies a single web service and the messages (or media types) it receives and returns. A web service that lets clients modify the terms of a loan could, for example, be identified by an operation named modifyTerms and indicate that the service receives and returns a LoanApplication message. Descriptors often provide a base URI for all web services in the descriptor. The metadata for individual operations (or resources) can extend or override this URI to define their own unique addresses. Usage policies may be associated with individual operations (or resources) or with all of the operations appearing in the descriptor. These policies identify such things as the protocols for authentication, data encryption, data signing, and reliable message delivery.

XML has become the dominant way to express service metadata. This information may be formally expressed through interface definition languages (IDLs) like WSDL and the Web Application Description Language (WADL). IDLs like these may be used by services with *RPC APIs* (18), *Message APIs* (27), or *Resource APIs* (38).

The primary reason most people use descriptors is to help client developers generate the code for *Service Connectors* (168). To this end, service metadata may be imported directly into developer tools from web servers or acquired from a *Service Registry* (220). The generated connectors provide an explicit interface that typically contains "business-oriented" methods. So, a typical connector might have a method like ModifyLoanTerms. The motivation is to let developers focus on higher-level concerns rather than lower-level protocols like HTTP. Descriptors are also used by many development environments to generate stubs for unit tests.

Considerations

Service developers should consider the following factors when thinking about using the *Service Descriptor* (175) pattern.

- **Relation to service contracts:** A Service Contract can be thought of as an agreement that specifies how clients and services may interact. Each service API style has its own perspective on this concept. The contracts for *RPC APIs* (18) and *Message APIs* (27) are usually defined with WSDL.

  Practitioners who use *Resource APIs* (38) often see the contract as being defined by the HTTP specifications, the media types used by each web service, and sometimes the URI patterns documented for the service. Developers who create this service API style may optionally use WSDL 2.0 or WADL to make this contract even more explicit and to also facilitate code generation of *Service Connectors* (168) and client-side workflows. However, adherents of REST typically argue that contracts like these are unnecessary because the HTTP specification already prescribes a uniform interface that encompasses application semantics, media types are supposed to be self-descriptive, and service addresses can be discovered at runtime through *Linked Services* (77). The notion of a consolidated contract that unites media types, service addresses, and application semantics to a higher business-oriented context is rejected. REST advocates often see little benefit in generating *Service Connectors* (168) and contend that descriptors cause clients to be tightly coupled to web services.

- **Service contracts and network efficiency:** Regardless of the selected web service API style, the service designer should consider the nature of the client-service interactions imposed by the contract. These interactions may be characterized as being "chatty" or "chunky." **Chatty contracts** are "fine-grained" and require the client to incur many network calls in order to complete a typical use case in the problem domain. For example, in the course of creating an order, a fine-grained service API might require the client to call one service to retrieve a customer address and another to acquire the contact information for that customer. In contrast, a coarse-grained interaction would return the customer address and contact information in a single *Request/Response* (54) interchange. The importance of this design strategy cannot be understated. Not only does it help to minimize network latency, it also mitigates the risks associated with network and server failures. The implication is that service contracts should not simply mirror the fine-grained interfaces of the objects used by the service to fulfill requests. Instead, a higher-level, coarse-grained interface over these objects should be implemented to improve network efficiency. This approach is known as the *Remote Façade* pattern [POEAA]. Service designers should apply the *Consumer-Driven Contracts* pattern (250) in order to arrive at the appropriate level of granularity

- **Coupling to Service Descriptors:** *Service Connectors* (168) that are generated from *Service Descriptors* are, by definition, tightly coupled to them and must be regenerated whenever a breaking change occurs on the descriptor. (For more on breaking changes, refer to the section What Causes Breaking Changes? in Chapter 7.) If the connector isn't regenerated, then the client may experience runtime errors on its next attempt to use the services listed in the descriptor. One may, however, avoid regeneration when messages are extended to receive optional data structures [see the *Dataset Amendment* pattern (237)]. This is possible because most code generation tools create connectors that ignore optional items. Connector regeneration can also be avoided when new services are added to the descriptor. In this case, the connector only needs to be regenerated if the client wants to use the new services.

  RPC APIs (18) can present special challenges since the information in the descriptor depends on the signatures of internal class methods (i.e., web service methods), and vice versa (see Figure 6.2). This means that whenever the signature of a web service method or a descriptor operation

Service
Descriptor

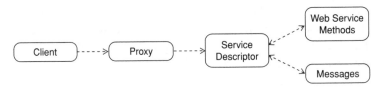

Figure 6.2 *Proxies generated from* Service Descriptors *must be re-created whenever a breaking change occurs on the descriptor. These breaking changes may be caused by changes to web service methods or by changes within the messages used by a service.*

changes, each must be updated, and the client's *Service Proxy* (168) must also be regenerated. In contrast, services with *Message APIs* (27) are less coupled to the signatures of web service methods. Regardless of the API style, client/descriptor coupling increases as the number of web services found in the descriptor rises.

- **Contract-First versus Code-First:** *Service Descriptors* may be created as stand-alone documents and used to generate service-side artifacts. They can also be automatically emitted by web service frameworks at runtime. The former approach is frequently called Contract-First, while the latter is called Code-First.

    Contract-First is closely associated with services that have *RPC APIs* (18) or *Message APIs* (27). With Contract-First, developers create descriptors as stand-alone XML files. Complex data structures are defined in files containing XML Schema Definition Language (i.e., XSDs), and *Service Descriptors* are created with WSDL files that include or reference the XSDs. Binding compilers can then be used to generate Service Interface Classes and *Data Transfer Objects* (94) for the programming language in which the service will be implemented (see Figure 6.3). Developers must then create a *Service Controller* (85) that implements the interface class. Developers creating *Resource APIs* (38) can leverage the Contract-First concept too. However, these programmers only generate *Data Transfer Objects* (94) from the media types defined in XML.

    The Contract-First approach should be considered when messages are designed by industry trade groups, or when the service owner has little control over message design. Service developers who embrace the Design-by-Contract [Meyer, Bertrand] philosophy often find this approach to be

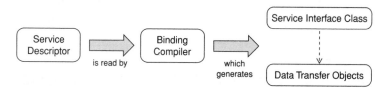

Figure 6.3 *A Binding Compiler may be used to generate Service Interface Classes and* Data Transfer Objects *(94) in a practice known as Contract-First. Developers must then create a* Service Controller *(85) that implements the interface class. Developers creating* Resource APIs *(38) can leverage this practice too, but may only generate* Data Transfer Objects *from the media types defined through XML.*

useful as well. Contract-First lets groups define interfaces that are independent of the code used to fulfill requests. Descriptors can be altered when necessary, Service Interface Classes are regenerated when these descriptors change, and the code in *Service Controllers* (85) is updated to accommodate these modifications.

The Contract-First approach has several benefits and disadvantages. While it gives developers significant control over message formatting and structure, they must have a good working knowledge of XML Schema Definition Language and WSDL. Fortunately, most Integrated Development Environments (IDEs) come equipped with graphical editors that simplify XSD and WSDL maintenance. However, once these artifacts are created, developers must often use arcane command-line utilities to generate the desired classes. Additionally, as of this writing, most binding compilers impose several constraints. For instance, most compilers are unable to produce Service Interface Classes for constructs like xsd:Restriction and xsd:Choice.

Service Descriptor

The Code-First approach may be used with *RPC APIs* (18), *Message APIs* (27), and *Resource APIs* (38). In this practice, classes known as *Service Controllers* (85) are created in languages like Java and C# whose methods are annotated with Routing Expressions. These annotations are used by the service framework to determine which controller methods should be invoked when requests are received. The framework may generate descriptors for the annotated controller when a client queries the base URI of the service, depending on the service API style (see Figure 6.4). Generation of WSDL for *RPC APIs* (18) and *Message APIs* (27) is widely supported in many frameworks. Some frameworks that support *Resource APIs* (38) reflect on the annotated classes and produce HTML help files describing the URI patterns and allowed HTTP verbs. There are also frameworks that support *Resource APIs* (38) which are capable of producing Atom Publishing Protocol (APP) Service Documents.

Figure 6.4 *In the Code-First practice, developers create annotated* Service Controllers *(85) in languages like Java and C#. The web service framework automatically generates descriptors for these controllers when clients query the base URI of the service.*

Of course, the Code-First approach has several benefits and drawbacks too. Developers don't need to maintain separate artifacts (i.e., XSDs, WSDL), nor do they have to become as familiar with these topics as do Contract-First practitioners. Code-First can be a very efficient and productive way to create services. Unfortunately, the developer may have to forfeit some control over message structure and formatting.

With Code-First, it is easy for clients to become coupled to internal classes that are exposed through the web service interface. So, if a web method exposes a *Domain Object* [POEAA] through annotation, then clients of this service will become dependent on that object's interface. Clients that use this service must therefore be updated and redeployed whenever the object's interface changes. Code-First practitioners also have to contend with circular references. Fortunately, many of these problems can be circumvented by using *Data Transfer Objects* (94).

- **The need for traditional documentation:** The use of service descriptors doesn't mitigate the need for good documentation. Client developers usually still need specifications to use services correctly. Whether a descriptor can be used by humans as documentation or for change management depends on the type of descriptor that is used. WSDL, for example, isn't really intended for human consumption.

Service
Descriptor

Example: *Web Services Description Language (WSDL)*

The following portrays a sample WSDL document. This fragment identifies three operations. Note that each has its own URI.

```
<wsdl:portType name="LoanServicePort">
  <wsdl:operation name="EvalEmploymentHistory">
    <wsdl:input wsaw:Action=
        "http://www.acmeLoans.org/EvalEmploymentHistory"
message="tns:EmploymentHistoryRequest" />
  <wsdl:output
message="tns:EmploymentHistoryResponse" />
  </wsdl:operation>

  <wsdl:operation name="CheckCredit">
    <wsdl:input wsaw:Action=
        "http://www.acmeLoans.org/CheckCredit"
message="tns:CheckCreditRequest" />
  <wsdl:output
message="tns:CheckCreditResponse" />
  </wsdl:operation>
```

```
<wsdl:operation name="DoBackgroundCheck">
  <wsdl:input wsaw:Action=
      "http://www.acmeLoans.org/DoBackgroundCheck"
message="tns:DoBackgroundCheckRequest" />
  <wsdl:output
message="tns:DoBackgroundCheckResponse" />
  </wsdl:operation>
</wsdl:portType>
```

This descriptor was created using WSDL 1.1, a specification that doesn't support all of the HTTP verbs. It can therefore only be used for *RPC APIs* (18) and *Message APIs* (27). WSDL 2.0 adds support for all HTTP verbs, and can therefore be used with *Resource APIs* (38) as well. It is also much simpler than 1.1 and has become a W3C recommendation. Unfortunately, at the time of this writing, there was sparse vendor support for 2.0. It may be some time before 2.0 becomes widely adopted since many organizations have invested so heavily in WSDL 1.1.

WSDL has been praised and criticized for many reasons. Many find WSDL to be overly complex. However, it is not meant to be directly created or read by humans. Instead, developers generally use specialized tools to work with WSDL. There have also been some problems with vendor compatibility.

Service Descriptor

While WSDL supports many transport bindings (e.g., HTTP, TCP, JMS, etc.), one cannot easily switch from one protocol to the other because the semantics for usage vary significantly. For example, services that use WSDL to bind to message queues behave quite differently from those that use HTTP. The former implies one-way messaging, while the latter uses *Request/Response* (54). Additionally, the former may require the client to use platform-specific libraries, while the latter is more interoperable.

Example: *Web Application Description Language (WADL)*

WADL was created as an application description language for RESTful services. It was offered as a member submission to the W3C in August 2009. While many have argued that REST doesn't need an IDL, it has, as of this writing, been used in several projects and software products. It remains to be seen if WADL will be adopted on a wider scale. The following provides a simple example of this meta-language.

```
<?xml version="1.0" encoding="UTF-8" standalone="yes"?>
<application
<resources base="http://acmeCorp.org">
```

```
<resource path="/{orderId}" >
  <param name="orderId" style="template" type="xsd:string"/>

  <method name="GET" id="getOrder">
    <response>
      <representation
        mediaType="application/vnd.acmeCorp.acmeOrder+xml"/>
    </response>
  </method>

  <method name="PUT" id="createOrder">
    <response>
      <representation
        mediaType="application/vnd.acmeCorp.acmeOrder+xml"/>
    </response>
  </method>
</resource>

</resources>
</application>
```

Asynchronous Response Handler

A client calls a web service.

▼───────────────────────────────────

How can a client avoid blocking when sending a request?

───────────────────────────────────▲

When a client calls a web service, the thread that initiated the request often blocks while waiting for a response. The time spent waiting for the response could, in many cases, be used to perform other tasks. Depending on the nature of the request and the efficiency of the service, the client could be kept waiting for some time. Some would suggest that the service should be reengineered to use an asynchronous pattern like *Request/Acknowledge* (59). This pattern can certainly help to minimize the time a client blocks, but that is not the primary motivation for using it. Indeed, moving to an asynchronous interaction style like Request/Acknowledge isn't easy, nor is it always recommended.

The semantics of synchronous and asynchronous conversational styles are entirely different. Neither the service nor the client developer can simply switch from one style to the other without significant effort. Consider an exchange in which a client sends a request to register for a conference. In the synchronous style, the client sends a request and receives an immediate response informing the user she's registered. In the asynchronous style, the client sends a request and receives an acknowledgment informing her that the request is being considered. The client may receive the final response by polling the service or waiting for a Callback Message. The synchronous style entails a single exchange of information between the client and service. The asynchronous style involves many more. How, then, can the client take advantage of the time a service processes its request without having to migrate to a completely asynchronous interaction style?

Asynchronous Response Handler

Dispatch requests on a separate thread of execution apart from the main client thread. Wait for the response on this thread while attending to other matters on the main thread.

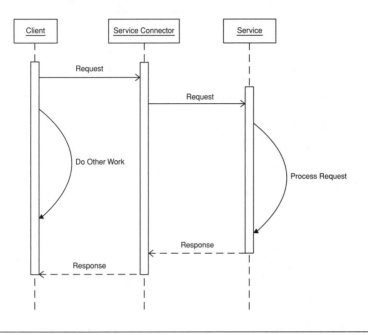

The *Asynchronous Response Handler* pattern specifically addresses the problem of blocking on the client thread that calls a service. It enables clients to do other things once the request has been sent. This pattern has two forms. The first is the *Polling Method,* and the second is the *Client-Side Callback.* The difference between the two is the way the *Service Connector* (168) handles the response. With the polling method, the client must periodically invoke a method on the connector to see if the response has been received. With the callback variation, the connector notifies a Callback Handler when the response has arrived.

In the *Polling Method* variation on the *Asynchronous Response Handler* (see Figure 6.5), the client first sends a request to the service by calling a special operation on the *Service Connector* (168). This causes the connector to spawn a thread that dispatches the request and waits for a response. Once this thread is started, the main thread receives control again and can attend to other work. The main client thread must call the connector's *Polling Method* periodically to

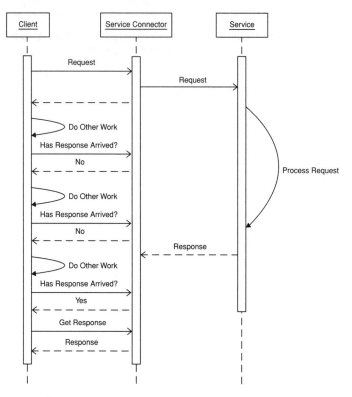

Figure 6.5 Polling Methods *are implemented on* Service Connectors *(168). The client calls a connector method, which spawns a new thread. This thread dispatches the request and waits for a response. The client must call the* Polling Method *periodically to determine if the response has arrived. The client can then pick up the response from another connector method.*

determine if a response has arrived. Once a response has been received, the next call to the *Polling Method* will provide an affirmative result. The client may then call another connector operation to acquire the response.

The tools used to generate *Service Connectors* (168) for *RPC APIs* (18) and *Message APIs* (27) can often be used to create *Polling Methods.* Java developers, for example, may use `wsimport` while C# developers can use `svcutil`. This pattern can also be used with *Resource APIs* (38), but developers usually have to manually create their own custom connectors. Fortunately, this is not hard to do.

With *Polling Methods,* the client must check on the response's arrival. If the client doesn't poll frequently enough, then there may be a significant delay between the time the response arrives and the time the client picks up on the response. Therefore, if the client would prefer to act on the response as soon as it arrives, one might consider using the *Client-Side Callback* variation of this pattern.

Client-Side Callbacks work much like *Polling Methods*. The difference is that the client doesn't have to poll the connector (see Figure 6.6). Instead, a Callback Handler is notified when the response arrives. This handler may be an instance of a concrete class, an anonymous class, or an anonymous method. A reference to the handler is provided to the connector when the client sends a request. The connector will then spawn a separate thread, which dispatches the request and waits for a response. Once this thread is started, the main client thread receives control and can work on other tasks. When the response arrives, the connector notifies the handler, which then pulls the response from the connector.

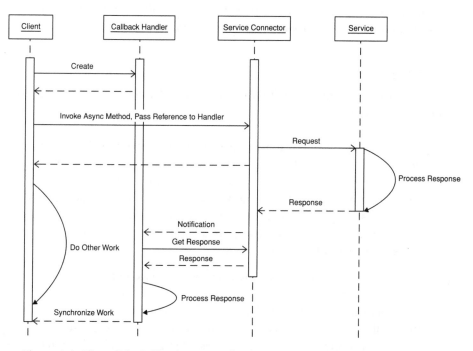

Asynchronous
Response
Handler

Figure 6.6 Client-Side Callbacks *are similar to* Polling Methods. *The difference is that the client doesn't have to poll the connector. When the client calls a connector method to send a request, it passes the connector a reference to a* Callback Handler. *The connector spawns a separate thread that dispatches the request and waits for a response. When a response is received, the callback handler is notified, and it pulls the response from the connector.*

If you want to process the response in the main thread rather than in the handler, you'll need to synchronize the handler thread with the main thread. This can be accomplished by passing the handler a reference to a shared data structure. When the handler receives the response, it can write its data to this shared structure after taking a lock on it. This prevents the main thread from accessing the structure while the handler is updating it.

Most frameworks used with *RPC APIs* (18) and *Message APIs* (27) make it easy to generate *Service Connectors* (168) that support this variation of the pattern. As is true for *Polling Methods,* this pattern can be used with *Resource APIs* (38), but custom connectors must be created.

The patterns described in this section have been discussed for many years and predate the concept of web services. One early example of how this pattern could be used with web services was provided at the International Conference on Web Services in 2003 in a paper titled "Design and Implementation of an Asynchronous Invocation Framework for Web Services" [Zdun, Voelter, Kircher]. The authors present two patterns named *Poll Object* and *Result Callback* that are used in the Apache Axis framework.

Considerations

Developers who use the *Asynchronous Response Handler* pattern should consider the following issues.

- **Not a remedy for long-running operations:** *Asynchronous Response Handlers* may be used when the service consistently completes in a short amount of time (i.e., less than a few seconds). If the service takes longer to complete, timeouts on the connector can occur and the response may be lost. If this becomes a frequent occurrence, the parties may want to consider using a pattern like *Request/Acknowledge/Poll* (62) or *Request/Acknowledge/Callback* (63).

- **An effective way to launch concurrent web service requests:** This pattern can be used to launch several concurrent requests. The client may, for example, need to call several services that have no dependencies. Rather than calling each one in sequence and waiting for the response, the client can submit several requests to be processed in parallel. The client may then poll for the responses or use a callback handler to consolidate the results. One must remember that the responses may not be returned in a predictable order.

- **Temporal coupling:** The *Asynchronous Response Handler* pattern is generally used with *Request/Response* (54). In this usage, it masks issues related to temporal coupling. The reason is that the underlying systems used by the service must be available when the client sends a request, and if the client crashes, the service will not be able to return a response because the connection has been lost. One may truly reduce temporal coupling by using the *Request/Acknowledge* pattern (59).

Example: *Polling Methods and RPC APIs*

Developer tools for the Java and .NET platforms make it easy to generate *Proxies* (168) that provide *Asynchronous Response Handlers* for *RPC APIs* (18) and *Message APIs* (27). The following code demonstrates how a Java client can poll for a response and perform other work in between the times it polls. This client is contacting an *RPC API* (18).

```
BargainAirService proxy = new BargainAirService();

BargainAir port = proxy.getBargainAirPort();

TravelOptionsMessage request = new TravelOptionsMessage();

// Populate request with data here

javax.xml.ws.Response<GetFlightSchedulesResponse> respBean =
        port.getFlightSchedulesAsync(request);

while(!respBean.isDone()) {
// do other things here
}

GetFlightSchedulesResponse response = respBean.get();

TravelOptionsMessage travelOptions = response.getReturn();
```

Asynchronous
Response
Handler

This client instantiates the proxy [i.e., *Service Connector* (168)], and then acquires a WSDL port reference. In the next several statements, the request message is constructed. After the request has been prepared, the method getFlightSchedulesAsync is called. This dispatches a request to the web service on a separate thread. It also immediately returns a response bean of the type javax.xml.ws.Response that extends java.util.concurrent.Future<T>. This enables the client to poll the *Service Connector* to determine when the response has arrived. When the service has returned a response, the client is able to retrieve it from the response bean. It must then call the getReturn method to acquire the unwrapped message.

Example: *Polling Methods and Resource APIs*

It takes a bit more work to support *Polling Methods* for clients of *Resource APIs* (38). The client developer must create a custom *Service Connector* (168) that waits for a response on a separate thread. This example starts by showing how a client might use a sample connector created in C#.

```
Connector connector = new Connector();

connector.PutRequest(
  "http://www.acmeCorp.org/products",
  product.ToXMLString() );

while ( !connector.ResponseReceived )
{
  // do other work
}

string productXML = connector.GetResponseAsString();
```

After the connector is instantiated, the target URI and the request contents are provided to the PutRequest method. The client can then poll for the response. Once the response has been received, the client can pick it up by calling the Get-ResponseAsString method. The implementation for the connector class is shown below.

Asynchronous Response Handler

```
public class Connector
{
    private HttpWebRequest request=null;
    private Thread thread=null;
    private bool responseReceived = false;
    private WebResponse response=null;

    public Connector(){;}

    public void PutRequest(string uri, string xml)
    {
        if ( null != thread) return;

        thread = Initialize(uri, xml);

        thread.Start();
    }
    private Thread Initialize(string uri_in, string xml)
    {
      responseReceived = false;

      Uri uri = new Uri(uri_in);

      request = (HttpWebRequest)WebRequest.Create(uri);
```

```
        request.Method = "PUT";

        UTF8Encoding encoding = new UTF8Encoding();
        byte[] byteArray = encoding.GetBytes(xml);

        request.ContentType = "text/xml";
        request.ContentLength = byteArray.Length;

        Stream stream = request.GetRequestStream();

        stream.Write(byteArray, 0, byteArray.Length);
        stream.Close();

        return new Thread(new ThreadStart(this.GetResponse));
    }

    private void GetResponse()
    {
        // The spawned thread blocks waiting for the
        //   response here
        response = request.GetResponse();
        responseReceived = true;
    }

    public bool ResponseReceived
    {
      get {return responseReceived; }
    }

    public string GetResponseAsString()
    {
      if (! responseReceived) // throw an exception;

      Stream stream = response.GetResponseStream();

      StreamReader reader =
        new StreamReader(stream, Encoding.GetEncoding("utf-8"));

      thread = null;

      return reader.ReadToEnd();
    }
}
```

When the client invokes the PutRequest method, the connector initializes
the request given data from the client. A new thread responsible for retrieving
the response from the service is started. This enables the flow of control to
return back to the client immediately so that it can do other work. Once the
response has arrived, it is saved into a private field, a Boolean field is set to indicate the response has arrived, and the thread terminates. The client can then
retrieve the response by calling the GetResponseAsString method.

Example: *Client-Side Callbacks and RPC APIs*

The following code demonstrates how a client can use a Proxy [i.e., *Service Connector* (168)] that supports *Client-Side Callbacks*. Notice how a reference to a Callback Handler is passed into an operation that supports asynchronous invocation.

```
BargainAirService proxy = new BargainAirService();
BargainAirPort port = proxy.getBargainAirPort();

TripReservationMessage req = new TripReservationMessage();

// populate the request message here

CallbackHandler callback = new CallbackHandler();

java.util.concurrent.Future<?> resp =
          port.reserveTripAsync(req, callback);
```

After the client has instantiated the proxy and acquired a WSDL port reference, it populates the request message. The client then instantiates a Callback Handler and passes that to a proxy method that supports asynchronous dispatching of requests. Note that the return of this method is of the type java.util.concurrent.Future<T>, a construct that may be used to check the results of an asynchronous operation, or even attempt to cancel it. In this example, I simply let the CallbackHandler do all of the work. When the client invokes the proxy method reserveTripAsync, the proxy automatically creates a new thread, sends the request to the service on that thread, and immediately allows the flow of control to return back to the client so that it will not be blocked. The proxy will also wait for the service's response on this new thread. When the response arrives, the proxy invokes the callback handler shown below.

Asynchronous Response Handler

```
public class CallbackHandler
    implements AsyncHandler<ReserveTripResponse>
{
    public void handleResponse(Response<ReserveTripResponse>
                                    callbackResponse)
    {
        ReserveTripResponse response = callbackResponse.get();

        TripReservationMessage reservation = response.getReturn();

        // Do something with the reservation …
    }
}
```

Note that the CallbackHandler class uses an AsyncHandler and Response bean of the type ReserveTripResponse. This is the name of the document wrapper generated by

JAX-WS for the response message returned by the reserveTrip service. Within this wrapper may be found the actual TripReservationMessage that we really want to work with. The method getReturn is used to extract that message from the document wrapper.

Example: *Client-Side Callbacks and Resource APIs*

The following example demonstrates how one might implement a C# *Service Connector* (168) that supports *client-side callbacks* for a *Resource API* (38).

```
public interface ICallbackHandler
{
    void Execute(WebResponse Response);
}

public class Connector
{
    private HttpWebRequest request=null;
    private Thread thread=null;
    private ICallbackHandler callback;

    public Connector(){;}

    public void PutRequest(string uri, string xml,
                    ICallbackHandler callback)
    {
        if ( null != thread) return;

        this.callback = callback;

        thread = Initialize(uri, xml);

        thread.Start();

    }
    private Thread Initialize(string uri_in, string xml)
    {
      // same code as shown in previous
      //  Resource Service Connector example
    }

    private void GetResponse()
    {
        // The spawned thread blocks waiting for the
        //   response here
        WebResponse response = request.GetResponse();
        callback.Execute(response);
    }
}
```

Asynchronous
Response
Handler

The PutRequest method of this class receives a reference to a class that implements the ICallbackHandler interface. When the client calls this method, the connector launches the GetResponse method on a separate thread. When the response is returned, the Callback Handler code listed below is executed.

```
public class CallbackHandler:ICallbackHandler
{
    public void Execute(WebResponse response)
    {
        Stream outputStream = response.GetResponseStream();

        StreamReader reader = new StreamReader(outputStream,
                                Encoding.GetEncoding("utf-8"));

        string productXML = reader.ReadToEnd();

        // do something with XML, for example, load into an XML DOM
    }
}
```

Asynchronous
Response
Handler

Service Interceptor

A client or service must implement common behaviors like authentication, caching, logging, exception handling, and validation.

How can common behaviors like authentication, caching, logging, exception handling, and validation be executed without having to modify the client or service code?

Services created for disparate functional domains like marketing, finance, customer management, and order fulfillment often require common behaviors like authentication, caching, logging, exception handling, and validation. One could code these behaviors directly within the client or service. This may be manageable when there are only a few services. However, it's likely that this code will be copied and pasted many times over, and this inevitably leads to maintenance problems.

One could use the *Template Method* pattern [GoF] and pull these common behaviors up into an abstract base class. With this approach, base classes are created to encapsulate generic behaviors that should be executed in a specific sequence by the service or client. These base classes execute common behaviors before or after specific events occur in their children. For example, a base service class could be designed to invoke a method that authenticates client credentials before sending the request to the child class. Likewise, a base *Service Connector* (168) could invoke a method that checks a local cache for recent responses before allowing the request to be dispatched to the service. Unfortunately, this pattern often results in code that becomes hard to maintain as the number of common behaviors increases. It can also be quite difficult for child classes to override, bypass, or add new generic behaviors.

Developers may therefore decide to abandon class inheritance and consider using object composition. With this strategy, common behaviors are extracted into small specialized classes where each class has a single responsibility. One could, for example, create one class for authentication, another for logging, and so forth. These classes are then instantiated and their methods are invoked only when needed by the service or client. While this simplifies maintenance, a "hard dependency" between the container object (i.e., client or service) and generic behaviors arises. In other words, the client or service must know what generic behaviors to implement. It would be better if the client and service were ignorant of such matters.

Service
Interceptor

Another common approach is to pull the cross-cutting behaviors out into their own services. In this case, requests are routed from one service to the next in a *Pipes and Filters* [EIP] architectural style. Therefore, if a client sends a request to an "order service," the call might first be directed to an authentication service, then to a logging service, and finally to the target service. While this strategy enables common behaviors to be executed, and also eliminates "hard dependencies," it is a more complex architecture that increases latency. A more pragmatic solution might leverage the *Pipes and Filters* concept while minimizing out-of-process calls.

Encapsulate cross-cutting behaviors within individual classes. Load these classes into pipelines that are managed by client or service frameworks.

Service Interceptor

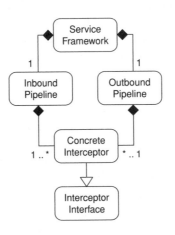

Service Interceptors are a specialization of the *Interceptor* pattern [POSA2] adapted for use with services and their clients. This pattern builds upon the *Pipes and Filters* concept. In this case, the common behaviors are loaded into pipelines that exist within the address space of the client or service. These pipelines are created and managed by a container framework like Apache's CXF, Microsoft's .NET, JAX-WS, JAX-RS, or Spring.

Developers can leverage standard *Interceptors* (i.e., filters) that are a part of the framework. Most frameworks, for example, provide interceptors that support behaviors like authentication and schema validation. Developers can also create custom interceptors to encapsulate and consolidate the logic for other generic behaviors. One might, for example, create distinct interceptors for logging, exception handling, and distributed (memory) cache management. In the latter scenario, one server-side interceptor could be created to save frequently accessed data to the distributed cache, while a second could be used to determine if a client's request can be fulfilled from the cache. Since common behaviors like these are consolidated into distinct classes, maintainability is promoted, and duplicate code is minimized. It's also easier to reuse these behaviors across multiple clients or services.

Each custom interceptor class must implement specific interfaces mandated by the container framework. Developers usually identify the interceptors that should be loaded and the sequence in which they should execute by providing instructions through configuration files. This makes it easy to add or remove behaviors after the client or service has been deployed. It also eliminates dependencies between the client or service and the common behaviors. If a new behavior is added, or an existing behavior is removed through a configuration change, the client or service need not be changed, rebuilt, or redeployed. The downside is that some of these configuration files can become quite lengthy and difficult to read. As an alternative to configuration, many frameworks also enable developers to annotate the methods of *Service Controllers* (85) or *Service Connectors* (168) with expressions that indicate the interceptors that should be loaded. While this is quite convenient and easier to read than configuration files, coupling is higher because the code must be changed whenever a behavior must be added or removed. The client or service may also have to be rebuilt and redeployed.

Service Interceptor

The client or service framework reads the configuration files or reflects upon the annotated classes at runtime in order to create an ordered list of interceptors, which are then loaded to an inbound or outbound pipeline (see Figure 6.7). The sequence in which they execute can usually be controlled with greater certainty through configuration. Regardless, when a client calls a service, the request passes through an outbound pipeline before it is received at the server. Once the request is received at the server, it goes through an inbound pipeline before it is dispatched to a request handler. In a similar fashion, when a service returns a response, that response is passed through an outbound pipeline before being marshaled to the client. On the client side, the response is sent through an inbound pipeline.

Frameworks often have a few common pipeline stages (see Figure 6.8). On the inbound service side, interceptors generally execute before or after requests are deserialized. Note that it is possible to circumvent service execution at any stage and return control to the client. On the outbound service side, interceptors may execute before or after the response is serialized. Client frameworks generally have similar pipeline stages.

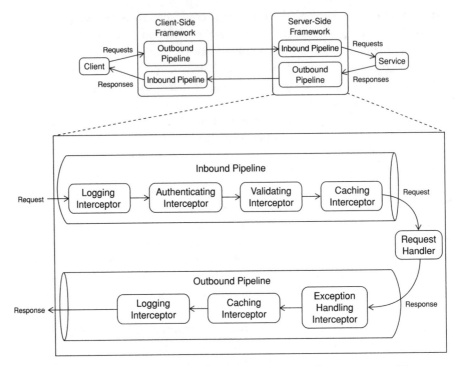

Figure 6.7 *Interceptors can be loaded into pipelines that are managed by client or server frameworks.*

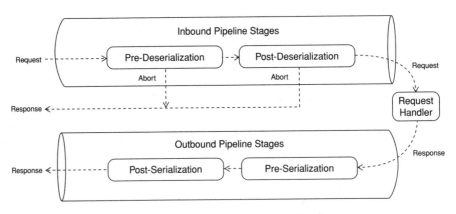

Figure 6.8 *Service frameworks generally segment pipeline processing into two primary stages. In practice, specific web service frameworks segment processing into finer stages.*

Example: *Intercepting Validators*

Runtime errors and wasted CPU cycles can be prevented, in part, when the data structures contained in requests are validated before the service is allowed to execute (see Figure 6.9). Many popular frameworks provide "built-in" interceptors that can be configured to validate requests against one or more XML or JSON schemas. Developers may also choose to create custom interceptors when there is a need to only validate select portions of these requests. This type of validation may leverage XPath.

JAX-RS enables developers to validate XML or JSON schemas through several means. The Apache CXF framework, for example, provides an extension to JAX-RS that enables developers to identify one or more schemas against which all services deployed to a given base URI should use. The fragment shown on the following page from a configuration file shows how this can be done with the jaxrs:schemaLocations element.

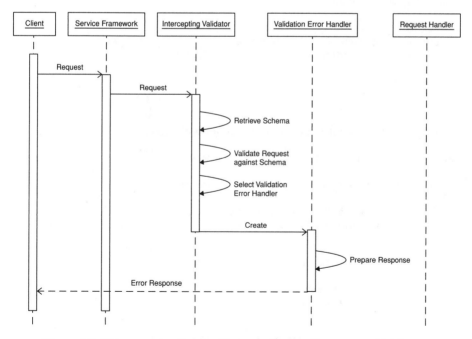

Service Interceptor

Figure 6.9 *This sequence diagram illustrates how an Intercepting Validator can circumvent service execution in the event of a validation error.*

```
<beans xmlns:util="http://www.springframework.org/schema/util">
  <jaxrs:server address="/">
    <jaxrs:schemaLocations>
      <jaxrs:schemaLocation>classpath:/schemas/Customer.xsd
        </jaxrs:schemaLocation>
      <jaxrs:schemaLocation>classpath:/schemas/Order.xsd
        </jaxrs:schemaLocation>
    </jaxrs:schemaLocations>
  </jaxrs:server>
</beans>
```

JAX-WS lets developers annotate *Service Controllers* (85) with the @SchemaValidation attribute to indicate that an intercepting validator should execute when a response is received. The framework validates the entire SOAP message against the schema found in the service's WSDL. The following code shows how a service developer can annotate a *Service Controller* to indicate that SchemaValidator should be used to handle validation exceptions.

```
@WebService
@SchemaValidation(handler = SchemaValidator.class)
public class WebServiceClass
{
  @WebMethod
  public RegisterForEventResponse RegisterForEvent
    (@WebParam RegisterForEvent request) throws GenericFault {

    // business logic here
  }
}
```

Service Interceptor

The class that handles the validation is shown below.

```
public class SchemaValidator extends ValidationErrorHandler
{
  public void warning(SAXParseException e) throws SAXException
  {
    // Allow warnings to be passed back in the packet
    packet.invocationProperties.put("Warning", e);
  }

  public void error(SAXParseException e) throws SAXException
  {
    // log error and return generic info to client
      // Prepare generic error response
  }

  public void fatalError(SAXParseException e) throws SAXException
  {
    // log error and return generic info to client    }
      // Prepare generic error response
  }
}
```

Example: *Intercepting Loggers*

Intercepting loggers may be loaded to the inbound service pipeline to record each request, and responses may be logged by interceptors loaded in the outbound pipeline. The simplest and often most efficient approach is to save this data directly to a file system. However, log files can consume a significant amount of server disk space. Additionally, it can be difficult to correlate requests and responses across log files or perform advanced queries when requests and responses are logged this way. Loggers can instead be configured to save requests and responses to database tables. This makes it much easier to perform queries that provide statistics like the average and peak response time per request type or per client. However, logging directly to a database can increase the overall response time of the service. One may instead achieve the same goal by using an Interceptor that writes the request to a queue before sending it to the (web service) handler. An asynchronous background process can then read this queue and log the necessary information to a database (see Figure 6.10).

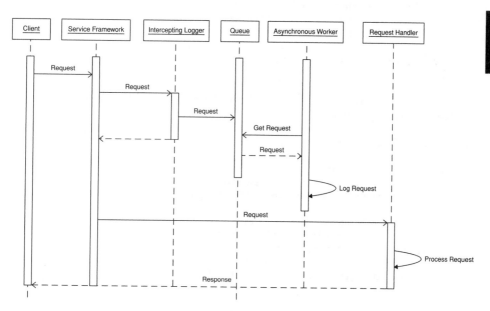

Figure 6.10 *Intercepting loggers often forward requests and responses through queues to asynchronous background workers that save this data to a database. This helps to minimize service response times and ensures that the data will be logged even if the database is unavailable.*

The following C# class encapsulates the logic used to log requests for services hosted by the WCF framework. The AfterReceiveRequest method executes after a request has arrived at the service. This example uses Microsoft's Enterprise Library Logging APIs to save the request.

```csharp
public class Logger : BehaviorExtensionElement,
                      IDispatchMessageInspector,
                      IServiceBehavior
{
  object IDispatchMessageInspector.AfterReceiveRequest(
              ref System.ServiceModel.Channels.Message request,
              IClientChannel channel,
              InstanceContext instanceContext)
  {
    LogEntry logEntry = new LogEntry();
    logEntry.Message = request.ToString();

    Logger.Write(logEntry);

    return null;
  }

  void IDispatchMessageInspector.BeforeSendReply(
              ref System.ServiceModel.Channels.Message reply,
              object correlationState)
  {
    // Response Logging could occur here
  }
```

The method ApplyDispatchBehavior is used to load the Logger class to the inbound service pipeline.

```csharp
// Logger class continued …

void IServiceBehavior.ApplyDispatchBehavior(
            ServiceDescription serviceDescription,
            ServiceHostBase serviceHostBase)
{
  foreach (ChannelDispatcher channelDispatcher
             in serviceHostBase.ChannelDispatchers)
    foreach (EndpointDispatcher dispatcher
               in channelDispatcher.Endpoints)
      dispatcher.DispatchRuntime.MessageInspectors.Add(this);
}
```

The Logger class inherits from BehaviorExtensionElement and must therefore implement the BehaviorType and CreateBehavior methods. This enables the class to be instantiated and loaded through configuration.

```
// Logger class continued ...

public override Type BehaviorType
{
  get { return typeof(Logger); }
}

protected override object CreateBehavior()
{
  return new Logger();
}
} // end of Logger class
```

The Logger class can be configured to load by updating the web.config file. Several steps must be completed in order to load the desired class. The service's behaviorConfiguration attribute must first be set to refer to an element in the behaviors section (i.e., the LoadInterceptors element). This element refers to a Logger behaviorExtension that identifies the class and assembly that contains the interceptor.

```
<system.serviceModel>
  <services>
    <service name="AcmeCorp.BargainAirService"
             behaviorConfiguration="LoadInterceptors">
      <endpoint address="" binding="basicHttpBinding"
             contract="AcmeCorp.IBargainAirService">
      </endpoint>
    </service>
  </services>

  <behaviors>
    <serviceBehaviors>
      <behavior name="LoadInterceptors">
        <Logger/>
        <!-Other interceptors could be listed here -->
      </behavior>
    </serviceBehaviors>
  </behaviors>

  <extensions>
    <behaviorExtensions>
      <add name="Logger"
           type="AcmeCorp.ServiceBehaviors.Logger,
                 AcmeCorp.ServiceBehaviors, Version=1.0.0.0,
                 Culture=neutral, PublicKeyToken=null"/>
    </behaviorExtensions>
  </extensions>
</system.serviceModel>
```

Example: *Intercepting Exception Handlers*

Unexpected errors may occur in the course of service execution. For example, a database connection may be lost right before the SQL can be executed. Rather than creating redundant try/catch blocks for unanticipated errors in each request handler, these exceptions can be caught by interceptors loaded to the outbound service pipeline (see Figure 6.11). This strategy can be used to consolidate the handling of unexpected errors. The exception-handling logic left in the handler should be specific to errors expected in the service.

The following example shows how interceptors can be used to trap unhandled errors so that clients only see generic errors rather than specific internal system errors. The ExceptionHandler class accomplishes this by using the exception name as a key to look up fault information from a memory-backed cache. If the key can't be found, a generic fault is created. While this example shows how SOAP faults can be trapped, it could also be used in *Resource APIs (38)* without much effort.

Service Interceptor

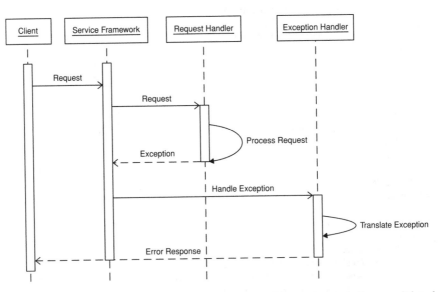

Figure 6.11 *The logic for unhandled or unanticipated exceptions can be consolidated within a common Intercepting Exception Handler. This enables the web service to concentrate on the exception-handling logic specific to the service's function.*

```
public class ExceptionHandler:IErrorHandler
{
  public bool HandleError(Exception error)
  {
    // log error here
    return true;
  }

  public void ProvideFault(Exception exception,
                           MessageVersion version,
                           ref Message fault)
  {
    string exceptionName = exception.GetType().Name;

    FaultInfo faultInfo = GetFaultInfoFromCache(exceptionName);

    if (null == faultInfo)
      faultInfo = CreateGenericFaultInfo();

    FaultException constructedFault =
      CreateFaultException(faultInfo);

    MessageFault msgFault =
      constructedFault.CreateMessageFault();

    fault = Message.CreateMessage(
            version, msgFault, constructedFault.Action);
  }

  private FaultInfo GetFaultInfoFromCache(string exceptionName)
  {
    // Access a memory cache.
    //  Details of this have been excluded.
    ExceptionCache exCache = ExceptionCache.Instance();
    return exCache.GetFaultInfo(exceptionName);

  }

  private FaultInfo CreateGenericFaultInfo()
  {
    return new FaultInfo("", "999,An error occurred");
  }

  private FaultException CreateFaultException(FaultInfo faultInfo)
  {
    FaultReason reason = new FaultReason(faultInfo.FaultReason);
    FaultCode code = new FaultCode(faultInfo.FaultCode);

    return new FaultException(reason, code);
  }
}
```

Service
Interceptor

Idempotent Retry

Every effort must be made to deliver a client's request to a service. The client-service interaction style may be *Request/Response* (54) or *Request/ Acknowledge* (59).

▼

How can a client ensure that requests are delivered to a web service despite temporary network or server failures?

▲

Not every request must be processed. For example, the consequences of not connecting to a restaurant-finder service are probably small. Some clients, however, must make every effort to ensure that requests are delivered. These clients must be prepared to handle many types of connectivity problems. For example, a client could successfully connect to a service and send a request only to see the connection drop while waiting for a response. When this happens, the client might assume that the request was lost and just resend it. However, unintended consequences could result if the service actually did process the request before losing the connection. If the client naively resends the request in this situation, the service might, for example, create two orders when the client only wanted one.

Another, more basic problem must be anticipated. The client might not be able to establish a connection with the service in the first place due to network or server problems. These issues may be temporary or chronic. If the client knew of alternative services, it could send requests to them as a fallback. Unfortunately, it might not know of any alternative services to choose from. The client could therefore deliver its requests to an intermediary responsible for routing requests to available targets. While this can provide delivery assurances, and can also help to reduce coupling with target services, it can be a rather complex and expensive approach too. This pattern also tends to increase the latency of responses. Therefore, using an intermediary to solve the basic problem of service connectivity may be an overly elaborate strategy.

Another option is to send requests to web services through message queues. Queues enable clients to send requests even when the remote systems aren't operational. Messages are stored in the remote queue until the target system decides to retrieve them. If the client can't connect to a remote queue, the client's queuing infrastructure usually saves the message to its own local queue and repeatedly attempts to send the message until it finally succeeds. While queues can be used to help mitigate some service connectivity problems, they are best reserved for use within a secured network, far behind the corporate firewall. One may mitigate some security concerns by establishing a queue entry point on a hardened gateway, but the business partner must use the same queuing technologies. If queues generally shouldn't be exposed beyond the corporate firewall, how can a client ensure that requests are delivered to a web service?

Networks are inherently unreliable. Connections will occasionally time out or be dropped. Problems will arise for innumerable reasons. Servers will be overloaded from time to time, and as a result, they may not be able to receive or process all requests. If a client can't connect to a service or loses a connection, or if the server reports that it is busy, sometimes the best solution is to simply try again.

Design the client such that common connectivity exceptions are caught. When a connection error occurs, reconnect to the service and resend the request. Limit the number of times such attempts are made. Include a unique identifier in each request so that the service can identify duplicate requests. Alternatively, send the request to a unique URI designated for the specific request.

Idempotent
Retry

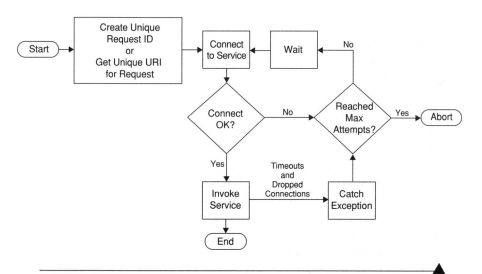

On first consideration, the *Idempotent Retry* pattern seems quite simple. Whenever a client calls a service, it must be prepared to catch several connectivity-related errors. If an error occurs, the client should try to reconnect to the service and resubmit the request as long as it does not exceed a maximum retry threshold. The client must abort further attempts once this limit has been passed. On closer analysis, we see that this pattern entails much more than this summary implies.

Clients must be prepared to catch and identify a number of connectivity errors. Connection failures and dropped connections may occur when server loads are high or servers fail, or when network problems arise. If a connection error occurs or the client cannot receive a response within a programmed or configured timeout period, the client's framework will abort the operation and may throw an exception. Timeouts help to ensure that the client won't block indefinitely. Client frameworks usually provide defaults that define how long they'll wait to establish a connection or receive a response. In most cases, developers will alter the default timeout value to a period that makes sense for the majority of their use cases.

In some cases, the client might not be able to connect to the service because it has an invalid URI. This situation often can't be reconciled when the service has an *RPC API* (18) or *Message API* (27) because the *Service Connectors* (168) employed by their clients frequently use fixed service URIs. In contrast, clients of *Resource APIs* (38) often know only a few "root" service addresses ahead of time. These clients frequently acquire links to related services [see the *Linked Services* pattern (77)] in each response. If a client attempts to access a linked service before the server has created or updated the underlying resources, then an error will occur. This scenario is known as a **race condition** because the server and client are racing against each other. If the client is faster, then the links provided in the previous exchange may be invalid. However, if the client waits awhile and tries again, the URIs will often be valid.

Clients detect connectivity errors in different ways. If the client uses a *Service Connector* (168), the error may be intercepted, converted, and thrown as a platform-specific exception by the connector. The client application must implement the appropriate exception-handling block to catch and identify these errors. Service connectors that are created for *Resource APIs* (38) often check for specific return codes. A resource service may, for example, return an HTTP code of 503 to say that it is busy, and provide a Retry-After header that specifies how long the client should wait before trying again. Once again, the connector may convert these status codes to more meaningful exceptions for the client. In any event, once the client has positively identified a temporary and recoverable connection-related error, it may initiate its retry logic.

Clients must determine how long to wait before attempting a retry. They may decide not to wait at all, or they might pause for a time. This delay time

Idempotent
Retry

may be set to be the same for all errors, or may vary depending on the type of error that occurred. The client must also determine how to implement a wait. If the client invoked the service on its main thread, the application would freeze if the thread were put to sleep. A better approach would be to invoke the service on a separate thread that may be put to sleep in between retries; this enables the main client thread to continue with its work. If the wait time is very long (i.e., minutes or hours), then this technique usually shouldn't be used. Instead, the information required to call the service may be persisted to a data store like a queue or database and picked up by an unattended background process at a later time. Regardless of how this information is stored, once this wait period has passed, the client or background process may try to connect to the service again. If it succeeds, then the request may be sent.

Clients should not naively initiate retries after connectivity failures. If a client assumes that a request may be resent after a lost connection, unintended side effects could occur. The service may have processed the request even though the connection was dropped. In order to assess whether or not unintended consequences will result, the client developer must determine if the request is supposed to be idempotent. An idempotent request is one that yields the same results no matter how many times the service is called. The simplest example is a request that deletes information. This type of request is idempotent because once the target of the delete is removed, it will always be deleted, and subsequent calls will yield the same results. Depending on the application protocols and specific server methods used, a create or update request may or may not be idempotent. For example, PUTs issued to *Resource APIs* (38) are supposed to be idempotent while POSTed requests are not. It is important to note that while the service may be required by the HTTP specification to exhibit idempotence, the developer must still implement the appropriate logic to ensure this quality. The service must therefore identify duplicate requests regardless of the server method issued by the client. This same recommendation holds true for *RPC APIs* (18) and *Message APIs* (27) as well. Clients using these last two API styles should always assume that create and update requests, or requests that don't fit neatly into the CRUD paradigm, are not idempotent.

Client developers must therefore pay special attention to requests that are supposed to be idempotent. Clients using *RPC APIs* (18) and *Message APIs* (27) often include unique request identifiers in requests so that services can identify duplicates (see Figure 6.12). These clients may generate their own unique identifiers, perhaps by using a Universally Unique Identifier (UUID). Clients may also fetch a set of unique identifiers that had previously been

Idempotent Retry

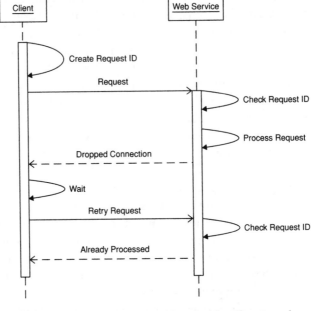

Figure 6.12 *Clients can inject unique identifiers into the request so that duplicate requests may be identified by the service on retry attempts.*

Idempotent Retry

generated. Regardless of the approach, these identifiers must be created or acquired by the client before connecting to the service. When a service receives a request, it can look at the request identifier to determine if the request was previously processed. If the identifier is new, the request will be processed; otherwise, an error response is returned.

Clients using *Resource APIs* (38) often take a different approach. The client may first send a query to a service asking for a unique URI that may be used for the upcoming request. The client will then POST the request and perform all retries against this URI (see Figure 6.13). If the request succeeds on any attempt, a success response code (e.g., HTTP status code 200) is returned. If the request was already processed, an error response is provided. The disadvantage with this approach is that an extra network round-trip is required in order to acquire the unique URI. This pattern, known as *Post-Once-Exactly* [Nottingham, Marc], provides yet another way to ensure idempotence when using the Retry pattern.

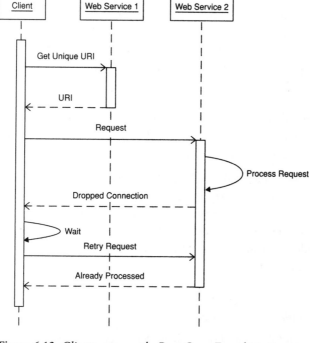

Figure 6.13 *Clients can use the* Post-Once-Exactly *pattern in conjunction with the basic Retry pattern to guarantee idempotent request behavior.*

Considerations

Developers should consider the following when using the *Idempotent Retry* pattern.

- **Minimum criteria for adoption:** The *Idempotent Retry* pattern need not be used when it's acceptable for the call to fail. Certain use cases and applications do not require every request to succeed. These applications accept the possibility that, from time to time, a service connection may fail or be dropped. For example, an application with a user interface may simply display an error message and let the user initiate the retry manually.

- **Retries fail too:** It should be evident that retries can fail. If a timeout, dropped connection, or other connectivity error occurs during a retry, then the client may try again. However, the client should not be allowed to retry indefinitely as this could tie up client resources. Therefore, a limit must be set on the number of times retries are allowed. This limit should be determined by the constraints of the use case under consideration.

Service owners should work with client developers to identify acceptable retry limits. Guidelines for maximum retries, for delay times between retries, and for maximum retry periods should be established. This information is typically maintained on the client side, but may also be dynamically provided by the server at runtime. For example, some services will tell clients to perform a retry after a certain period of time if they are too busy to handle a client's request.

- **Dealing with client-side crashes:** Developers should consider the possibility that the client may crash in between retries. If the request takes a "long" time to create, then it may be worthwhile to persist the request to a data store (e.g., database or queue) before initiating the retry loop. This means that code must also be written to retrieve the request after a crash and reinitiate the retry.

Idempotent Retry

Example: *Simple Retry Manager*

This example in C# shows how a client can inject a *Service Connector* (168) into a class that manages retries. Once the retryManager has been instantiated, the number of retries that will be allowed and the time to wait between retries is set by the call to SetRetryParameters. Note that the client would usually retrieve the retry parameters from a configuration file or database. The call to the retryManager's SetRetryReturnCodes method sets a list of HTTP return codes that are used by the retryManager to determine when a retry should occur. SetConnectionErrors sets a list of connectivity exceptions that cause the retryManager to attempt a retry. The retryManager calls the service when the Execute method is invoked. The details of the product and RetryErrorListRepository classes have been omitted. You should assume that the request contains a unique identifier.

```
ServiceConnector connector = new ResourcePoster();
connector.Initialize(someUri, product.ToXMLString());

IRetryManager retryManager = new RetryManager();

// set the number of retries and wait time between retries
retryManager.SetRetryParameters(3, 1000);

retryManager.SetRetryReturnCodes(
  RetryErrorListRepository.GetHttpErrorList());
```

```
retryManager.SetConnectionErrors(
  RetryErrorListRepository.GetConnectErrors());

retryManager.SetConnector(connector);

retryManager.Execute();
```

The following is the base class for the *Service Connector* (168) in this example.

```
public abstract class ServiceConnector
{
  public abstract void Execute();

  protected int DefaultTimeout
  {
    get { return // read from config file or cache; }
  }

  protected string TargetURI{ get; set;}

  protected string Request{ get; set;}

  protected string Response{ get; set;}

  public void Initialize(string uri, string request)
  {
    this.TargetURI = uri;
    this.Request = request;
  }

  public string GetResponse()
  {
    return this.Response;
  }
}
```

The following class encapsulates the logic used to POST data to a URI. This class inherits from ServiceConnector.

```
public class ResourcePoster:ServiceConnector
{
  public override void Execute()
  {
    base.Response = null;

    ValidateInput();

    HttpWebRequest request = InitializeRequest();
```

```
    GetResponse(request);
  }

  private void ValidateInput()
  {
    if (String.IsNullOrEmpty(base.TargetURI))
      throw new Exception("targetURI cannot be null or empty");

    if (String.IsNullOrEmpty(base.Request))
      throw new Exception(
        "requestAsXMLString cannot be null or empty");
  }

  private HttpWebRequest InitializeRequest()
  {
    HttpWebRequest request = null;

    Uri uri = new Uri(base.TargetURI);

    request = WebRequest.Create(uri) as HttpWebRequest;

    request.Method = "POST";
    request.ContentType = "text/xml";
    request.Timeout = base.DefaultTimeout;

    UTF8Encoding encoding = new UTF8Encoding();

    byte[] byteArray = encoding.GetBytes(base.Request);

    request.ContentLength = byteArray.Length;

    WriteRequestToStream(request, byteArray);

    return request;
  }

  private void WriteRequestToStream(HttpWebRequest request,
                                    byte[] byteArray)
  {
    Stream stream = request.GetRequestStream();
    stream.Write(byteArray, 0, byteArray.Length);
    stream.Close();
  }

  private void GetResponse(HttpWebRequest request)
  {
    WebResponse response = request.GetResponse();

    StreamReader reader =
      new StreamReader(response.GetResponseStream(),
                       Encoding.GetEncoding("utf-8"));
```

Idempotent Retry

```
    base.Response = reader.ReadToEnd();
  }
}
```

The RetryManager class encapsulates the logic that implements the Idempotent Retry pattern. This example runs on the thread of the caller, so when it pauses in HandleRetryError, the caller's thread will block. This class can be easily loaded and executed on a separate thread so that the client isn't blocked; this is left as an exercise for the reader.

```
public class RetryManager : IRetryManager
{
  public const int HTTP_OK = 200;

  IList<WebExceptionStatus> connectionErrors = null;

  bool doRetry = true;
  int maxTries=0;
  int tryCount = 0;

  int waitTime=0;
  ResourceErrors retryErrorList = null;
  ServiceConnector serviceConnector = null;

  int responseCode = HTTP_OK;

  public RetryManager() { }

  public void SetRetryParameters(int maxRetries,
                                  int waitTimeBetweenRetries)
  {
    maxTries = maxRetries;
    waitTime = waitTimeBetweenRetries;
  }

  public void SetRetryReturnCodes(ResourceErrors errorList)
  {
    retryErrorList = errorList;
  }

  public void SetConnectionErrors(
      IList<WebExceptionStatus> connectErrors)
  {
    connectionErrors = connectErrors;
  }

  public void SetConnector(ServiceConnector connector)
  {
    serviceConnector = connector;
  }
```

```
public void Execute()
{
  tryCount = 0;
  doRetry = true;

  while (doRetry)
  {
    try
    {
      responseCode = HTTP_OK;

      serviceConnector.Execute();

      doRetry = false;
    }
    catch (Exception ex)
    {
      // log exception here

      if (!(IsRetryError(ex))) throw;

      HandleRetryError(ex);
    }
  }
}

private bool IsRetryError(Exception exception)
{
  if (!(exception is WebException)) return false;

  WebException webException = (WebException)exception;

  if (null != webException.Response)
  {
    HttpWebResponse response =
      (HttpWebResponse)webException.Response;

    this.responseCode = (int)response.StatusCode;

    return retryErrorList.ContainsKey(this.responseCode);
  }

  WebExceptionStatus status = webException.Status;

  return connectionErrors.Contains(status);
}

private void HandleRetryError(Exception ex)
{
  tryCount++;
```

Idempotent Retry

```
    if (tryCount == maxTries)
    {
      doRetry = false;
      return;
    }

    Thread.Sleep(waitTime);
  }
}
```

Example: *WS-Reliable Messaging*

WS-Reliable Messaging (WS-RM) is a protocol that defines a standard XML-based vocabulary that can be implemented by service frameworks to provide message delivery assurances similar to traditional messaging systems. WS-RM implementations provide the capability to retry sending messages on failed attempts, and also make it possible for the developer to define rules which determine how many times the message is delivered. One can instruct a framework to send a message exactly once, at most once, at least once, and so on. Developers can also configure their systems to ensure that messages are received and processed in the exact order they were sent. This being said, the implementations for WS-RM can vary greatly, and not every framework is capable of handling dropped connections.

Idempotent Retry

There are two entities involved in WS-RM. These include the "RM Source" and the "RM Destination." Both of these agents exist on the client and service side. When a client sends a request to a service, it functions as the RM Source, and the service acts as the RM Destination. When the service returns a response, the responsibilities are swapped. The presence of these agents is largely hidden from the developer. The RM Source is responsible for starting and terminating a "Reliable Messaging Session." When an RM session is initiated, both sides of the communication initialize a cache into which copies of messages are saved. Different platforms implement this cache in different ways. Some implementations use durable, persistent message stores. Others use local (i.e., nondistributed) memory-backed caches.

RM conversations are initiated when the client's RM Source sends a CreateSequence message to the service. The RM Destination on the service responds with a CreateSequenceResponse message that includes a unique SequenceID that is used by the client to identify all of the messages that will be submitted in the sequence. From that point on, each message sent by the client will contain a sequence header that includes the sequence identifier and a message number. The value of the first message number is always 1, and the value for each subsequent message number is incremented by 1. The RM Source also saves a copy of each message sent in its cache.

The RM Destination keeps track of each message that it receives by saving copies into its own cache. Depending upon the "Delivery Semantics" defined in the service's policy the RM Destination may or may not immediately dispatch messages forward to the actual service implementation code. If, for example, the service has defined that all messages must be delivered in order, and the RM Destination receives messages 1, 2, and 4, the RM Destination will hold on to message 4 until it has received message 3. Once the RM Destination has received message 3, it will forward messages 3 and 4 on to the service implementation. Given this, you should see that there may be a time delay on the RM Destination side before the message is actually delivered to the web service method. It should be noted that the aforementioned delivery semantics are not a part of the WS-Reliable Messaging specification. Instead, they may be implemented differently on each platform.

There are other times when the RM Destination will not send a message forward to the service. This behavior occurs when the service has a policy of "Exactly-Once" delivery and it receives duplicate messages. In order to enforce this policy, the RM Destination looks in its cache for a message with a matching SequenceID. If it receives a new message and finds a message with a matching SequenceID in the cache, it knows that it has a duplicate message and will usually just discard the message.

Idempotent Retry

The RM Destination will periodically send a SequenceAcknowledgement message back to the RM Source. The purpose is to let the RM Source know what messages have been received. Rather than sending one acknowledgment for each message, the RM Destination minimizes network traffic by batching these acknowledgments up into one message. When the RM Source receives a SequenceAcknowledgement, it inspects it to see which messages the RM Destination has reported as being missing. For each message the RM Destination reports to be missing, the RM Source retrieves those messages from its cache and resubmits them. Note that the service uses its own RM Source agent to communicate with the client's RM Destination so that the same delivery assurances are provided for responses.

The following configuration file entry shows how WS-RM can be enabled for WCF Services. Here you can see that a binding named ReliableHttpBinding is created to support reliable messaging over HTTP. All messages must be delivered in order.

```
<bindings>
  <customBinding>
    <binding name="ReliableHttpBinding">
      <reliableSession ordered="true"
                       acknowledgementInterval="00:00:00.2000000"
                       maxRetryCount="3"/>
      <httpTransport/>
    </binding>
  </customBinding>
</bindings>
```

The service designer must also modify the service configuration information as is shown below.

```
<service name="AcmeCorp.Shipping"
  behaviorConfiguration="AcmeCorp.defaultBehavior">

  <endpoint address="" binding="customBinding"
            contract="AcmeCorp.IShipping"
            bindingConfiguration="ReliableHttpBinding">
  </endpoint>
</service>
```

When the service is published, the following policy assertions appear in the service's WSDL. Notice how the acknowledgment interval has been carried over from the declaration, and the delivery semantics indicate ExactlyOne, which means that duplicates will be dropped.

```
<wsp:Policy wsu:Id="CustomBinding_IShipping_policy">
  <wsp:ExactlyOne>
    <wsp:All>
      <wsrm:RMAssertion xmlns:wsrm=
          "http://schemas.xmlsoap.org/ws/2005/02/rm/policy">
        <wsrm:InactivityTimeout Milliseconds="600000" />
        <wsrm:AcknowledgementInterval Milliseconds="200" />
      </wsrm:RMAssertion>
      <wsaw:UsingAddressing />
    </wsp:All>
  </wsp:ExactlyOne>
</wsp:Policy>
 .
 .
 .
<wsdl:binding name="CustomBinding_IShipping" type="tns:IShipping">
  <wsp:PolicyReference URI="#CustomBinding_IShipping_policy" />
  .
  <!-- wsdl operations declared here -->
  .
</wsdl:binding>
```

A Quick Review of SOA Infrastructure Patterns

There are many definitions for Service-Oriented Architecture (SOA). Some see it as a style of technical design that enables heterogeneous systems to be integrated through reusable business functions (i.e., services). Others consider SOA to be a methodology that helps companies identify, create, deploy, integrate, and govern the life cycle of any software asset that provides a useful service to the organization or its business partners. This section provides a brief overview of a few infrastructures that are frequently mentioned by SOA practitioners. It is important to note that none of these are required to create a SOA.

Please keep in mind that the services in a SOA are not constrained to using HTTP. In fact, software components that use standards, technologies, and protocols like JMS, MSMQ, TCP, UDP, and named pipes can all be "service-enabled" and included in a SOA.

The Service Registry

One of the central infrastructures commonly used in SOA is the *Service Registry*. A **registry** is a central repository that stores metadata for service-related artifacts that embody the standards for a given corporation. The goal is to promote reuse of these artifacts and facilitate governance. Registries typically house the following types of artifacts.

- Reusable messages and complex type definitions defined with the XML Schema Definition Language.

- Reusable policies defined through WS-Policy. Policies define the rules for how clients should be authenticated, how messages should be encrypted, and other similar concerns.

- WSDL documents that identify the required communication protocols (i.e., HTTP, JMS, etc.), input and output message types, policies, and addresses for each service.

Registries frequently enable users to version artifacts. This being said, they are not meant to replace Software Configuration Management (SCM) and version control tools like Perforce, Git, or Subversion.

Developers may create composite applications by importing registry metadata into their development environment at design time. This ensures that applications will use approved services and policies. Developers can also create

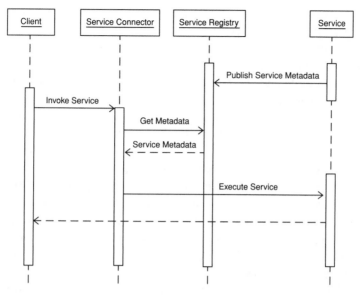

Figure 6.14 Service Registries *store metadata for service-related artifacts that embody the standards for a given company. The goal is to promote reuse of these artifacts and facilitate governance. Registry metadata may be imported at design time in order to create composite applications that use approved services. They are also queried by* Service Connectors *(168) at runtime so that client applications can locate, connect, and use registered services.*

SOA
Infrastructure
Patterns

and publish their own "composite services" that use registered services. Information from the registry is frequently used by specialized *Service Connectors* (168) at runtime so that client applications can locate, connect, and use registered services (see Figure 6.14).

The Enterprise Service Bus

The *Enterprise Service Bus* (ESB, a.k.a. bus) is another infrastructure pattern that figures prominently in SOA. One articulation of the concept appears in the *Message Bus* pattern [EIP]. ESBs have three primary objectives:

- Message routing

- Message translation

- Protocol translation and transport mapping

First and foremost, ESBs function as *Message Routers* [EIP] that forward requests to services and shuttle responses back to clients. The intent is to provide clients a means to invoke services while minimizing the client's dependencies on specific service implementations. ESBs provide a layer of indirection that enables services to be added, upgraded, replaced, or removed while minimizing the impact on client applications. This is possible because clients send messages to the bus rather than communicating directly with target services. In other words, the client's dependencies shift to the bus. Clients frequently send messages through *Virtual Services* [IBM, ESB Patterns]. These look like the actual target services to clients, but simply provide a common endpoint that receives messages. Clients may also use special *Channel Adapters* [EIP] to connect to the bus. ESBs route messages to the appropriate service according to predefined rules. There are many ways to construct these rules. ESB administrators may, for example, use SOAPAction or WS-Addressing headers, URI templates, or content found deep within the message. These rules are often retrieved from *Service Registries* (see Figure 6.15).

Clients that communicate with services through ESBs typically have to use a standard set of messages often referred to as the *Canonical Data Model* [EIP]. The advantage with this approach is that you won't need to create specialized services designed to process requests from specific client applications. Since all clients are forced to use the canonical model, a single service can be created to process all requests. Unfortunately, this shifts the burden over to the client, and clients may have to use a *Message Translator* [EIP] to convert their messages to the canonical form. This logic can be encapsulated within a *Service Connector* (168) that translates the client's message to the canonical form, then sends the transformed message to the bus. Once the bus has received a message, it may

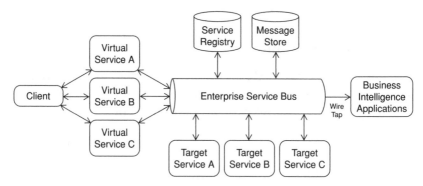

Figure 6.15 *ESBs provide a layer of indirection that enables services to be added, upgraded, replaced, or deprecated while minimizing the impact on client applications.*

use a *Message Translator* to convert the canonical message to the format defined in the service's contract. This enables the service's contract and canonical data model to vary independently. A similar process is used to convert service responses to the canonical form, and finally to the structures used by clients (see Figure 6.16).

A third key function performed by ESBs is protocol translation and transport mapping. This feature may be employed when the target service uses a protocol or transport that is foreign to the client. A .NET client application may, for example, submit requests over HTTP to a *Virtual Service* [IBM, ESB Patterns] hosted by an ESB. If the target service uses a different protocol like JMS, the ESB would convert the message and use the JMS APIs to connect to the service.

Sophisticated ESBs perform many other useful functions. For example, they frequently provide *Guaranteed Delivery* [EIP] of messages. If a target service is unavailable, the ESB may persist the message to a *Message Store* [EIP] and try

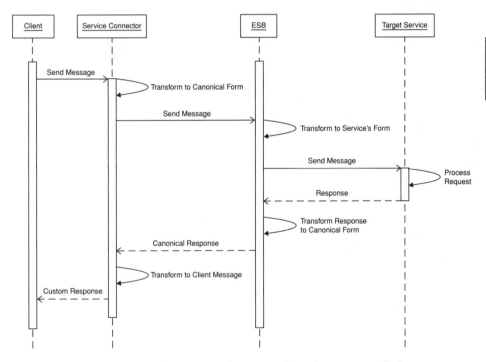

Figure 6.16 *Clients that communicate with services through ESBs typically have to use a standard set of messages that are defined independent of all services and client applications. The bus may use a* Message Translator *[EIP] to convert the canonical request to the format defined in the service's contract.*

to send the message at a later time by using the *Idempotent Retry* pattern (206). ESBs may also perform other generic functions like authentication, authorization, and logging on behalf of target services. This removes the responsibility from the target service, and ensures that policies are consistently enforced throughout the company. Since the bus "sees" all of the messages carried between clients and services in real time, a *Wire Tap* [EIP] can be established to forward information from the bus to business intelligence applications.

The Orchestration Engine

ESBs often route messages to services that connect to *Orchestration Engines*. These are centralized infrastructures that direct the activities of long-running or complex workflows (see Figure 6.17). The activities, or tasks, found in these workflows are often performed by services, though they need not be web services that use HTTP. Workflows are typically created with graphical tools or meta-languages like BPEL.

Orchestration Engines manage the lifetime of workflow or process instances. Workflows are instantiated when messages are sent to *Workflow Connectors* (156). Once a workflow has been initialized, the engine controls which activities in the workflow are executed, and also decides when the workflow should

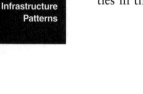

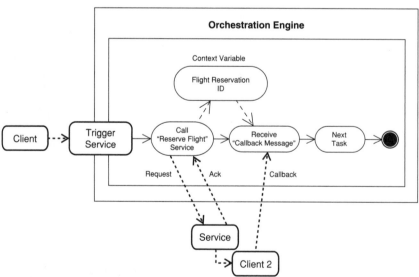

Figure 6.17 Orchestration Engines *provide centralized infrastructures that direct the activities of long-running or complex workflows.*

be suspended or terminated. Workflows can execute a simple sequence of tasks, they can use conditionals to select different paths in the workflow, and they can also control loop iteration. More impressive is their ability to manage parallel task execution.

Orchestration Engines can easily handle the fundamental service interaction patterns. For example, if a task calls a service that uses the *Request/Acknowledge* (59) interaction, the workflow may poll for a response or wait for a callback message. If a Callback Service is used to receive a response, the engine will route the callback message back to the specific workflow instance that initiated the call. For more information on orchestration, see *Patterns for Orchestration Environments* [Manolescu]. In-depth coverage of Workflow Patterns is also provided at http://workflowpatterns.com/ [van der Aalst, et al].

Service Registries, ESBs, and *Orchestration Engines* are sophisticated infrastructures. Vendor-backed solutions can be quite expensive, but free, open source offerings have also become available in recent years. The features and maturity of these products can vary drastically. Some organizations choose to build their own custom infrastructures. This, however, can often be more costly than vendor solutions if you tally up the total costs of development and ongoing maintenance.

SOA
Infrastructure
Patterns

Chapter 7

Web Service Evolution

Introduction

Service developers strive to maintain Backward Compatibility whenever a service is changed. This condition exists when the service can successfully process requests from clients that submit older versions of messages or media types. Backward compatibility also means that a client won't break if the service returns a response using an updated data structure that the client may not fully comprehend. Services can also be Forward Compatible. A client may, for example, send "version 2" of a message, but the service may only know how to process data found in the first version because it hasn't been altered to work with the newer message structure. This is a common occurrence when structures are defined by external parties. If the service can still process the request without crashing, it may be considered Forward Compatible [Orchard].

Backward and forward compatibility are quite difficult to achieve. A service can only be forward-compatible if it is able to ignore new content. This means that, while the service cannot process data that it is not yet aware of, it should still be able to process the remainder of the request. As a practical matter, service owners tend to spend the majority of their time worrying about backward compatibility. The key problem that all service designers should be aware of is that services can cause clients to break whenever the data structures they receive or send are changed.

While changes to the internal logic of a service can certainly cause clients to break, most of the focus in this chapter is on how changes to a service's contract (see Chapter 2) affect backward compatibility. We'll look at the factors that cause breaking changes, and briefly review two common versioning strategies. We'll also see how *RPC APIs* (18) can be designed to become less brittle and more flexible, and we'll review an approach that lets all services, regardless of API style, to be augmented so that they may receive and process new data. Finally, we'll present an approach that helps all message recipients to become more resilient, and another that ensures services will continue to meet the needs of clients. This chapter concludes with a brief look back at how many of the patterns in this book either support or hinder service evolution. Table 7.1 presents an overview of the patterns in this chapter.

Table 7.1 *Patterns for Web Service Evolution*

Pattern Name	Problem	Description
Single-Message Argument (234)	How can a web service with an RPC API (18) become less brittle and easily accommodate new parameters over time without breaking clients?	Design each service operation such that it only receives a single message parameter that contains all of the data for a request.
Dataset Amendment (237)	How can a service augment the information it sends or receives while minimizing the probability of breaking changes?	Append optional data to existing request and response data structures.
Tolerant Reader (243)	How can clients or services function properly when some of the content in the messages or media types they receive is unknown or when the data structures vary?	Design the client or service to extract only what is needed, ignore unknown content, and expect variant data structures.
Consumer-Driven Contracts (250)	How can a web service API reflect its clients' needs while enabling evolution and avoiding breaking clients?	Client developers write integration tests that express the client's expectations of a service API. These tests are given to the service owner, who incorporates them into the service's test suite.

What Causes Breaking Changes?

A **breaking change** is any change that forces client developers to update their code or change configurations. Clients that fail to makes the necessary changes may experience runtime exceptions. The most common causes for breaking changes include

- Moving services to different domains
- Changing the URI patterns clients use to address services

- Structural changes to media types or messages

- And *Service Descriptor* (175) changes

Among other things, the section titled How the Patterns Promote Service Evolution at the end of this chapter provides tips on how the first two issues can be mitigated. This section focuses on the last two bullet items.

Structural Changes to Media Types or Messages

Service developers must consider how clients may be affected by changes made to the data structures exchanged with clients. In many cases, the required media types or messages will be formally defined through a meta-language such as XSD or JSON Schema. In other cases, these agreements will simply be listed on a web page. Developers should be aware of what actions on these data structures may cause breaking changes. Several of these are listed below:

- Removing or renaming qualified elements or attributes

- Changing the data types of qualified elements or attributes

- Changing elements or attributes from being optional to being required

- Changing the order in which elements occur in a data structure

- Changing the hierarchical relationships between complex data structures

- Adding elements to the middle of a strict sequence of elements

- Changing the namespace of a data structure or its child structures

- Deprecating data structures

- Changing character encodings

Clients must be able to predict the layout and data types used in service data structures. Changes like those that are listed above can make the processing rules used by clients obsolete and cause them to break. The effect of some of these changes can, however, be mitigated by using the *Tolerant Reader* pattern (243).

The service's expectations regarding what information is required and what is optional can be explicitly defined through "machine-readable" meta-languages like XSD and JSON Schema. These expectations might also be described in text-based documents (e.g., Word, HTML, etc.) aimed at developers. Regardless of how these expectations are expressed, once the parties have agreed to

What Causes
Breaking
Changes?

"the contract," and the service has been deployed, they can rarely be changed without causing some disruption. Several common-sense guidelines should therefore be considered. A service should, for example, never change an optional request or response item to become required after it is released. This action usually results in a breaking change. Conversely, a service can usually loosen restrictions and change a required request item to become optional in later releases without incurring breaking changes.

Another factor to consider is whether or not data structure items should occur in a strict sequence. Consider an address structure that contains a street name, city, state or territory, postal code, and country code. The order in which these items occur really shouldn't matter. Unfortunately, many tools encourage the service designer to define structures that impose a specific sequence. It is worth noting that *Data Transfer Objects* (94) that use data-binding instructions can map data to or from message structures without imposing such strict sequences. The service designer must, however, be familiar with how to use her platform's APIs and annotations to enable this outcome. For the greatest degree of flexibility, the Data Transfer Object may avoid data-binding altogether and instead leverage the *Tolerant Reader* pattern (243).

Some *Resource APIs* (38) use generic multipurpose media types like Atom Publishing Protocol (APP) or Microformats. These types are relatively static and change infrequently. Some contend that when these structures and protocols are used, the probability of a breaking change is remote. However, generic protocols like APP frequently carry domain-specific structures (e.g., products, customers, inventory, etc.). With APP, one must embed proprietary types within the APP content element. If a breaking change occurs on a type carried in this element, APP cannot insulate the client from the effects.

What Causes
Breaking
Changes?

Service Descriptor Changes

RPC APIs (18) and *Message APIs* (27) frequently use WSDL as a *Service Descriptor* (175) to explicitly enumerate related services (i.e., logical operations) and to formally identify the data types received and returned by each operation. *Resource APIs* (38) may use the Web Application Description Language (WADL) or WSDL 2.0 for similar reasons. Artifacts created with these meta-languages are considered to be backward compatible if the descriptor contains all of the logical operations found in the prior interface, and alterations made to the referenced data structures do not cause breaking changes. New operations may therefore be added without breaking clients.

The following list identifies a few descriptor changes that can cause problems for clients.

- Changing the descriptor's namespace.

- Removing (i.e., deprecating) or renaming service operations (WSDL) or logical identifiers (e.g., WADL method IDs).

- Changing the order of parameters in a logical operation.

- Removing or renaming operation parameters. This includes changing the service's response to or from a null response.

- Changing operation input or response types.

- Changing service bindings (WSDL only).

- Changing service addresses.

- Asserting new policies (e.g., requiring a new form of client authentication or encryption).

One issue with descriptors is caused by the fact that they are meant to group a set of logically related operations. While a consolidated listing of related operations can be useful to clients for code generation, this approach also increases client-service coupling. Problems may arise when a breaking change occurs on a single operation appearing in the descriptor. Such a change may require clients to regenerate their *Service Connectors* (168) even when they don't care about the affected operation. Clients can choose to ignore the upgrade if they never call the affected service. However, if they eventually wish to use these services, then the connectors must be regenerated. The degree of client-service coupling for these services can therefore be decreased by minimizing the number of operations appearing in a single descriptor.

It is worth noting that *Linked Services* (77) provide much of the same information that appears in *Service Descriptors,* albeit in a "late-bound" fashion at runtime. The client must always be synchronized to know how to search Link Relations and Service Documents (re: Atom Publishing Protocol). It is possible that the service owner could remove or rename relation types or accepted media types and not coordinate these changes with the client. This, of course, may cause clients to break.

What Causes
Breaking
Changes?

Common Versioning Strategies

Services should be expected to change. New services may be added while others are deprecated. The data structures they exchange may be altered as well. As we saw in the preceding section some actions cause breaking changes while others are backward compatible. Services may also be altered in ways that are not immediately apparent. For example, the algorithm a service uses to calculate shipping costs may change. To summarize, some service changes are overt and are related to the Service Contract (see Chapter 2) while others are subtler. Either type may call for a new release and version identifier.

Versioning techniques are used to identify service releases that encompass distinct features and data structures. Versions provide information to help clients decide what release to use. The service owner may decide to support one version at a time, or they might support multiple versions if clients migrate at different rates. In the latter case, the service owner may have to maintain multiple code-bases. This, of course, is a scenario that should be avoided, but is often necessary to support business requirements.

A formal versioning strategy enables clients to clearly identify older versions of service artifacts (e.g., messages, media types, descriptors, etc.) from newer ones. To this end, a variety of techniques may be employed. The traditional approach has been to identify major and minor releases along with revision numbers. Major releases are rolled out when breaking changes occur on the service contract or when the functionality of a service has changed significantly. Minor releases generally correspond to optional upgrades (e.g., new logical service operations) or to significant fixes or additions that do not incur breaking changes [e.g., *Dataset Amendments* (237)]. Service releases with revision numbers may be used to identify a logical grouping of bug fixes that are less significant than what might be found in a minor release. Clients usually only opt-in to using major or minor service releases. As you might conclude, the decision regarding what should incur a major, minor, or revision release varies per organization. Service owners must therefore create a versioning strategy that is tailored to their needs and the needs of their clients.

Common
Versioning
Strategies

Example: *A Client That Requests a Specific Version*

The following shows how a client using a *Resource API* (38) may leverage *Media Type Negotiation* (70) to request a specific version of a proprietary media type.

```
GET http://acmeCorp.org/products
Accept application/vnd.acmeCorp.product+json;version=2.1
```

This request indicates that the client would like to receive a product data structure that has a major version of 2 and a minor version of 1. The assumption is that the service is able to produce multiple versions of this media type.

Example: *Versioning by Date*

Another common versioning strategy uses dates. The following URI shows how a company might use this approach to version the data structures used by a *Message API* (27).

```
http://www.acmeCorp.org/2011/10/14/Messages.xsd
```

This URI provides a unique identifier for a namespace containing message definitions. It indicates that Messages.XSD was released on October 14, 2011. This technique is typically used to identify a major release; the XSD itself may also incorporate changes for minor releases. This practice provides an effective way to identify schemas that clients and services should use when validating the data structures they exchange.

Common
Versioning
Strategies

Single-Message Argument

A web service receives data through an *RPC API* (18). Service developers are using a Code-First strategy [see the *Service Descriptor* pattern (175)].

How can a web service with an *RPC API* (18) become less brittle and easily accommodate new parameters over time without breaking clients?

RPC APIs (18) can be especially brittle. These services often have long parameter lists. If the need ever arises to add or remove parameters, one usually can't avoid a breaking change. Service operations with these kinds of "flat APIs" are inherently inflexible and fragile. Consider the following service signature.

```
@WebMethod(operationName = "ReserveRentalCar")
public RentalOptions ReserveRentalCar (
  @WebParam(name = "RentalCity")  String RentalCity,
  @WebParam(name = "PickupMonth") int PickupMonth,
  @WebParam(name = "PickupDay")   int PickupDay,
  @WebParam(name = "PickupYear")  int PickupYear,
  @WebParam(name = "ReturnMonth") int ReturnMonth,
  @WebParam(name = "ReturnDay")   int ReturnDay,
  @WebParam(name = "ReturnYear")  int ReturnYear,
  @WebParam(name = "RentalType")  String RentalType
)
{
  // implementation would appear here
}
```

Single-
Message
Argument

Perhaps you might want to offer the renter the ability to supply an airport or postal code as an alternative to selecting the RentalCity. These parameters could be added to the end of this list, and many clients wouldn't need to be updated because most auto-generated *Service Proxies* (168) can ignore parameters they don't recognize as long as they occur at the end of an argument list. Regrettably, the service's signature starts to become disorganized. It would be better if we could insert new parameters alongside the RentalCity so that the options for the rental location are all kept together. Unfortunately, a breaking change usually occurs whenever new parameters are inserted into the middle of the list. In situations like these, several tough questions must also be answered. Should the service owner create a new service, retire the old one, and coax clients onto the new service? Should he instead create a new service and keep the older one to maintain backward compatibility? Neither option seems appealing.

If we had anticipated the need to add new rental location parameters, we might have moved RentalCity to the end of the argument list so that all new parameters for this topic would follow. However, this shuffling of parameters would do little to alleviate our problems because the same situation would likely occur time and again. How can an *RPC API* (18) become more flexible and support the introduction of new parameters in a way that is backward compatible?

Design each service operation such that it only receives a single message parameter that contains all of the data for a request.

The *Single-Message Argument* pattern suggests that service developers who use a Code-First strategy [see the *Service Descriptor* pattern (175)] should refrain from creating signatures with long parameter lists. Signatures like these typically signal the underlying framework to impose a strict ordering of parameters. This, in turn, increases client-service coupling and makes it more difficult to evolve the client and service at different rates. *RPC APIs* (18) can instead be designed to receive a single message argument. These messages may contain primitive data types (e.g., integers, strings, etc.) or compound structures that may be used to group logically related data. Each child element in the message may be required or may be optional, the allowed values can be constrained or open-ended, and the order in which data is serialized can be explicitly prescribed or be allowed to vary. Each compound structure with the containing message may, of course, contain other structures as well. Their content may be required or not, constrained or open-ended, and the serialization order may vary as well.

By deliberately pushing all arguments down into a single message argument, the service designer has the opportunity to exert a greater degree of control over how the message is formatted and serialized for transmission. Developers can extend messages with ease by applying the *Dataset Amendment* pattern (237), and may also reuse the structure across multiple services.

Example: *An Operation on an RPC API Receives a Single Message*

The ReserveRentalCar service can be altered to receive a single message.

```
@WebMethod(operationName = "ReserveRentalCar")
public RentalOptions ReserveRentalCar (
  @WebParam(name = "RentalCriteria") RentalCriteria request
)
{
  // implementation would appear here
}
```

The message received by this service is a RentalCriteria *Data Transfer Object* (94). Getters and setters were omitted to keep the example brief.

```
@XmlAccessorType(XmlAccessType.FIELD)
@XmlType(name = "RentalCriteria")
@XmlRootElement(name = "RentalCriteria")
public class RentalCriteria {
  @XmlElement(name="RentalLocation",required=true)
  public RentalLocation rentalLocation;

  @XmlElement(name="PickupDate",required=true)
  public PickupDate pickDate;

  @XmlElement(name="ReturnDate",required=true)
  public ReturnDate returnDate;

  @XmlElement(name="VehicleCriteria")
  public VehicleCriteria vehicleCriteria;
}
```

Single-Message Argument

The RentalLocation *Data Transfer Object* (94) provides a point of extensibility. This structure can be extended by adding new optional parameters without incurring breaking changes (for more information, see the section What Causes Breaking Changes? earlier in this chapter).

```
@XmlAccessorType(XmlAccessType.FIELD)
@XmlType(name = "RentalLocation")
@XmlRootElement(name = "RentalLocation")
public class RentalLocation {
  @XmlElement(name="City") public String city;
  @XmlElement(name="AirportCode") public String airportCode;
  @XmlElement(name="ZipCode") public String zipCode;
}
```

Dataset Amendment

A web service has many clients. The service may define message structures through proprietary protocols, or by using open standards like XML.

How can a service augment the information it sends or receives while minimizing the probability of breaking changes?

Clients often request changes to data structures after a service has been released. In an effort to avoid breaking changes, the service owner may decide to introduce new services (i.e., request handlers) that process client-specific messages or media types (for more on breaking changes, see the section What Causes Breaking Changes? earlier in this chapter). *Message APIs* (27) and *Resource APIs* (38) are quite flexible in that they usually can accommodate new structures without breaking clients. A *Resource API* (38) may, for example, use *Media Type Negotiation* (70) to route requests to handlers that are capable of processing client-specific data structures. Services that have *Message APIs* (27) can likewise receive and route client-specific requests to new handlers with minimal impact to existing clients. Unfortunately, service logic is often duplicated when individual services are created for each client application. In an effort to simplify service logic, the service owner might try to encourage all client owners to adopt the data requirements of the requestor. Regrettably, the service owner may encounter resistance if the new structures are irrelevant or incompatible with their needs.

Service owners that use XML to exchange data might consider using Extension Points to allow for Wildcard-Content [Orchard]. This technique makes it possible to add new data structures to existing XML-based messages or media types without having to update published schemas or create additional service handlers to support the new client requirements. Any party (i.e., client or service) that receives a structure with an Extension Point can ignore the data in the extension if it doesn't recognize its content; otherwise, it can go ahead and process it. The following Java class provides an example of this pattern:

Dataset Amendment

```
@XmlAccessorType(XmlAccessType.FIELD)
@XmlType(name = "Product",
  propOrder = {"CatalogueId", "Extensions"})
@XmlRootElement(name = "Product")
public class Product {
  @XmlElement(name="CatalogueId",required=true)
  public String CatalogueId;
```

```
@XmlElement(name="Extensions",required=false)
public ExtensionElement Extensions;
}

@XmlAccessorType(XmlAccessType.FIELD)
@XmlRootElement(name = "ExtensionElement")
public class ExtensionElement {
  @XmlAnyElement(lax=true)
  public Object Extensions;
}
```

The associated XSD for this code looks like this:

```
<xs:complexType name="Product">
  <xs:sequence>
    <xs:element name="CatalogueId" type="xs:string" />
    <xs:element name="Extensions" type="tns:extensionElement"
                minOccurs="0" />
  </xs:sequence>
</xs:complexType>

<xs:complexType name="extensionElement">
  <xs:sequence>
    <xs:any processContents="lax" />
  </xs:sequence>
</xs:complexType>
```

**Dataset
Amendment**

While this practice is common, many have found that it can be problematic. The first issue relates to how the structures within Extension Points are validated. Implementers may constrain the allowed data structures by using the namespace attribute. They may also use the processContents attribute (re: www.w3.org/TR/xmlschema-1/#Wildcards) to prescribe how the content of the extension should be validated. The problem with this approach is that such restrictions tend to trigger many validation exceptions. Consequently, logic which catches and handles each validation error must be created, and this results in a rather inefficient and inelegant way to drive service logic. The service owner may therefore decide to let the content of each extension be unconstrained. This means that the service can't predict what data types may be found in an extension until it is parsed. Adding to this complexity is the possibility that extensions may contain their own extensions. The service (or client) must therefore parse each extension in turn, figure out what it contains, and have a strategy for dealing with whatever it finds. Strategies to parse and validate Extension Points may be realized in many ways (e.g., programmatic logic, XPath, Schematron) and encapsulated in *Request Mappers* (109), but other challenges remain.

Another problem with Extension Points pertains to the problem of **nondeterminism.** This occurs when an XML processor (i.e., client, service, or validating

XML parser) can't figure out when a document or document fragment terminates. A complex type may, for example, define a sequence of elements that contains an optional telephone number element followed by an Extension Point. If the client sends the telephone number, the processor can't know if that should be the last element or if the wildcard content in the extension might follow. One solution is to make everything that precedes the extension a required element, but this fundamentally alters the rules for how data is exchanged. The parties could instead identify the extension as being a required element and mark it off with Sentry Elements [Obasanjo] that surround the extension and act as delimiters. This means that the sender must always provide an extension, but the contents of it may be left blank. While this solves the problem of nondeterminism, the party receiving this structure still has no way to predict what it might find.

These problems are not unique to data exchange formats like XML. Many of these same issues must be addressed with other formats as well. How can service messages, regardless of the format, support extensibility in a way that is explicit and self-descriptive, yet does not break clients that use older structures?

▼

Append optional data to existing request and response data structures.

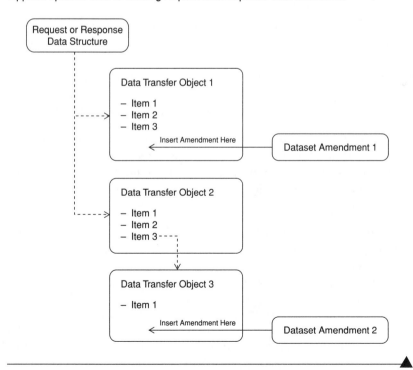

Dataset
Amendment

The *Dataset Amendment* pattern suggests that service owners should append primitive data or complex data structures to any *Data Transfer Object* (94) as optional data. Web services can be designed to easily recognize and process amendments when they appear in requests. Since amendments are optional, breaking changes on the client side are generally avoided because most popular service frameworks skip validation of these elements and hide them from the client application. Still, their contents are frequently preserved by the framework (e.g., WCF stores unanticipated data in an ExtensionDataObject). If, for example, the client updates a structure (i.e., message or media type) received from a service, and this structure contains an amendment with content the client doesn't recognize, the client can send the updated structure back to the originating service or to another service that recognizes the amendment, and the receiver will be able to deserialize and access the preserved amendment with ease.

Amendments to existing messages or media types are often described in a minor release. This makes it possible for services or clients that use validating parsers to deliberately select an appropriate validation scheme (e.g., XSD) for the version they understand.

Considerations

Service developers should consider the following before using the *Data Amendment* pattern.

Dataset Amendment

- **Optional data:** The prerequisite for using this pattern is that the client's data must be optional. The service should be able to successfully process the request whether or not an amendment can be found in the request.

- **Doesn't eliminate client-specific structures:** This pattern does not eliminate the need to create and maintain data structures for specific clients. It does, however, provide the opportunity to evaluate how these structures might be consolidated into common messages and media types that are used by all clients.

- **Ability to leverage data binding:** Since the new structures are explicitly defined as being a part of the parent message or media type, one can take advantage of data-binding technologies to automatically deserialize or serialize information in these structures. This helps to simplify data handling on both the client and service sides.

- **Potential for cluttered data structures:** This pattern should be used with restraint because it can result in bulkier transmissions that carry data that may be irrelevant to many parties. Service designers may decide to accommodate client-specific needs by using this pattern in between major releases. However, every effort should be made to work with all parties to make the *Dataset Amendments* a formal part of the next major release. This does not, however, mean that the content in the amendment should be required.

• **Use with abstract types:** Service owners should be careful about introducing Dataset Amendments that are logically equivalent to other amendments. As an example, the service owner might create two customer *Data Transfer Objects* (94) which are structurally different in order to appease two different client developer groups. This will, of course, increase service complexity and reduce ease of maintenance. If the service owner cannot sway the clients to adopt a common approach, then the owner may consider using *Abstract Data Transfer Objects* (105) in the amendment. This variation on the *Data Transfer Objects* pattern can be used to define "base types" for a family of structures used in requests or responses. For example, whenever an XSD contains a reference to an abstract type, the sender may insert a concrete type derived from that type. This creates an effect similar to polymorphism. New types can be added over time without requiring the client to be updated.

Example: *A Data Transfer Object That Supports Amendments*

The following C# code shows how a *Data Transfer Object* can support amendments. The Order attribute on the FlightPreferences DTO is a platform-specific trick that forces it to be appended to the parent DTO. The more important attribute is the IsRequired value.

Dataset
Amendment

```
[DataContract]
public class TripReservation
{
  [DataMember]
  public string ReservationId{get;set;}

  [DataMember]
  public ReservationStatus Status{get;set;}

  [DataMember]
  public TripItinerary Itinerary{get;set;}

  //****************************************
  // Data Amendment/ Minor release starts here ...
  //****************************************
```

```
    [DataMember(Order = 999, IsRequired = false)]
    public FlightPreferences FlightPreferences{get;set;}

    // Other amendments would occur here
}


[DataContract]
public class FlightPreferences
{
    // An enumerated type indicating
    //  the traveler's preferences for aisle or window

    [DataMember(Name = "SeatPreference", IsRequired = false)]
    public SeatPreferences SeatPreference {get;set;}

    // An enumerated type indicating the traveler's
    // preferences for Economy, Business, or First-Class seating

    [DataMember(Name = "TravelClass", IsRequired = false)]
    public TravelClass TravelClass {get;set;}
}
```

Dataset Amendment

Tolerant Reader

A client or service expects changes to occur in a message or media type it receives.

How can clients or services function properly when some of the content in the messages or media types they receive is unknown or when the data structures vary?

Rarely can a single software release produce messages or media types that address all future needs. Indeed, Agile practices have taught us that it is more effective and realistic to adhere to the concept of Emergent Design. The idea is to deliver small incremental pieces of functionality over time, and let the system design evolve naturally. Unfortunately, this introduces the possibility for breaking changes as data items are added to, changed, or removed from the message (for more on breaking changes, refer to the section What Causes Breaking Changes? earlier in this chapter). Message designers can prevent many issues if they understand what causes breaking changes. For example, an optional message element should never become required in future releases. *Consumer-Driven Contracts* (250) can also help services ensure that client needs will be met when messages change. In any case, message designers must be allowed to make changes. The problem is that client developers may not be able to keep up with these changes. How can a client continue to process service responses when some of the content is unknown or the data structures vary?

Service designers often have to deal with message variability as well. For example, some message structures may be owned and designed by business partners, industry consortiums, or trade groups. In situations like these, service developers may not be able to keep up with client applications that adopt newer message versions. The service must therefore be forward-compatible and accept content that it may not fully understand.

These scenarios suggest that clients should anticipate changes in service responses, and services should, under certain conditions, expect changes in client requests.

Design the client or service to extract only what is needed, ignore unknown content, and expect variant data structures.

Tolerant
Reader

Tolerant Readers gracefully handle change and the unknown. This concept was described in the first part of the *Robustness Principle* [RFC 1122], also known as *Postel's Law*:

Be liberal in what you accept

Tolerant Readers extract only what is needed from a message and ignore the rest. Declarative (e.g., XPath) or imperative approaches (i.e., static or dynamic code) can be used to surgically extract the data of interest. It should go without saying, but *Tolerant Readers* must always know the names and data types of the message items they are interested in.

Schema validators can be overly conservative, and often throw exceptions when the cause of the error can be addressed by the reader. Rather than implementing a strict validation scheme, *Tolerant Readers* make every attempt to continue with message processing when potential violations are detected. Exceptions are only thrown when the message structure prevents the reader from continuing (i.e., the structure cannot be interpreted) or the content clearly violates business rules (e.g., a money field contains nonmonetary values). *Tolerant Readers* also ignore new message items (i.e., objects, elements, attributes, structures, etc.), the absence of optional items, and unexpected data values as long as this information does not provide critical input to drive downstream logic.

Considerations

Client and service developers should consider the following issues.

- **Data access:** Developers should consider when data can be extracted from a message without having to traverse hierarchies. For example, a reader might be able to use an XPath query like //order instead of /orders/order. There will always, of course, be occasions when knowledge of a hierarchy provides the requisite context to process a message. For example, information about a spouse might only make sense in relation to an employee structure (e.g., /employee/spouse). It is worth noting that a reader can also ignore all hierarchies below the "context node" and still acquire the desired item (e.g., /employee//spouse).

    Tolerant Readers should let sibling items in a data structure (e.g., XML elements in a complex type) occur in any sequence when the business rules permit. One common scenario in which this cannot be done occurs when the sequence of message items implicitly indicates the order in which data should be processed.

Tolerant Readers can ignore namespaces when processing XML. For example, the XPath expression `//*[local-name()='order']` is able to acquire an `order` node regardless of the associated namespaces.

- **Preservation of unknown content:** While *Tolerant Readers* should extract and use only those parts of the message they are interested in, they should also attempt to preserve unknown content when the message must be passed on to other systems or back to the original sender. The reason is that these parties may be interested in the very same data which the reader doesn't care about. There are many ways to accomplish this goal. The easiest way is to simply save the original message (in a memory-based variable), then pass it on to the next party. Some frameworks that use data binding provide special constructs that make it easy for recipients to get what they need out of a message while also preserving unknown content. An example of this is found in the `ExtensionDataObject` of Microsoft's WCF.

- **The second part of Postel's Law:** There is a second part to Postel's Law. It states, *"(be) conservative in what you send"*. This means that all message senders should make every effort to conform to the agreed-upon protocols for message composition because a message sender that commits a gross violation of the "message contract" can cause significant problems, even for a *Tolerant Reader*. One such example occurs when the message sender fails to submit a required element or uses the wrong data type for some item. Message senders can therefore facilitate effective communications by using schema validation before sending a message. This stands in stark contrast to the *Tolerant Reader,* which typically avoids schema validation altogether.

Tolerant Reader

- **Use with Data Transfer Objects:** *Data Transfer Objects* (94), a.k.a. DTOs, are frequently used to decouple *Domain Models* [POEAA] or internal APIs from message structures, and vice versa. One variation on this pattern allows these classes to be annotated with data-binding instructions that direct the recipient's framework to map message content to or from one or several DTOs. Since the developer doesn't have to write parsing logic, it becomes much easier to get or set message data. Unfortunately, binding annotations cause the *Data Transfer Objects* to become tightly coupled to the messages structures. The end result may be that a recipient which uses DTOs (with data binding) may have to regenerate and redeploy these classes whenever a message changes. This doesn't mean that DTOs with data binding should never be used. However, developers should consider limiting their use to situations where the constituent parts of a message are relatively static and are modified through *Dataset Amendments* (237).

Alternatively, *Data Transfer Objects* can be created without data-binding instructions. These DTOs are *Tolerant Readers* in their own right. An example of this approach is provided in the code example that follows.

- **Consumer-driven contracts:** Client developers who create Tolerant Readers to receive service responses should demonstrate how the reader is supposed to behave through a suite of unit tests. These tests can be given to the service owner to help ensure that the client's expectations will be met. For more information, see the *Consumer-Driven Contracts* pattern (250).

Example: *A Tolerant Reader That Extracts Address Information*

This example shows how a *Tolerant Reader* written with Java and JAX-RS can be designed to extract and validate only the message content that is required. The source XML message looks like this:

```
<CustomerInfo>
  <CustomerAccount>
    <BillingAddress street="123 Commonwealth Ave"
                    city="Boston" state="MA" zip="12345" />
  </CustomerAccount>

  <ShippingAddress street="234 State Street"
                   city="Boston" state="MA" zip="67890" />

  <ExtraStuffThatIsIgnored>
    <item id="678" count="1" />
    <item id="876" time="2" />
  </ExtraStuffThatIsIgnored>
</CustomerInfo>
```

The saveAddresses service shown below receives an InputStream from the client and passes it to the constructor of XPathParser, a class that encapsulates common XPath processing logic. The implementation details for this class have been omitted because they are tangential to the key concepts I wish to impart for this pattern. Anyway, once an XPathParser has been acquired, the service calls static methods on the BillingAddress and ShippingAddress classes in order to populate *Data Transfer Objects* (94) of the same name. Information from these DTOs is saved to a database; the logic for this has also been left out.

```
@Path("/addresses")
public class TolerantReader {
```

Tolerant Reader

```
@POST
@Consumes("appication/xml")
public Response saveAddresses(InputStream stream) {

   try{

      XPathParser parser = new XPathParser(stream);

      BillingAddress billAddress =
         BillingAddress.Get(parser);

      ShippingAddress shipAddress =
         ShippingAddress.Get(parser);

      // Save address information to a database here

   }
   catch(Exception x){
      ; // handle errors here
   }

   return
     Response.status(Status.OK).type("text/plain").build();
 }
}
```

The BillingAddress and ShippingAddress *Data Transfer Objects* (94) mentioned above extend a class named Address. This class is shown below.

```
public abstract class Address {
  private String id;
  private String street;
  private String city;
  private String state;
  private String zip;

  public String getId() {
    return id;
  }

  public void setId(String value) {
    this.id = value;
  }

  public String getStreet() {
    return street;
  }

  public void setStreet(String value) {
    this.street = value;
  }
```

Tolerant
Reader

```
public String getCity() {
  return city;
}

public void setCity(String city) {
  this.city = city;
}

public String getState() {
  return state;
}

public void setState(String state) {
  this.state = state;
}

public String getZip() {
  return zip;
}

public void setZip(String zip) {
  this.zip = zip;
}
}
```

The DTOs shown below are the *Tolerant Readers* in this example. They have been designed to tolerate changes in data structures and accept, for whatever the business reason might be, the absence of individual address items (e.g., street, city, state, zip code). You should therefore assume that getNodeValueAsString does not throw an XPathExpressionException when an item can't be found, but instead returns an empty string.

Tolerant Reader

```
public class BillingAddress extends Address {
  public static BillingAddress Get(XPathParser parser)
  {
    BillingAddress address = new BillingAddress();

    try{

      address.setId(
        parser.getNodeValueAsString(
          "//BillingAddress/@id"));

      address.setStreet(
        parser.getNodeValueAsString(
          "//BillingAddress/@street"));

      address.setCity(
        parser.getNodeValueAsString(
          "//BillingAddress/@city"));
```

```
        address.setState(
          parser.getNodeValueAsString(
            "//BillingAddress/@state"));

        address.setZip(
          parser.getNodeValueAsString(
            "//BillingAddress/@zip"));
      }
      catch(Exception ex){
        // handle error here
      }

      return address;
    }
}


public class ShippingAddress extends Address {
  public static ShippingAddress Get(XPathParser parser)
  {
    ShippingAddress address = new ShippingAddress();

    try{

      address.setId(
        parser.getNodeValueAsString(
          "//ShippingAddress/@id"));

      address.setStreet(
        parser.getNodeValueAsString(
          "//ShippingAddress/@street"));

      address.setCity(
        parser.getNodeValueAsString(
          "//ShippingAddress/@city"));

      address.setState(
        parser.getNodeValueAsString(
          "//ShippingAddress/@state"));

      address.setZip(
        parser.getNodeValueAsString(
          "//ShippingAddress/@zip"));
    }
    catch(Exception ex){
      // handle error here
    }

    return address;
  }
}
```

Tolerant
Reader

Consumer-Driven Contracts

By Ian Robinson

A service has several clients, each with different needs and capabilities. Service owners know who their clients are, and client developers can establish a channel for communicating their expectations of the service's API to service owners. Such interactions typically occur within an enterprise or corporate environment.

> How can a web service API reflect its clients' needs while enabling evolution and avoiding breaking clients?

Service APIs are often used by multiple clients in different contexts, but designing a web service interface to support these different usages can be difficult. If an API is too coarse-grained, its use will be limited to a very specific context. If it is too granular, clients will often have to supplement it with functionality or data sourced from elsewhere. Getting the balance right depends on understanding how clients expect to use the service. A client's needs and capabilities around message types and representation formats, as well as the mechanisms used to invoke procedures and access resources, can vary from client to client; these needs and capabilities should drive the design and evolution of the service API.

A good service API decouples clients from the internal implementation of a service. But if the clients' expectations of an API are not taken into account when designing the service, the resultant interface can inadvertently leak a service's internal domain details. This is particularly true when wrapping a legacy system with a service API. In the struggle to make legacy functionality accessible through a web service interface, system and infrastructure details can make their way into the service API, thereby forcing the client to couple itself to the underlying system, and to what are often a lot of extraneous system-specific reference data, method signatures, and parameter values. *Data Transfer Objects* (94), *Request Mappers* (109), and *Response Mappers* (122) can help to prevent internal details from leaking to clients, but they do nothing to help service developers understand what clients really need or how they expect to use a service.

The use of Extension Points can help to make message and media type schemas backward- and forward-compatible. Extension points allow additional

Consumer-Driven Contracts

elements and attributes to be added to a message or resource representation at certain predefined places in the schema. But while extension points enable compatibility, they do so at the expense of increased complexity. By adding container elements to a message, they undermine the expressive power that comes from a simple schema. New clients often bring with them additional needs, many of which require the service API to evolve. If a service has to change to accommodate new requirements, it should do so in a way that doesn't break existing clients. Maintaining backward and forward compatibility between different versions of a service API helps localize the cost and impact of change. When an API changes in a way that is neither backward- nor forward-compatible with previous versions of the API, there is a risk that it will introduce breaking changes (for more on breaking changes, refer to the section What Causes Breaking Changes? earlier in this chapter). Altering, testing, and rereleasing an updated client in lockstep with the modified service API results not only in the cost of change increasing, but also in it being shared between service and client owners.

Some service developers, in an attempt to prevent a service from having to change, try to design a comprehensive service API that encompasses all current as well as all future client needs and capabilities. These speculative APIs seek to protect against having to be modified at a later date by "getting things right the first time." But no matter how much time and effort is invested in analysis and design up front, a service may still have to modify its published API if a missed requirement comes to light or an unanticipated change emerges sometime after the service is released. Such modifications reintroduce the risk of breaking existing clients.

Consumer-
Driven
Contracts

On top of these design issues, service owners need to understand the relationships between services and clients so that they can diagnose problems, assess the impact of variations in service availability, and plan for evolving individual services in response to new or changed business requirements. In this context, service owners can benefit from understanding which clients currently use their service, and how they use it. Knowing which clients currently use a service API helps a service owner plan changes to the API and communicate those changes to client developers. Understanding how clients currently use an API helps service developers test changes to the API, identify breaking changes, and understand the impact of those breaking changes on each client.

Documentation can help communicate service and client requirements, and so smooth the evolutionary growth of a service. Documentation that describes each version of an API, its status, whether live, deprecated, or retired, and any compatibility issues can help client designers understand how to use an API and what to expect when the service changes. Client owners, in turn, can document how their client expects to use the service, and which versions of an API it uses.

But unless the documentation is generated from code and schema artifacts, and regenerated every time those artifacts change, it can quickly become out of date and of little value. What the parties really need are a set of automated integration tests.

Client developers write integration tests that express the client's expectations of a service API. These tests are given to the service owner, who incorporates them into the service's test suite.

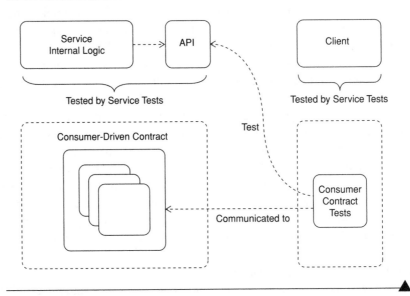

Consumer-Driven Contracts

The *Consumer-Driven Contract* pattern helps service owners create service APIs that reflect client needs; it also helps service owners evolve services without breaking existing clients. Service owners receive integration tests from each client and incorporate these tests into the service's test suite. The set of integration tests received from all existing clients represents the service's aggregate obligations with respect to its client base. The service owner is then free to change and evolve the service just so long as the existing integration tests continue to pass. Breaking tests help service developers identify breaking changes, understand the impact of those changes on existing clients, and communicate the changes and their impact to the relevant client owners.

Consumer-Driven Contracts can be used at several different stages in the service development life cycle. During the design stage they can be used to shape an API by capturing in code examples how it might be used. During the development stage, they help decouple development activities in different work streams, while at the same time establishing a shared understanding of service and client responsibilities. At this stage, client developers work against stub implementations of a service API, and then share their integration tests with the service owner. Finally, *Consumer-Driven Contracts* can be used after a service has gone live, to record how specific clients actually use a service.

Client owners implement consumer contracts in the form of integration tests. These tests are usually written against a stub version of the service. When the contracts are given to the service owner, these stub implementations are replaced with a real service instance; the assertions, however, remain the same.

Tests can focus on several different aspects of the service contract.

- **Content:** These tests check for the presence of certain elements and attributes in messages and resource representations. They may also assert the data types of specific values, and even check that more complex invariants hold; that, for example, a <status> of rejected is always accompanied by a <reason>. Though the examples here focus on XML-formatted messages and resource representations, the *Consumer-Driven Contract* pattern is equally applicable to formats such as JSON and proprietary formats like Google's Protocol Buffers.

- **Processing context:** Such tests assert the presence or absence of certain headers. A client may expect, for example, that an ETag header always accompany cacheable responses.

- **Behavior:** These tests communicate the client's expectations regarding the service's behavior, as evidenced by response codes, headers, and response data. Such tests may check that calculations are correct, that changes to state result in an event being published, or that the steps in a workflow proceed as expected.

- **Quality of service:** These tests communicate expectations around things such as response times, exceptions, security protocols, and compression and encryption algorithms.

The *Consumer-Driven Contract* pattern is a natural complement to the *Tolerant Reader* pattern (243). Clients acting as Tolerant Readers can use consumer contracts to communicate exactly which parts of a service API they use. When a contract test fails in the service test suite as a result of an essential breaking change to the API, the service owner can identify the relevant client from the test, and thereafter negotiate a plan for supporting or migrating the client.

Consumer-
Driven
Contracts

Considerations

When using *Consumer-Driven Contracts,* developers and service owners should consider the following issues.

- **Stub and real service implementations:** Client developers typically write their consumer contract integration tests against a fake implementation of a service. At this stage, the tests are not real integration tests; they test neither the service nor the client's behavior. Rather, they simply communicate the client's expectations of the service. For them to be useful as consumer contracts, the tests should make it easy for service developers to substitute a real service instance for the client's use of a fake. The tests realize their full value when they are handed over and run in a service (rather than client) test suite; that is, when they are run against a real service instance. This technique is different from clients using integration and certification environments to certify a product for use, though it can be used to complement such procedures.

- **Exchanging and versioning contracts:** Service and client owners should establish a means for exchanging tests and resolving contract disputes. Tests should be version-controlled so that owners can identify when a contract changed, and for what reason. Tests received from different clients should be clearly identified and versioned independently of one another. Many of today's version control systems can import dependencies from external repositories, thereby allowing different consumer contracts to be pulled into a service test suite. Subversion, for example, provides support for external definitions. Git has the powerful concept of submodules.

- **Enforce contracts with every change to a service:** Contract tests should be run with every change to a service, regardless of whether the change occurs to the API or in the internal service logic. Automated, self-checking tests can be incorporated into a continuous integration pipeline, where they will be executed with every check-in of service code.

- **Modifying contracts:** Tests written in the early stages of a service's design and development are different from those written once a service API has been published. The former helps to shape the API, but may be modified as service and client owners negotiate the scope and composition of the API. The latter makes assertions about a published API and should not, therefore, be changed while that API is being used.

- **Platform dependencies:** Contracts are often written as unit tests in a particular programming language. This can introduce unwelcome platform dependencies for service developers if the platform used to develop the contract is different from the platform used to develop the service. Schema languages such as Schematron can be used to write platform-independent tests for XML.

- **Scope and complexity:** The *Consumer-Driven Contract* pattern is applicable where service owners can identify their clients, and clients can establish a channel for sending contracts to service owners. This is usually the case in enterprise web service environments, but may also apply in situations where independent software vendors can solicit representative use cases and tests from clients. No matter how lightweight the mechanisms for communicating and representing expectations and obligations, service and client owners must know about, agree on, and adopt a set of channels and conventions, all of which add to the complexity of the delivery process.

- **Test strategies:** A comprehensive consumer contract suite of tests will cover exceptional as well as happy-path uses of the service API. Though focused primarily on unit testing, many of the patterns described in *xUnit Test Patterns, Refactoring Test Code* [Meszaros, Gerard] can be applied to these unusual cases. The book also describes several patterns, such as *Test Double,* which help decouple test routines and the service under test from other dependencies.

- **Long-running, asynchronous services:** Services that use the *Request/ Acknowledge/Poll* pattern (62) or *Request/Acknowledge/Callback* (63) pattern can be difficult to test in a reliable and timely fashion end-to-end. Nonetheless, consumers can still express their expectations of an acknowledgment, a polled response, or a callback using XPath assertions, a Schematron rules document, or similar. The book *Growing Object-Oriented Software, Guided By Tests* [Freeman, Pryce] describes several strategies for testing asynchronous code. Nat Pryce, one of the authors of that book, also provides several interesting ideas at www.natpryce.com/articles/ 000755.html.

- **Reasonable expectations:** Consumer contracts express a client's expectations of a service API, but these expectations must be reasonable and capable of being fulfilled. Allowing consumer contracts to drive the specification of a service API can sometimes undermine the conceptual integrity of that API. Service integrity should not be compromised by unreasonable demands falling outside the scope of the service's responsibilities.

Consumer-
Driven
Contracts

Example: *A Consumer Contract for Service Behavior Implemented in C#
and NUnit*

This example shows a simple consumer contract for a news service *Resource
API* (38). The contract has been written by developers of one of the service's clients, and then given to the service owner who has incorporated it, together with
other consumer contracts, in the service's continuous integration pipeline to
form a consumer-driven contract.

```csharp
[TestFixture]
public class NewsServiceConsumerContract
{
  private IIntegrationContext context;
  private HttpResponseMessage response;

  [SetUp]
  public void Init()
  {
    context = CreateContext();

    string xml =
        @"<entry xmlns=""http://www.w3.org/2005/Atom"">
            <title>Lilliput Siezes Blefuscudian Fleet</title>
            <id>urn:uuid:897B5900-7805-4A61-BC63-03691EEE752D</id>
            <updated>2011-06-01T06:30:00Z</updated>
            <author><name>Jonathan Swift</name></author>
            <content>Lilliput's Man-Mountain this morning...</content>
        </entry>";

    HttpContent content = new StringContent(xml);
    content.Headers.ContentType =
      new MediaTypeHeaderValue("application/atom+xml");

    response = context.Client.Send(new HttpRequestMessage
      {
          Method = HttpMethod.Post,
          RequestUri = context.TargetUri,
          Content = content
      });
  }

  [TearDown]
  public void Dispose()
  {
    context.Dispose();
  }
```

```
[Test]
public void ResponseIncludes201CreatedStatusCode()
{
  Assert.AreEqual(HttpStatusCode.Created, response.StatusCode);
}


[Test]
public void ResponseIncludesLocationHeader()
{
  Assert.IsNotNull(response.Headers.Location);
}


[Test]
public void ResponseBodyIncludesAnEditedElement()
{
  XPathNavigator message = new XPathDocument(
    response.Content.ContentReadStream).CreateNavigator();
  Assert.AreEqual(1, message.Select("//*[local-name()='edited']").Count);
}

//Helper methods omitted
}
```

These contract tests have been written using the NUnit test framework. The
setup for each test uses an HTTP client to POST a news article to the service. The
tests then assert that the service has successfully created the article, assigned it a
URI, and added an edited timestamp. The XPath expression used to select the
edited element is quite forgiving of structure—it looks for the element at any
depth in the response, ignoring any XML namespaces.

The tests use a pluggable IIntegrationContext to set up the HTTP client. Client
developers create an implementation of IIntegrationContext whose HTTP client is
configured with a fake *Service Connector* (168). Service developers replace this
implementation with one that lets the client communicate with a service running in a local or remote host environment. When the tests run in the service
test environment, the IIntegrationContext implementation used there connects the
client to a real service instance. The IIntegrationContext interface is shown below.

```
public interface IIntegrationContext : IDisposable
{
  HttpClient Client { get; }
  Uri TargetUri { get; }
}
```

When developing the consumer contract, the client developers create a
FakeNewsServiceIntegrationContext that returns an HTTP client configured with a

fake response. This fake response exhibits the behavior expected of the service by the client, as shown below.

```csharp
public class FakeNewsServiceIntegrationContext : IIntegrationContext
{
  private readonly Uri targetUri;
  private readonly HttpClient client;

  public FakeNewsServiceIntegrationContext()
  {
    targetUri = new Uri("http://localhost/news/articles/");

    string xml =
      @"<entry xmlns=""http://www.w3.org/2005/Atom""
          xmlns:app=""http://www.w3.org/2007/app"">
          <app:edited>2011-06-01T06:30:00Z</app:edited>
        </entry>";

    HttpContent content = new StringContent(xml);
    content.Headers.ContentType =
      new MediaTypeHeaderValue("application/atom+xml");

    HttpResponseMessage response = new HttpResponseMessage
      {
        StatusCode = HttpStatusCode.Created,
        Content = content
      };
    response.Headers.Location =
      new Uri("http://localhost/news/articles/123");

    HttpClientChannel endpoint = new FakeEndpoint(response);
    client = new HttpClient {Channel = endpoint};
  }

  public HttpClient Client
  {
    get { return client; }
  }

  public Uri TargetUri
  {
    get { return targetUri; }
  }

  public void Dispose()
  {
    //Do nothing
  }
}
```

Consumer-
Driven
Contracts

The NewsServiceConsumerContract fixture creates an appropriate IIntegrationContext by calling the CreateContext factory method before each test. CreateContext instantiates an IIntegrationContext instance based on a couple of settings in a configuration file. The code for CreateContext is shown below.

```
private IIntegrationContext CreateContext()
{
  string contextAssembly =
    ConfigurationManager.AppSettings["ContextAssembly"];
  string contextImplName =
    ConfigurationManager.AppSettings["ContextImplName"];

  if (contextAssembly == null)
  {
    Type testHostType = Type.GetType(contextImplName);
    return (IIntegrationContext) Activator.CreateInstance(testHostType);
  }

  return (IIntegrationContext) Activator.CreateInstance(
    contextAssembly, contextImplName);
}
```

When the consumer contract is run in the client's test environment, the CreateContext method returns a FakeNewsServiceIntegrationContext instance. When the tests are incorporated into the service test suite, the service developers can reconfigure the test fixture to return a NewsServiceIntegrationContext that connects the client to a real service instance. The code for NewsServiceIntegrationContext is shown below.

```
public class NewsServiceIntegrationContext : IIntegrationContext
{
  private readonly ServiceHost service;

  public NewsServiceIntegrationContext()
  {
    service = CreateNewsService();
    service.Open();
  }

  public HttpClient Client
  {
    get { return new HttpClient(); }
  }

  public Uri TargetUri
  {
    get { return new Uri("http://localhost:8888/news/articles/"); }
  }
```

```
public void Dispose()
{
  service.Close();
}

private ServiceHost CreateNewsService()
{
  //Implementation omitted
  }
}
```

NewsServiceIntegrationContext controls the lifetime of a service instance. Here the service instance is running in a locally hosted environment. An alternative implementation of InvoiceServiceIntegrationContext might connect the client to a service instance running in a remote host environment. The Client property returns a simple HTTP client, which the consumer contract uses to POST a news article to the service.

Example: *A Consumer Contract for Message Structure Implemented Using ISO Schematron*

Consumer-
Driven
Contracts

Code-based consumer contracts work well when both the client and the service are developed on the same platform. Many organizations, however, use multiple development platforms. In such circumstances, it is not always possible or feasible to exchange code-level contracts. This example shows a consumer contract written using ISO Schematron, a powerful validation language. Using an XSLT-based Schematron processor, a service owner can apply a Schematron document to the messages produced by a service to validate their conformance to the contract.

Schematron is a rule-based XML schema language for checking a document's structure and its conformance to complex business rules. Schematron rules use XPath assertions to select XML elements and attributes and check that their values conform to the business rules specified by the schema author. As shown in Figure 7.1, a Schematron rules document, which in this instance has been written by the client developers, is transformed into an intermediate XSLT and applied to the XML to be validated. The skeleton implementation of Schematron, which is available from the Schematron site, includes an XSLT preprocessor that transforms the rules document into an XSLT transform. This transform is applied to the XML to be validated, creating another XML document that describes the validation results.

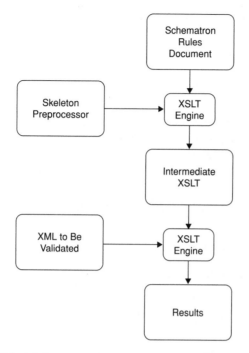

Figure 7.1 *A Schematron preprocessor uses a Schematron rules document to create a validating transform. This intermediate XSLT is applied to the document to be validated.*

The Schematron schema shown below validates that the necessary elements are present in an invoice. The schema is authored by a client owner and then given to a service owner to form a consumer contract.

```xml
<?xml version="1.0" encoding="UTF-8"?>
<schema xmlns="http://purl.oclc.org/dsdl/schematron">
  <title>Invoice contract for client example.org</title>
  <pattern>
    <rule context="//*[local-name()='Invoice']">
      <assert test="count(.//*[local-name()='InvoiceId']) = 1" >Expected
        InvoiceId</assert>
      <assert test="count(.//*[local-name()='WorkOrder']) = 1" >Expected
        WorkOrder</assert>
      <assert test="count(.//*[local-name()='Billed']) &gt; 0" >Expected at
        least one Billed element</assert>
    </rule>
    <rule context="//*[local-name()='Billed']">
```

```
      <assert test="count(.//*[local-name()='BillCode']) = 1" >Expected
        BillCode</assert>
      <assert test="count(.//*[local-name()='Time']) = 1" >Expected
        Time</assert>
   </rule>
 </pattern>
</schema>
```

This schema checks that an InvoiceId element, a WorkOrder element, and at least one Billed element are present in the context of an Invoice element. It also checks that each Billed element contains BillCode and Time elements. As with the code contract from the previous example, the XPath here is forgiving of depth and namespace.

On receiving the schema, the service owner incorporates it in a unit test.

```
[Test]
public void ApplySchematronConsumerContract()
{
  XmlReader message = CreateInvoiceMessage();
  ValidationResult result = Validate("Invoice.schematron.xml", message);

  Assert.IsTrue(result.Success, result.ToString());
}
```

The ApplySchematronConsumerContract test calls a Validate helper method to execute the Schematron pipeline using the supplied consumer contract.

Consumer-
Driven
Contracts

```
private ValidationResult Validate(string schematronUri, XmlReader message)
{
  //Generate intermediate XSLT
  Stream xsltStream = new MemoryStream();
  XslCompiledTransform xsl = new XslCompiledTransform();
  xsl.Load("iso_svrl_for_xslt1.xsl");
  xsl.Transform(schematronUri, null, xsltStream);
  xsltStream.Seek(0, SeekOrigin.Begin);

  //Generate results XML
  Stream resultStream = new MemoryStream();
  XslCompiledTransform xslt = new XslCompiledTransform();
  xslt.Load(XmlReader.Create(xsltStream));
  xslt.Transform(message, null, resultStream);
  resultStream.Seek(0, SeekOrigin.Begin);

  XElement results = XElement.Load(resultStream);
  IEnumerable<XElement> failedAsserts =
    results.Descendants(XName.Get(
      "failed-assert", "http://purl.oclc.org/dsdl/svrl"));
```

```
  return new ValidationResult {Success = failedAsserts.Count().Equals(0),
    Errors = failedAsserts};
}
```

The Validate method applies the skeleton preprocessor (iso_svrl_for_xslt1.xsl, which is supplied with the Schematron implementation available on the Schematron site) to the supplied rules document in order to generate an intermediate XSLT document. The method then validates the supplied message by transforming it with this intermediate XSLT. If there are any failed assertions in the output of this transformation, they are wrapped in a ValidationResult object. The code for ValidationResult is shown below.

```
public class ValidationResult
{
  public bool Success { get; set; }
  public IEnumerable<XElement> Errors { get; set; }
}
```

How the Patterns Promote or Hinder Service Evolution

This section briefly summarizes how many of the patterns in this book promote or hinder service evolution.

- *RPC API* (18):

  - RPC APIs tend to create tight dependencies between clients and the procedures (i.e., handlers) used to process requests. Developers can make it easier to evolve the service if they use the *Single-Message Argument* pattern (234). These messages can be easily extended to support new customer requirements through the *Dataset Amendment* pattern (237).

  - Service owners can support different versions of a given service, but this may confuse client developers. Older services can be deprecated in favor of newer ones, but the service owner must coordinate with client developers to determine the timing of such events.

- *Message API* (27):

  - This pattern makes it very easy to add new message types, especially when the service doesn't use a *Service Descriptor* (175). The logic used to process these messages can be easily rolled out without affecting clients that use older message versions.

  - Messages can be easily extended to support new customer requirements through the *Dataset Amendment* pattern (237).

- *Resource API* (38):

  - This pattern makes it very easy to support new media types and representation formats. *Media Type Negotiation* (70) can be used to meet new customer data requirements while simultaneously supporting older data requirements.

  - New service logic can be introduced quite easily by providing clients new URIs. If a URI must be deprecated, the service can return HTTP codes in the 3xx range or use a URI Rewrite engine.

  - Media types can often be extended to support new customer requirements through the *Dataset Amendment* pattern (237).

- *Request/Response* (54):

  – Responses can contain *Linked Services* (77).

  – This interaction style introduces strong temporal coupling between the client and service.

- *Request/Acknowledge* (59):

  – Acknowledgments can contain *Linked Services* (77). Clients may use this information to poll for continuing updates or to acquire the final response. By including this information as *Linked Services*, the client avoids becoming coupled to specific service URIs.

  – Clients can pass URIs for callback services and relay services in with the initial request. This helps to minimize the service's coupling to specific services owned by the client (or its partners), and enables the client owner to easily add or change callback/relay service URIs and associated logic over time. However, the messages and media types must be known by all parties ahead of time.

- *Linked Service* (77):

  – This pattern lets clients use new or altered services without becoming coupled to the service's address. The client must, however, know how to parse each response to find information on the services it is interested in. It must also understand the requisite messages or media types, and must know what server methods (i.e., GET, PUT, POST, DELETE) should be used at various times.

The Patterns
and Service
Evolution

- *Data Transfer Object* (94):

  – This pattern effectively decouples the client from internal objects, database tables, and so on that are used to fulfill client requests. This makes it possible to evolve the client and internal resources at different rates.

  – Data Transfer Objects that rely on data-binding technologies increase coupling between the DTO and message structures, making it harder to evolve both.

  – The *Abstract Data Transfer Object* (105) variation on this pattern may be used to define a base type for a family of related structures.

- *Request Mapper* (109):

  - Request Mappers let service owners support new customer data require-
    ments without forcing the change onto all clients. This pattern also helps
    to minimize the need to create separate services that process specific cli-
    ent messages.
  - Service evolution can be promoted through this pattern when it is used
    with *Message APIs* (27) and *Resource APIs* (38).

- *Response Mapper* (122):

  - Response Mappers provide a level of indirection between clients and the
    internal objects, database tables, and so on used to create responses.
    This lets the client and internal resources evolve at different rates.
  - Specialized mappers can be created for specific clients.
  - Response Mappers can be used to produce URIs for *Linked Services* (77).
  - Service evolution can be promoted through this pattern when it is used
    with *Message APIs* (27) and *Resource APIs* (38).

- *Datasource Adapter* (137):

  - Datasource Adapters generally result in a tight coupling among the cli-
    ent, service, and underlying resources (e.g., database table, domain
    object), thereby making it harder to evolve them at different rates.
  - Developers can sometimes change service metadata to alter the service's
    behavior without requiring clients to be updated as well. One might, for
    example, be able to alter the SQL used by an adapter to insulate the cli-
    ent from column name changes on a table.

- *Operation Script* (144), *Command Invoker* (149), *Workflow Connector*
  (156), and *Orchestration* (224):

  - Services that implement or use these patterns provide a simplified inter-
    face or *Façade* [GoF] over a complex set of activities. Since the client is
    dependent on the service interface, the service owner can often change
    the algorithms used to manipulate the objects or tables referenced by the
    service without affecting the client.

- *Service Connector* (168):

  - The logic within connectors can often be altered to accommodate service changes while leaving the client application unaffected.

  - Connectors hide service URIs from clients, making it easier to change service addresses as the need arises.

  - Connectors that are generated from *Service Descriptors* (175) often need to be re-created when the descriptor changes.

- *Service Descriptor* (175):

  - Service owners can augment descriptors to support different service versions, but this may confuse client developers. Older services can be deprecated in favor of newer services, but the service owners should usually coordinate with client developers to determine the timing of such events.

  - Breaking changes on descriptors usually require *Service Proxies* (168) to be regenerated. The rollout of these changes often has to be carefully coordinated with the client owners. (For more on breaking changes, see the section What Causes Breaking Changes? earlier in this chapter.)

  - Descriptors used in *RPC APIs* (18) are automatically regenerated when the API is created through the Code-First practice. This often requires *Service Proxies* (168) to be regenerated.

  - Messages defined in descriptors can be easily extended to support new customer requirements through the *Dataset Amendment* pattern (237).

- *Service Interceptor* (195):

  - Service Interceptors make it easy to add new generic behaviors without having to update the client or service implementations. One can easily add new rules for logging, authentication, data validation, data encryption, message signing, caching, exception handling, and other similar functions.

- *Service Registry* (220):

  - Registries can be used to support a formal governance process that guides service design from inception through retirement.

  - Developer tools can frequently use registries to acquire up-to-date service metadata.

  - *Service Connectors* (168) can contact registries at runtime in order to acquire recent service metadata.

The Patterns and Service Evolution

- *Enterprise Service Bus* (221):
  - By functioning as a *Mediator* [GoF], an ESB insulates clients from the actual services used to fulfill their requests. This can make it easier to add or change services as the need arises. However, the cost is often higher complexity, higher latency, and increased capital expenditures. While clients become less coupled to the real services that process requests, they often become tightly coupled to the bus. Additionally, developers may have to spend additional time creating *Message Translators* [EIP].

- *Tolerant Reader* (243):
  - This pattern enables the message recipient to become more robust despite the fact that messages may contain unknown content and data structures.

- *Consumer-Driven Contract* (250):
  - Consumer-Driven Contracts are the union of all client expectations. Service owners can use this pattern to understand how their clients are affected when a service changes. This pattern also enables service developers to gain insight into how services must be altered in order to meet the needs of all clients.

The Patterns
and Service
Evolution

Appendix

Reference to External Patterns

The following convention is used in this appendix to reference external patterns:

Pattern Name [Reference]

The name of the pattern is followed by a cross reference to the Works Cited in the Bibliography or to a web document.

External Patterns

The patterns follow:

Adapter [GoF]

Converts a class interface to another interface, thereby making it possible for classes that were previously incompatible to interact. *Adapters* are sometimes called *Wrappers* because they encapsulate and hide the actual objects used to fulfill client requests.

Command [GoF]

An object which encapsulates the logic used to process client requests. These objects may be executed immediately, enqueued for deferred processing, persisted, and logged.

Command Message [EIP]

A message which indentifies a logical operation the client would like to invoke. Command messages also provide input data to these operations.

Content-Based Router [EIP]

Examines message content to determine where a message should be sent for further processing. This pattern is often used when the logic for a logical operation is spread across physical locations.

Correlation Identifier [EIP]

A unique identifier carried within a message that allows clients to match responses with requests. This pattern is typically used with the *Request/ Acknowledge* pattern (59).

A.k.a. *Request Identifier*

Related: *Asynchronous Completion Token*, see

www.cs.wustl.edu/~schmidt/PDF/ACT.pdf

Data Transfer Object [POEAA]

This pattern is used with distributed object technologies like CORBA and DCOM in order to optimize network traffic. *Data Transfer Objects* (DTOs) are objects that encapsulate a set of related data that must be marshaled between different processes.

Dependency Injection [www.martinfowler.com/articles/injection.html]

A pattern which separates the selection and instantiation of objects from the clients that use these objects. Clients rely on an assembler to create the necessary objects, and then communicate with these objects through common interfaces. This eliminates direct dependencies between the client and the objects they use.

Related: *Inversion of Control* (IoC)

Document-Literal-Wrapped

[www.ibm.com/developerworks/webservices/library/ws-whichwsdl/]

A WSDL pattern that specifies how *RPC APIs* (18) should format SOAP messages. This pattern makes it relatively easy to validate messages against XSDs. It accomplishes this by wrapping all procedure arguments within a separate complex element whose name equals the target procedure name.

Document Message [EIP]

A message which carries a business document like a purchase order or invoice. The receiver decides how the document should be processed based upon its content and type.

Domain Layer [DDD]

Domain logic is "business logic." Therefore, a *Domain Layer* is that part of an application or system which contains business logic. This layer may include *Domain Models* and *Table Modules* [POEAA]. A *Domain Layer* may also be divided further. It may, for example, have a *Service Layer* [POEAA] containing web services that control the activities of Domain Objects.

Domain Model [POEAA]

An object model where each class encapsulates the data and behavior (i.e., business logic) of significant entities in the problem domain.

Event Message [EIP]

A message which carries data about a topic of interest to the receiver. The receiver decides how the message should be processed based upon its content and type.

A.k.a. *Notification*

Façade [GoF]

Provides a high-level interface to a subsystem. This interface hides the details of the subsystem, thereby making it easier to use.

Factory Method [GoF]

An interface containing methods for object instantiation. Classes which implement the interface encapsulate logic to instantiate the required classes, thereby decoupling clients from these algorithms.

Front Controller [POEAA]

Receives all requests for a given web domain and invokes *Commands* [GoF] based on request contents.

Gateway [POEAA]

An object which encapsulates the logic used to access an external system.

Related: *Adapter* [GoF], *Façade* [GoF], *Mediator* [GoF]

Interceptor [POSA2]

Allows requests and responses to be manipulated before or after the target service processes the request. Each *Interceptor* (a.k.a. *Filter*) may be added to a "handler chain." The client and service are unaware of the filter's presence.

Mapper [POEAA]

An object that allows two objects to share data while keeping them independent of each other. The objects that are referenced by the *Mapper* are totally unaware of it.

Mediator [GoF]

An object that lets a set of objects communicate while keeping them independent of one another. Objects notify the mediator of interesting events, and the mediator propagates this information to the other objects. The objects used by the *Mediator* must therefore be aware of its existence.

Message [EIP]

A data structure that packages information which may be exchanged between two systems. While the EIP catalogue primarily uses this term to refer to structures exchanged over messaging systems (e.g., queues), it is also used to refer to information conveyed over HTTP.

Message Bus [EIP]

Software infrastructure that lets applications send and receive messages without becoming directly coupled to each other. The *Message Bus* is the base pattern for the *Enterprise Service Bus* (221).

Message Router [EIP]

Receives a message and forwards it to other processors (a.k.a. *Filters*) based upon some set of conditions. The EIP catalogue goes into great detail on several variations of this pattern (e.g., *Content-Based Router, Dynamic Router,* etc.).

Message Store [EIP]

Stores message data to a central location that can be queried.

Normalizer [EIP]

Used to process requests that are formatted differently yet are semantically equivalent. Normalizers route requests to *Message Translators* [EIP]. The request is often passed through several process boundaries.

One-Way Message Exchange [www.w3.org/TR/soap12-part3/]

The WSDL specification describes this as a type of interaction in which a service receives a request but doesn't return a response.

A.k.a. *In-Only* [www.w3.org/TR/wsdl20-adjuncts/#in-only]

Related: *Fire-and-Forget*

Operation Script [POEAA]

Contains application logic that directs the activities of entities (i.e., objects) in a *Domain Model* [POEAA]. Each script typically fulfills a use case in an application domain. Operation Scripts are different from *Transaction Scripts* [POEAA] in that they delegate most of their work to domain objects.

Pipes and Filters [EIP]

An architectural style in which a large process is broken down into independent steps called *Filters*. Messages are passed between processing steps by way of the pipes (e.g., queues).

Post Once Exactly [http://tools.ietf.org/html/draft-nottingham-http-poe-00]

A mechanism that lets clients POST a request multiple times while ensuring the request will only be processed once.

Prototype [GoF]

A design approach in which frequently used objects, or *Prototypes,* are created ahead of time. These objects are typically managed by a class known as a *Registry.* Clients contact the registry to request copies of Prototypes. The registry responds by returning a cloned (i.e., copied) instance of the desired class.

Proxy [GoF]

Proxies control access to other objects, components, and services. They behave as surrogates or stand-ins for the actual entities the client wishes to use. Proxy interfaces are identical to the interfaces found on the target objects, components, and services. From the client's perspective, a proxy looks much like the target entity. When a client invokes a proxy method, the proxy formats and forwards the request to the target entity.

Related: *Remote Proxy* [GoF]

Record Set [POEAA]

An in-memory data structure containing tabular data.

Remote Proxy [GoF]

An object that acts as a surrogate for an entity that exists in a remote address space.

Related: *Proxy*

Service Layer [POEAA]

Provides a distinct API which establishes a clear boundary between client applications and domain-specific logic. The *Service Layer* is actually a part of the *Domain Layer* [DDD]. Services often fulfill client requests by coordinating the actions of Domain Objects and *Table Modules* [POEAA]. They may also use workflow engines, code libraries, commercial packages, and legacy applications.

Singleton [GoF]

Restricts instantiation of a class to one instance, and provides a common interface which lets clients access this instance.

Table Module [GoF]

A class that controls access to a database table or view. Each table module encapsulates the logic which manages CRUD (Create, Read, Update, Delete) activities against the target table or view.

Template Method [GoF]

A method which provides an outline for a generic algorithm. The specific logic executed within each step of the algorithm is determined by the concrete classes that are instantiated.

Transaction Script [POEAA]

Organizes business logic by procedures (i.e., scripts). Each procedure contains logic which directly accesses the target resource (e.g., database, file).

Glossary

ActiveX controls—

http://msdn.microsoft.com/en-us/library/aa751972(VS.85).aspx

AJAX—_See_ Asynchronous JavaScript and XML

Anonymous Class—A temporary class that has no name (i.e., identifier). Anonymous classes are defined and instantiated through in-line expressions with the new operator.

Anonymous Method—A convention found in languages like C#, JavaScript, and PHP where a block of code (i.e., function, method) can be passed into a method as a parameter. Unlike traditional methods, these do not have names.

_A.k.a._ anonymous function

Apache Software Foundation Projects—

Project	Associated URL
The Apache Software Foundation	www.apache.org/
Apache web services projects	http://ws.apache.org/
Axis2: A Web Services/SOAP/WSDL engine	http://ws.apache.org/axis2/
An HTTP Client	http://hc.apache.org/httpclient-3.x/
JXPath: An XPath interpreter	http://commons.apache.org/jxpath/
Apache CXF: An open source framework used to host web services (SOAP/WSDL and RESTful/HTTP) and classic remoting technologies (e.g., CORBA objects)	http://cxf.apache.org/
HTTPD: The Apache web server	http://httpd.apache.org/
Log4J: A logging utility	http://logging.apache.org/log4j/

Project	Associated URL
Apache ODE: An Orchestration Engine that uses the WS-BPEL standard	http://ode.apache.org/
Apache ServiceMix: An open source ESB	http://servicemix.apache.org/home.html
Apache Subversion: An open source centralized version control system	http://subversion.apache.org/
Apache Struts: An open source framework that implements the MVC pattern	http://struts.apache.org/
Apache Thrift: An RPC framework for cross-language service development originally developed by Facebook and contributed to Apache	http://thrift.apache.org/
Apache XMLBeans: An XML data-binding technology	http://xmlbeans.apache.org/

ASCII—The American Standard Code for Information Interchange.

http://en.wikipedia.org/wiki/ASCII

ASP.NET MVC—A Microsoft framework which implements the MVC pattern.

www.asp.net/mvc

Asynchronous JavaScript and XML (AJAX)—A number of client-side scripting techniques which leverage asynchronous background calls to web services. These techniques promote dynamic and rich web applications, and allow data to be retrieved or updated without having to load an entire web page.

Atom Publishing Protocol—An XML vocabulary used to create and update web-based resources over HTTP.

http://tools.ietf.org/html/rfc5023

Basic Authentication—Describes a simple mechanism to encode and transmit client credentials (i.e., username and password) over HTTP. This protocol is not considered a secure mechanism for client authentication.

http://tools.ietf.org/html/rfc2617

Black-box Reuse—A form of software reuse in which the implementation details of a class or component are opaque and cannot be altered by the client developer. Developers code to the public interface of these entities. Components that use this form of reuse are typically distributed as binary libraries.

BPEL—*See* Business Process Execution Language

BSD Sockets API—A "low-level" C library for interprocess communications over TCP/IP.

http://en.wikipedia.org/wiki/Berkeley_sockets

BSON—A framework that provides binary-encoded serialization of JSON-like data structures.

http://bsonspec.org/

Business Process Execution Language (BPEL)—An open standard which defines processes as a set of interactions with web services.

Cache—Software infrastructures that typically store data in memory or file systems for use across multiple client requests. Caches help to minimize redundant queries and computations by storing data from recent client requests. If the results for a query can be found in a cache, then data is returned from that cache. Caches may be implemented as client-side caches, intermediary caches, and server caches. Network utilization can be optimized and server load can be greatly reduced when data is served from caches that are close to the client.

Related: Proxy Server, Reverse Proxy

Castor—An XML data-binding framework for Java.

www.castor.org/xml-framework.html

Common Object Request Broker Architecture (CORBA)—A set of vendor-independent standards for distributed-object communications. CORBA technologies allow software components to be consumed by client applications created for disparate computing platforms (i.e., operating systems, programming languages, etc.).

www.omg.org/gettingstarted/corbafaq.htm

Composition—Object composition occurs when a class contains or uses other objects. For example, an `Order` object might contain a collection of `Order_Item` objects.

Service composition is similar. Composite services are created by assembling smaller, simpler services into larger, more complex processes. Composite services can invoke external services directly. The *Workflow Connector* pattern (156) and *Orchestration Engine* pattern (224) may also be used to create composite services.

Related: Conversations

Conversation—The exchange of topically related messages between two or more parties, possibly including intermediaries and crossing organizational boundaries. Conversations are usually initiated to carry out business tasks.

CORBA—*See* Common Object Request Broker Architecture

CRUD—An acronym which means "Create, Read, Update, Delete". These are the common logical operations performed by database-centric applications.

Daemon—A software program that runs as an unattended background process.

Data Binding—Software infrastructure that maps data in XML, JSON, or proprietary formats to objects. Once mappings have been defined, the associated data-binding framework can deserialize source data structures to objects, and vice versa.

Dataset—A collection of data. Datasets are often created as tabular data structures, but may also use other forms (e.g., jagged arrays).

Deadlock—Occurs when two clients acquire locks on different resources, then attempt to acquire locks on the resources being held by the other. The clients remain at an impasse because they must wait for the other to release its locks.

Denial of Service (DoS)—A malicious attack that seeks to render target servers unavailable or unresponsive. One of the most common ways to do this is to flood the target web servers with invalid requests. This makes it difficult for servers to handle legitimate client traffic, and often consumes an excessive amount of server resources (e.g., memory, CPU, etc.).

Deserialize—The inverse of serialization. The act of converting data from a byte stream into a local data structure (e.g., class) that can be acted upon by a service.

A.k.a. Unmarshal

Digest Authentication—Describes a mechanism to encode and transmit client credentials (i.e., username and password) over HTTP. This protocol is considered to be more secure than Basic Authentication because of its use of MD5 hash functions to encrypt client credentials.

http://tools.ietf.org/html/rfc2617

Distributed Component Object Model (DCOM)—Microsoft's proprietary standard for distributed-object communications. DCOM lets software components be consumed by client applications written in different programming languages. It was often difficult to use these components on non-Microsoft platforms.

Distributed Transaction—A distributed transaction exists when multiple networked resources (e.g., databases, queues, caches, file systems, etc.) are enlisted in a single "all-or-nothing transaction." In other words, all of the operations against the resources must complete successfully, or all operations must be reversed.

WS-* services may use the WS-AtomicTransaction [WS-AT] specification to implement distributed transactions through a Two-Phase Commit Protocol (2PC). In the first phase, services are invoked and a transaction coordinator enlists each service into the global transaction. When a service completes, it casts a vote to commit or abort its work. The transaction coordinator collects these votes at the end of phase one. If even one service votes to abort, the coordinator instructs all services to roll back their work in the second phase. However, if all services voted to commit, the coordinator instructs them to commit. 2PC requires services to maintain resource locks, typically database locks, for the duration of the transaction. For this reason, it is best used for transactions that are relatively short in duration. Additionally, since it requires a high degree of trust between clients and services, it is usually reserved for use within secure corporate networks.

DLL—*See* Dynamic Link Library

Document Object Model (DOM)—A language-independent mechanism for representing and manipulating XML, HTML, and XHTML documents. DOM parsers load entire documents into memory and permit random access to any node in the document through programmatic means or declarative XPath scripts.

www.w3.org/DOM/

Domain Name System (DNS)—An Internet standard for naming, locating, and addressing networked computers and services on the Internet or within secure intranets. Networked computers are associated with domains, and DNS records are replicated to distributed databases.

Domain Object—Individual classes within a *Domain Model* [POEAA] that encapsulate the data and behavior of logical entities in a specific business domain.

A.k.a. Entities [DDD], *Reference Objects* [DDD], *Business Object*

DoS—*See* Denial of Service

Dynamic Link Library (DLL)—A proprietary Microsoft standard for encapsulating code libraries as deployable binary units that can be reused by different client applications.

EBCDIC—Extended Binary Coded Decimal Interchange Code.

http://en.wikipedia.org/wiki/Ebcidic

Endianness—The rules which define how a specific computing platform orders the bytes of 16-, 32-, or 64-bit words stored in memory.

A.k.a. Byte Order

Extensible Markup Language (XML)—

www.w3.org/XML/

Extensible Stylesheet Language Transformations (XSLT)—An XML-based language that defines how content from XML can be converted into other formats and data structures.

www.w3.org/TR/xslt

Extensible XML Application Markup (XMAL)—A proprietary XML-based language from Microsoft. When used with Windows Workflow (WF), it lets developers describe business process workflows, much like WS-BPEL.

http://msdn.microsoft.com/en-us/library/ms735921(VS.90).aspx

Fail-Over—The ability to automatically switch over to a back-up resource (e.g., server, computer disk, network, etc.) when a critical error occurs on the primary resource.

Fault Message—A SOAP standard which lets services convey error information to clients through responses.

Related: SOAP

Firewall—A network device that can be configured to permit, deny, encrypt, decrypt, and forward requests to servers and services based upon a set of rules defined by network administrators.

Git—A free and open sourced version control system originally developed by Linus Torvalds. It is considered a distributed repository because it does not require a central server. For more information, see http://git-scm.com/.

Git Submodules—Provides the means to import dependencies from external repositories into Git. For more information, see

www.kernel.org/pub/software/scm/git/docs/git-submodule.html

Google Protocol Buffers—An efficient protocol for serializing structured data in a language- and platform-neutral manner.

http://code.google.com/apis/protocolbuffers/

Governance—The processes used by organizations to manage software changes so that "Quality of Service" (QoS) standards are ensured, legal contracts and regulations are upheld, and business goals are achieved.

Hypermedia—Text-based data formats which contain links to other resources (e.g., images, audio, video, documents, files, and executable programs).

Hypertext Transport Protocol (HTTP)—

www.w3.org/Protocols/rfc2616/rfc2616.html, www.w3.org/Protocols/ HTTP/AsImplemented.html, www.iana.org/assignments/http-status-codes

Interface Definition Language (IDL)—A meta-language used to define the public interfaces of software components. Each interface defines a contract that identifies the operations clients may call, the input arguments for each operation, and the related return types. Clients bind to this contract, and communicate with the software components through these interfaces. This insulates clients from the implementation details of the component. Components may run locally in the consumer's process, or remotely on another machine.

Related: CORBA, DCOM

Internet Information Services (IIS)—Microsoft's web server.

www.iis.net/

Java API for RESTful Web Services (JAX-RS)—A Java API used to create RESTful services and *Resource APIs* (38).

http://jcp.org/en/jsr/detail?id=311, https://jsr311.dev.java.net/

Java API for XML Processing (JAXP)—Provides XML parsers for DOM, SAX, and StAX interfaces. Also provides an XSLT interface.

http://jcp.org/en/jsr/detail?id=206

Related: Document Object Model, Simple API for XML

Java API for XML Web Services (JAX-WS)—A Java API used to create web services that have *RPC APIs* (18) or *Message APIs* (27).

http://jcp.org/en/jsr/detail?id=224, https://jax-ws.dev.java.net/

Java Architecture for XML Binding (JAXB)—Provides mechanisms to map XML data to Java objects. Once mappings have been defined, the framework has the information it needs to deserialize XML to objects, and to serialize object data to XML documents.

https://jaxb.dev.java.net/

Related: XML Data Binding

Java Message Service (JMS)—A Java API for message queuing.

http://java.sun.com/products/jms/docs.html

JavaScript Object Notation (JSON)—A lightweight and platform-independent data-interchange format.

www.ietf.org/rfc/rfc4627.txt?number=4627, www.json.org/

JSON RPC—A specification for encoding remote procedure calls through JSON. For more information, see

http://json-rpc.org/.

JSON Schema—A vocabulary used to declare JSON data structures.

http://tools.ietf.org/html/draft-zyp-json-schema-02)

JUnit—A unit testing framework for Java. For more information, see

www.junit.org/.

Latency—The time it takes for a service to provide a response or acknowledgment. Latency is affected by many factors including network utilization, server load, data payload size, data compression, and much more.

Late Binding—Runtime resolution of a service's address, accepted media types, and the server methods used to dispatch requests. Late binding can be accomplished through many patterns including *Linked Services* (77) and *Media Type Negotiation* (70). *Service Connectors* (168) and *Service Registries* (220) may also be used to resolve service URIs.

Load Balancing—A variety of software and hardware techniques used to distribute requests across one or more servers. When load balancing is used, clients don't communicate directly with the web servers. Instead, the load balancer intercepts each request and uses an algorithm to determine which server in the "server farm" (a.k.a. cluster) should handle the request. The goal is to spread the work evenly across the servers.

Lost-Update Problem—Occurs when two clients attempt to update the same resource at roughly the same time. Consider the case where client A and client B both retrieve data on customer C at the same time. Let's say client A updates and saves this record, then client B does the same. If client A immediately reads the data on customer C again, it may appear as though their update was lost because they now see client B's updates.

Man-in-the-Middle Attack (MITM)—Occurs when a third party intercepts communications between a client and service. In the case of web services, the malicious party co-opts the TCP connection between the client and the server. The end result is that the client has a connection to the middleman, which also has a connection to the target service. The middleman may silently eavesdrop on the conversation to acquire information, or inject commands to alter the flow of the conversation.

Media Type—Used to categorize data formats exchanged over the Internet. Examples include plain text files, images, sound and video files, and even software programs. Media types have two parts, referred to as the Content-type and Subtype.

www.iana.org/assignments/media-types/

A.k.a. MIME, Content Type

Message Transmission Optimization Mechanism (MTOM)—Defines how SOAP data may be serialized as binary data in a way that minimizes the size of message payloads. Considered a WS-* specification.

www.w3.org/TR/2005/REC-soap12-mtom-20050125/

Microformat—A set of simple data formats that can be used in a variety of applications.

http://microformats.org/

Microsoft Enterprise Library—A set of DLLs that provide common behaviors such as logging, authentication, caching, and so forth.

http://msdn.microsoft.com/en-us/library/ff648951.aspx

Microsoft Interface Definition Language (MIDL)—A proprietary Interface Definition Language used with Microsoft's implementation of RPC.

http://msdn.microsoft.com/en-us/library/aa367091(VS.85).aspx

Microsoft Message Queuing (MSMQ)—Microsoft's implementation of queuing middleware.

http://msdn.microsoft.com/en-us/library/ms711472(VS.85).aspx

Multipurpose Internet Mail Extension (MIME)—Originally used to define standard data types that could be attached to emails. Examples include plain text files, images, sound and video files, and even software programs. MIMEs are now used to identify standard media types that can be exchanged by RESTful web services.

www.iana.org/assignments/media-types/

Related: Media Type

Nondeterministic Content Models—Occurs when an XML processor can't figure out when the end of an element or document occurs.

NUnit—A .NET port of the JUnit testing framework. For more information, see

http://nunit.org

Object Relational Mapper—Object Relational Mappers (ORMs) move data between relational databases and object models. They free developers from having to create SQL and manage database transactions.

Related: Domain Model, Active Record, Data Mapper [POEAA]

Open Data Protocol (OData)—A Microsoft specification that extends Atom Publishing Protocol. This protocol defines mechanisms for querying and updating resources exposed over HTTP. (www.odata.org/)

Open Systems Interconnection (OSI) Model—A standard that defines common layers used by networked systems.

www.itu.int/rec/dologin_pub.asp?lang=e&id=T-REC-X.200-199407-I!!PDF-E&type=items

Origin Server—The web server from which specific response data originates. This term is used to differentiate web servers from web caches (e.g., proxies) which can also provide response data.

Pipeline—A chain of independent processors (a.k.a. Filters) that are arranged into a sequence where the output from one element is provided as the input to the next. This concept was first articulated by Douglas McIlroy.

Related: Pipes and Filters [EIP]

Plain Old XML (POX)—Refers to any use of XML which avoids standards like SOAP. Developers that use POX messages often avoid XML Schema as well. The argument is that use of such standards tends to bloat the message payload.

Plug-In—A program that can be downloaded from a server on-demand. These programs are typically hosted in applications like web browsers, email clients, mobile devices, or consumer appliances (e.g., multimedia and gaming stations, GPS devices, etc.). They often run in a "sandbox" and cannot directly access the hardware subsystems of their host.

Postel's Law—This principle was posited by John Postel, a computer scientist and pioneer who played a significant role in the development of the Internet and its standards. Postel's Law has been found in many Request For Comments (RFCs) as early as RFC 760 in 1980 (re: http://tools.ietf.org/html/rfc760, section 3.2). RFC 1122 (re: http://tools.ietf.org/html/rfc1122#page-12) suggests that one should "Be liberal in what you accept, and conservative in what you send". Other wordings for this principle have arisen over time. For more information, see The Postel Center, www.postel.org/postel.html.

Proxy Server—*See* Reverse Proxy

Race Condition—This situation can occur when messages are processed asynchronously. It happens when the completion time of two parallel tasks in a logical workflow cannot be predicted. Since the tasks execute in parallel, they are racing to provide input to downstream tasks. This can be a problem if subsequent tasks expect to receive output from these tasks in a specific sequence.

Regression Test—Practices used to ensure that any changes made to software do not introduce runtime exceptions or cause unexpected program results. Regression tests are typically created through a combination of unit tests and functional tests.

Related: Governance

Remote Procedure Call (RPC)—Remote Procedure Call Protocol Specification Version 2.

www.ietf.org/rfc/rfc1831.txt

Representational State Transfer (REST)—An architectural style that is defined by a specific set of constraints. REST calls for layered client/server systems that employ stateless servers, liberal use of caching on the client, intermediaries, and server, a uniform interface, and optionally, code-on-demand. For more information, see Fielding in the Works Cited in the Bibliography.

Reverse Proxy—Receives Internet traffic addressed to internal web servers. Provides Network Address Translation (NAT) which converts public addresses to private internal addresses, load balancing, caching capabilities, and data compression.

Robustness Principle—*See* Postel's Law

Ruby on Rails—An open source web development framework

http://rubyonrails.org/

SAX—*See* Simple API for XML (SAX)

Scalability—The capacity of a "logical system" comprising one or more servers to maintain acceptable response times and throughput as load increases.

Schematron—A rules-based meta-language which makes it possible to check an XML document's structure and its conformance to complex business rules.

www.schematron.com/

Secure Sockets Layer (SSL)—*See* Transport Layer Security (TLS)

Serialize—The act of converting data from a local in-memory data structure (e.g., class) to a stream of bytes that can be transmitted over the network. These objects are often, but not always, deserialized by the receiver (web service or client) in the same form.

A.k.a. Marshal.

Related: Deserialize

Service Composition—*See* Composition

Servlet—A Java programming language construct commonly used to handle web service requests.

http://java.sun.com/j2ee/tutorial/1_3-fcs/doc/Servlets2.html

Session—A bounded exchange of information between a client and server. Sessions begin when the client first opens a connection to the server. They are terminated when the client deliberately disconnects or when the server decides a client's session has been inactive for too long. The server typically allocates memory that is used to store client data. This data may be accessed by web services across multiple requests.

Related: Session Variables

Session Variables—Memory allocated on a server for a specific client session. Once this memory is allocated, it is usually held until the client explicitly releases it or the client's session times out.

Related: Session

Simple API for XML (SAX)—Originally a Java-only API, but now available in multiple programming languages. SAX parsers read forward through XML documents and trigger events when elements, attributes, or other content is found. These events are triggered in custom classes created by developers. Each callback method that receives a SAX event contains code to extract data from the element or attribute which triggered the event. Since XML documents are traversed in a forward-only fashion, nodes that have passed cannot be accessed again. SAX parsers also prohibit manipulation of XML document data. However, these parsers are a memory-efficient alternative to the XML DOM and are often used in high load scenarios.

www.saxproject.org/

SOAP—This term was originally coined as an acronym for "Simple Object Access Protocol." However, with SOAP 1.2, this translation was dropped. The term "SOAP," in its current usage, has no translation.

www.w3.org/TR/soap/

Software Configuration Management (SCM)—A set of activities and software used to manage changes to software products. SCM encompasses version control, reporting, and work-item management. Some SCM tools also manage automated builds and provide defect tracking.

Related: Governance

Spring—A multipurpose open source framework.

www.springsource.org/about

SSL—*See* Secure Sockets Layer, Transport Layer Security

Subversion—*See* Apache Subversion

Subversion External Definitions—Provides the means to import dependencies from external repositories into Subversion. For more information, see

http://svnbook.red-bean.com/en/1.1/ch07s04.html

svcUtil—A tool that generates proxies for .NET clients.

http://msdn.microsoft.com/en-us/library/aa347733.aspx

Transport Layer Security (TLS)—Used to ensure data privacy over unsecure networks.

http://tools.ietf.org/html/rfc5246

Related: Secure Sockets Layer

Unicode Transformation Format (UTF)—For information on UTF-8, see

http://tools.ietf.org/html/rfc3629

UTF-16, see

http://tools.ietf.org/html/rfc2781

Unified Modeling Language (UML)—A standard set of graphic notations and diagramming techniques used to create logical and physical models which depict various aspects of software systems.

www.uml.org/

Uniform Resource Identifier (URI)—A set of characters that identifies an abstract or physical resource which is usually network addressable.

www.ietf.org/rfc/rfc3986.txt

Universally Unique Identifier (UUID)—A 128-bit value that is guaranteed to be globally unique across space and time.

http://tools.ietf.org/html/rfc4122

URI Rewrite—A technique typically used to make URIs more readable and friendly to search engines. URI Rewriting can also be used when a server administrator wishes to redirect requests from one address to a new URI.

URI Template—Defines the rules for constructing URIs.

http://tools.ietf.org/html/draft-gregorio-uritemplate-04

www.ibm.com/developerworks/web/library/wa-uri/

URL Encoding—A practice in which a URI is converted to a format which can be transmitted using the ASCII character set even when the URI uses non-ASCII characters. Spaces are normally replaced with the + sign, and "unsafe" ASCII characters are replaced with the % sign.

WCF—*See* Windows Communication Foundation

Web Application Description Language (WADL)—A meta-language that provides a generic approach to describe any web resource.

www.w3.org/Submission/wadl/

Web Distributed Authoring and Versioning (WebDAV)—Extends HTTP with a set of methods and behaviors that allow remote users to edit and maintain resources. This protocol is used in many applications, including the Subversion version control system.

http://tools.ietf.org/html/rfc4918

Web Services Addressing (WS-Addressing)—Specifies how information about message senders and receivers may be provided in SOAP messages. Considered a WS-* specification.

www.w3.org/TR/ws-addr-core/

Web Services Atomic Transactions (WS-AT)—Describes how web services can be used in distributed transactions. Considered a WS-* specification.

http://docs.oasis-open.org/ws-tx/wsat/2006/06

Related: Distributed Transaction

Web Services Business Process Execution Language (WS-BPEL)—A meta-language that lets developers describe control-flow logic for business processes where each task is a web service. Considered a WS-* specification.

www.oasis-open.org/committees/tc_home.php?wg_abbrev=wsbpel

Web Services Description Language (WSDL)—An XML-based meta-language used to describe the interfaces of web services that send and receive SOAP messages. Considered a WS-* specification.

www.w3.org/TR/wsdl

Web Services Discovery (WS-Discovery)—Describes how clients may send SOAP messages to a multicast group in order to acquire service addresses. Considered a WS-* specification.

http://docs.oasis-open.org/ws-dd/ns/discovery/2009/01

Web Services Interoperability Basic Profile (WS-I Basic Profile)—A set of standards that seeks to ensure interoperability across disparate web service frameworks.

www.ws-i.org/Profiles/BasicProfile-1.1-2004-08-24.html

Web Services Interoperability Organization (WS-I)—An organization that establishes standards for web service interoperability.

www.ws-i.org/

Web Services Interoperability Technology (WSIT)—An open source project, originally backed by Sun, which sought to ensure that Java frameworks using WS-* standards would be compatible with Microsoft's WCF framework.

http://download.oracle.com/docs/cd/E17802_01/webservices/webservices/reference/tutorials/wsit/doc/index.html

Web Services Policy Framework (WS-Policy)—A generic framework that describes how the capabilities, characteristics, constraints, and requirements for a web service can be described to clients. Considered a WS-* specification.

www.w3.org/TR/ws-policy/

Web Services Reliable Messaging (WS-RM)—This specification defines how clients and services can collaborate to ensure that messages are delivered in the correct sequence and the correct number of times. Considered a WS-* specification.

www.oasis-open.org/committees/tc_home.php?wg_abbrev=wsrm

Web Services Security (WS-Security)—A set of protocols that prescribe how message integrity and privacy can be ensured. Considered a WS-* specification.

www.oasis-open.org/committees/tc_home.php?wg_abbrev=wss

White-box Reuse—A form of software reuse in which the client developer has access to the internal implementation of the code and can change it.

Windows Communication Foundation (WCF)—Microsoft's framework for web services. This framework supports RESTful web services and SOAP/WSDL services.

http://msdn.microsoft.com/en-us/netframework/aa663324.aspx

Windows Service—*See* Daemon

Wsimport—A tool that generates JAX-WS artifacts for Java clients.

https://jax-ws.dev.java.net/jax-ws-ea3/docs/wsimport.html

X.509 Certificate—A Public Key Infrastructure (PKI) standard used to represent client credentials. These certificates are typically provided by third-party certificate authorities (e.g., VeriSign) who ensure the identity of clients.

www.ietf.org/rfc/rfc2459.txt

XML—*See* Extensible Markup Language (XML)

XML Path Language (XPath)—A query language used to search XML documents.

www.w3.org/TR/xpath/

XML Schema—A meta-language which lets developers define the structure, content, and semantics of XML documents. XML processors can validate XML documents against these schemas.

www.w3.org/XML/Schema

XMAL—*See* Extensible XML Application Markup (XAML)

XSLT—*See* Extensible Stylesheet Language Transformations (XSLT)

Bibliography

Works Cited

[Brown 1]

Brown, Kyle. *Asynchronous Queries in J2EE.*

www.javaranch.com/journal/2004/03/AsynchronousProcessingFromServlets.html

[Brown 2]

Brown, Kyle. *Web Services Value Type Inheritance and Interoperability.*

www.javaranch.com/journal/2004/03/AsynchronousProcessingFromServlets.html

[DDD]

Evans, Eric. *Domain Driven Design* (Addison-Wesley, 2003).

[EIP]

Hohpe, Gregor, and Bobby Woolf. *Enterprise Integration Patterns: Designing, Building, and Deploying Messaging Solutions* (Addison-Wesley, 2003).

[Fielding]

Fielding, Roy T. *Architectural Styles and the Design of Network-based Software Architectures.* Doctoral dissertation. University of California Irvine, 2000.

www.ics.uci.edu/~fielding/pubs/dissertation/top.htm

[Fowler]

Fowler, Martin. *Mocks Aren't Stubs.*

http://martinfowler.com/articles/mocksArentStubs.html

[Freeman, Pryce]

Freeman, Steve, and Nat Pryce. *Growing Object-Oriented Software, Guided by Tests* (Addison-Wesley, 2010).

[GoF]

Gamma, Erich, Richard Helm, Ralph Johnson, and John M.Vlissides. *Design Patterns, Elements of Reusable Object-Oriented Software* (Addison-Wesley, 1995).

[IBM, ESB Patterns]

https://www.ibm.com/developerworks/wikis/display/esbpatterns/ESB+and+Connectivity+Patterns

[Manes]

Manes, Anne Thomas. *SOA is Dead; Long Live Services.* January 2009.

http://apsblog.burtongroup.com/2009/01/soa-is-dead-long-live-services.html

[Manolescu]

Manolescu, Dragos A. *Patterns for Orchestration Environments.*

http://hillside.net/plop/2004/papers/dmanolescu0/PLoP2004_dmanolescu0_0.pdf

[Meyer, Bertrand]

Meyer, Bertrand. "Applying Design by Contract." In *Computer* (IEEE) 25(10): October 1992, pp. 40–51.

http://se.ethz.ch/~meyer/publications/computer/contract.pdf

[Meszaros, Gerard]

Meszaros, Gerard. *xUnit Test Patterns, Refactoring Test Code* (Addison-Wesley, 2007).

[Newcomer, Lomow]

Newcomer, Eric, and Greg Lomow. *Understanding SOA with Web Services* (Pearson Education, 2005).

[Nottingham, Marc]

Nottingham, Marc. *Post-Once-Exactly.* March 2005.

http://tools.ietf.org/html/draft-nottingham-http-poe-00

[OASIS Ref Model]

The OASIS Reference Model for Service Oriented Architecture 1.0. October 2006.

http://docs.oasis-open.org/soa-rm/v1.0/soa-rm.pdf

[Obasanjo]

Obasanjo, Dare. *Designing Extensible, Versionable XML Formats.* July 2004.

www.xml.com/pub/a/2004/07/21/design.html

[Orchard]

Orchard, David. *Versioning XML Vocabularies.* December 2003.

www.xml.com/pub/a/2003/12/03/versioning.html

[POEAA]

Fowler, Martin. *Patterns of Enterprise Application Architecture* (Addison-Wesley, 2002).

[POSA2]

Schmidt, Douglas C., Michael Stal, Hans Rohnert, and Frank Buschmann. *Pattern-Oriented Software Architecture Volume 2: Patterns for Concurrent and Networked Objects* (Wiley, 2000).

[Richardson, Ruby]

Richardson, Leonard, and Sam Ruby. *RESTful Web Services* (O'Reilly Media, Inc., 2007).

[Robinson]

Robinson, Ian. *Consumer Driven Contracts: A Service Evolution Pattern.*

http://martinfowler.com/articles/consumerDrivenContracts.html

[Snell]

Snell, James. *Asynchronous Web Service Operations using JMS.* October 2004.

www.ibm.com/developerworks/webservices/library/ws-tip-altdesign1/

[van der Aalst, et al.]

van der Aalst, Wil, Arthur ter Hofstede, Bartek Kiepuszewski, and Alistair Barros. Workflow Patterns.

http://workflowpatterns.com/

[Waldo, Wyant, Wollrath, Kendall]

Waldo, Jim, Geoff Wyant, Ann Wollrath, and Sam Kendall. *A Note on Distributed Computing.* 1994.

http://labs.oracle.com/techrep/1994/abstract-29.html

[Zdun, Voelter, Kircher]

Zdun, Uwe, Markus Voelter, and Michael Kircher. *Design and Implementation of an Asynchronous Invocation Framework for Web Services.*

http://citeseerx.ist.psu.edu/viewdoc/summary?doi=10.1.1.2.1270

Related Books, Papers, and Articles

Barros, Alistair, Marlon Dumas, and Arthur ter Hofstede. *Service Interaction Patterns: Towards a Reference Framework for Service-Based Business Process Interconnection.*

www.workflowpatterns.com/documentation/documents/
ServiceInteractionPatterns.pdf

Brewer, Dr. Eric A. *Towards Robust Distributed Systems.*
www.cs.berkeley.edu/~brewer/cs262b-2004/PODC-keynote.pdf

Burke, Bill. *RESTful Java* (O'Reilly Media, Inc., 2010).

Bustmante, Michele Leroux. *Learning WCF* (O'Reilly Media, Inc., 2007).

Fielding, Roy T. *REST APIs Must Be Hypertext Driven.* October 2008.
http://roy.gbiv.com/untangled/2008/rest-apis-must-be-hypertext-driven

Fielding, Roy T. *It is okay to use Post.* March 2009.
http://roy.gbiv.com/untangled/2009/it-is-okay-to-use-post

Hansen, Mark D. *SOA Using Java Web Services* (Pearson Education, 2007).

Hohpe, Gregor. *Correlation and Conversations.* May 21, 2004.
www.eaipatterns.com/ramblings/09_correlation.html

Josuttis, Nicolai M. *SOA in Practice* (O'Reilly Media, Inc., 2007).

Kanneganti, Ramarao, and Prasad Chodavarapu. *SOA Security* (Manning
Publications Co., 2008).

Lowy, Juval. *Programming WCF* (O'Reilly Media, Inc., 2007).

Luckham, David, and Brian Frasca. *Complex Event Processing in Distributed
Systems.* Program Analysis and Verification Group, Computer Systems Lab,
Stanford University, August 18, 1998.

Neto, I.S., and F. Reverbel. *Lessons Learned from Implementing WS-
Coordination and WS-AtomicTransaction.* Computer and Information Science,
2008. ICIS 08. Seventh IEEE/ACIS International Conference, May 14–16,
2008, pp. 367–372.

http://ieeexplore.ieee.org/Xplore/login.jsp?url=http%3A%2F%2Fieeexplore.
ieee.org%2Fiel5%2F4529779%2F4529780%2F04529847.pdf%3Farnumber
%3D4529847&authDecision=-203

Newcomer, Eric. *Understanding Web Services* (Addison-Wesley, 2002).

Resnick, Steve, Richard Crane, and Chris Bowen. *Essential Windows Communication Foundation* (Pearson Education, 2008).

Wirfs-Brock, Rebecca, and Allan McKean. *Object Design: Roles, Responsibilities, and Collaborations* (Addison-Wesley, 2002).

Wirfs-Brock, Rebecca. *Responsibility Driven Design.*

www.wirfs-brock.com/Design.html

Index

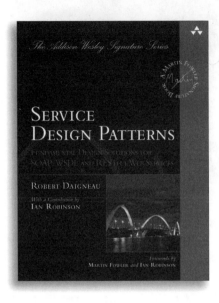

FREE Online Edition

Your purchase of **Service Design Patterns** includes access to a free online edition for 45 days through the Safari Books Online subscription service. Nearly every Addison-Wesley Professional book is available online through Safari Books Online, along with more than 5,000 other technical books and videos from publishers such as Cisco Press, Exam Cram, IBM Press, O'Reilly, Prentice Hall, Que, and Sams.

SAFARI BOOKS ONLINE allows you to search for a specific answer, cut and paste code, download chapters, and stay current with emerging technologies.

Activate your FREE Online Edition at www.informit.com/safarifree

> **STEP 1:** Enter the coupon code: RMYFXBI.

> **STEP 2:** New Safari users, complete the brief registration form.
>   Safari subscribers, just log in.

If you have difficulty registering on Safari or accessing the online edition, please e-mail customer-service@safaribooksonline.com

Web Service API Styles	Pick One . . .	*RPC API* (18) *Message API* (27) *Resource API* (38)

Client-Service Interaction Styles	Pick One . . .	*Request/Response* (54) *Request/Acknowledge* (59)
	Pick Zero or More . . .	*Media Type Negotiation* (70) *Linked Service* (77)

Request and Response Management	Pick Zero or More . . .	*Service Controller* (85) *Data Transfer Object* (94) *Request Mapper* (109) *Response Mapper* (122)

Web Service Implementation Styles	Pick One . . .	*Transaction Script* (134) *Datasource Adapter* (137) *Operation Script* (144) *Command Invoker* (149) *Workflow Connector* (156)